PRAISE FOR *MÉTIS MATRIARCHS*

"A nuanced account of the lives of Métis women and their vital roles as they helped guide their families and communities through generations of transitions." —MICHEL HOGUE, author of *Metis and the Medicine Line*

"*Métis Matriarchs* is a thoughtful collection of essays that explore the agency of Métis women, both past and present, in maintaining the cultural and economic survival of their communities." —HEATHER DEVINE, Professor Emerita, Department of History, University of Calgary

"Richly detailed, deeply researched, and beautifully written portraits of resilient, tenacious, resourceful, and determined women who provided for and protected their families and communities, and who worked to preserve and promote Métis culture, history, and art. They were healers, midwives, artists, farmers, teachers, and more. They were beacons of stability and keepers of memory and culture during years of colonial intrusion and upheaval. They were makers of Canadian history." —SARAH CARTER

"*Métis Matriarchs* is the book we've all been waiting for—the authors of these lovingly crafted and researched essays are re-positioning women and bringing them to the forefront of our history, experience, and way of life." —BRENDA MACDOUGALL

"I loved spending time with these magnificent Métis women—subjects and authors alike. We have been waiting a long time to raise up the Métis women icons who have been a vital but often overlooked part of our story. They're gathered here: listen!" —KIM ANDERSON, author of *Life Stages and Native Women* and *A Recognition of Being: Reconstructing Native Womanhood*

University of Regina Press designates one title each year that best exemplifies the guiding editorial and manuscript production principles of long-time senior editor Donna Grant.

Métis Matriarchs

Agents of Transition

edited by
Cheryl Troupe &
Doris Jeanne MacKinnon

University of Regina Press

© 2024 Cheryl Troupe and Doris Jeanne MacKinnon

All rights reserved. No part of this work covered by the copyrights hereon may be reproduced or used in any form or by any means—graphic, electronic, or mechanical—without the prior written permission of the publisher. Any request for photocopying, recording, taping, or placement in information storage and retrieval systems of any sort shall be directed in writing to Access Copyright.

Printed and bound in Canada. The text of this book is printed on 100% post-consumer recycled paper with earth-friendly vegetable-based inks.

Cover art: Photo courtesy of Musée Héritage St. Albert, Alberta
Cover design: Duncan Noel Campbell, University of Regina Press
Interior layout design: John van der Woude, JVDW Designs
Copyeditor: Rachel Taylor
Proofreader: Rachel Ironstone
Indexer: Judy Dunlop

Library and Archives Canada Cataloguing in Publication

Title: Métis matriarchs : agents of transition / edited by Cheryl Troupe & Doris Jeanne MacKinnon.
Names: Troupe, Cheryl, 1972- editor | MacKinnon, Doris Jeanne, editor
Description: Includes bibliographical references and index.
Identifiers: Canadiana (print) 20240383826 | Canadiana (ebook) 20240383842 | ISBN 9781779400123 (hardcover) | ISBN 9781779400116 (softcover) | ISBN 9781779400130 (PDF) | ISBN 9781779400147 (EPUB)
Subjects: LCSH: Métis women. | LCSH: Métis women—Social life and customs.
Classification: LCC FC129.W6 M47 2024 | DDC 305.48/897—dc23

10 9 8 7 6 5 4 3 2 1

University of Regina Press, University of Regina
Regina, Saskatchewan, Canada, S4S 0A2
TEL: (306) 585-4758 FAX: (306) 585-4699
WEB: www.uofrpress.ca

We acknowledge the support of the Canada Council for the Arts for our publishing program..We acknowledge the financial support of the Government of Canada. / Nous reconnaissons l'appui financier du gouvernement du Canada. This publication was made possible with support from Creative Saskatchewan's Book Publishing Production Grant Program.

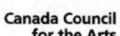 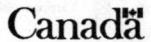 

Dedicated to the Métis matriarchs whose stories are shared here, and those whose stories have yet to be shared.

Contents

Acknowledgements **xi**
Introduction. Métis Matriarchs: Agents of Transition **xiii**

One. **Marie Rose Delorme Smith** 1
"Buckskin Mary—Queen of the Jughandle" (1861–1960)
by Doris Jeanne MacKinnon

Two. **Remembering and Retelling the Legacies
of Métis Women in Alberta** 29
The Life and Memories of Victoria Belcourt Callihoo
by Madalyn Mandziuk

Three. **Josette Lagacé Work** 63
Strong and Elastic as Steel
by Vanessa Winn

Four. **Caroline McNabb and Culturally Adaptive
Practices of Métis Kinship** 101
by Jade McDougall

Five. "She Did Lead a Rough Life,
but She Lived a Good Life"   133
The Life of Julia Lamotte
by Gabrielle Legault

Six. On Becoming Sovereign   157
Generations of Métis Matriarchal Resistance
by Janice Cindy Gaudet

Seven. Métis Matriarchs in
kāministikominahikoskahk (Cumberland House)   195
mîkisistahikêwin—Beading Together the Generations
by Allyson Stevenson

Eight. Activating Lessons of Care from Family Matriarchs   223
The Social and Political Work of Nora Cummings
by Cheryl Troupe

Conclusion   261
About the Contributors   269
Bibliography   271
Index   291

Acknowledgements

The editors acknowledge the insights and dedication of the authors who shared their stories of the matriarchs featured in this collection. We are humbled by their dedication in seeking out and telling the stories shared by, in many instances, family members. All authors approached with humility and care as they sought out, recorded, and respectfully shared their insights in relating the life stories of the Métis women featured herein. These stories are representative of the many stories that remain untold about the contributions of Métis women to their communities both during the height of the fur trade and into the transitional period that followed where the Métis assumed critical roles in the development of new economies in the Prairie west. We acknowledge and anticipate the vast array of stories that remain untold about those contributions.

We also acknowledge the important insights shared by the anonymous readers which served to strengthen and deepen the discussions found in this collection. We acknowledge the assistance of editor Patrick Farrell in ensuring the integrity of the narrative. Finally, we acknowledge the University of Regina Press. We are humbled by and appreciate the Press's recognition of the value of this collection in our collective understanding of Métis women as matriarchs in their families and communities.

Introduction

Métis Matriarchs: Agents of Transition

Métis communities have been and continue to be defined by family networks, kinship relationships, and the responsibilities and obligations these entail. In the nineteenth and early twentieth centuries, communities organized around extended family groupings, where families worked, hunted, and lived together along kinship lines. Kinship relationships created obligations and responsibilities to one another and extended the network of those who could be relied upon in times of need. Familial relationships between individuals living and working together and across a broad geography helped maintain culture and tradition, making it easier for families to adapt to new environments and social, economic, and political change. Kinship provided stability and ensured interaction in these community-oriented societies. In many instances, the kinship relationships between women bound these communities together.[1]

Métis women, generally those of advanced age, held a place of authority within extended family systems and were seen as matriarchs, respected for their age, experience, and reputations. Métis family stories and oral histories, like some of those shared in this collection, are replete with examples of older Métis women—aunties and grannies—who were matriarchs within their extended families.[2] Indigenous scholar Kim Anderson notes that these older women provided leadership and governance across their communities. She argues that "men may have had specific roles that were more visible in terms of politics and governance, but this does not negate the vital role that women—and particularly older women—held in managing their communities."[3] These women provided formal and informal family and community leadership and were often sought for counsel and decision making in social, economic, and political matters. They helped mediate family affairs, making decisions for the family's well-being. In many instances, matriarchs exhibited a clearly defined economic authority, acting in business affairs for their families, often supporting their families through domestic, farm, and ranch labour or artistic production. They fulfilled a family and community responsibility, acting as healers and midwives and providing care to children and adults in their immediate and extended families. They knew the protocols and processes for preparing the dead for funeral and burial. They acted as cultural teachers, contributing to child rearing and passing on cultural values, stories, practices, and traditions. Often, they raised at least one of their grandchildren, and many remained independent, maintaining their households well into old age. In many instances, these Métis matriarchs also ensured that religious services were observed and the community's children were baptized.

Matriarchs knew family histories and genealogies. In closely knit extended families, it was essential to understand how individuals were related to one another so that marriages could be casually arranged and kinship networks remained strong. It was also the role of matriarchs to informally, and sometimes more formally, monitor the actions and behaviours of family and community members, ensuring that social transgressions were known and dealt with and community values upheld. Through these activities, family matriarchs provided collective social control and stability to their families and community at a time when Métis faced increased pressure to assimilate and adapt. In fulfilling their roles, Métis matriarchs were both mothers of the nation and agents of transition, providing cultural continuity and stability and holding families and communities together through a period of immense change.

This collection is a series of qualitative case studies that follow a biographical approach. It explores the lives of several Métis matriarchs who lived in parts of what is now Western Canada at different moments in the past. These stories provide glimpses into these women's everyday lives helping us understand change and consistency in Métis family roles and responsibilities and revealing the strength of Métis women throughout the course of their lives. Collectively, these case studies reveal how Métis women emerged in varied social, economic, political, and geographic contexts as "agents of transition," playing critical roles in navigating the changes brought about by increasing settlement and state control, situating their actions in the larger historical context of development of Western Canada in the nineteenth century and beyond.

Using the concept of matriarchy demonstrates how women of a certain age and stature navigated the changing world around them. This framing allows readers to see the essential work of Métis women in new ways, including the ways they enacted maternal values of caretaking, nurturing, conflict resolution, and negotiation held by the extended family, grounding themselves and their actions in their cultural knowledge and understanding of the influential role they filled as matriarchs. These women were active agents of change adapting to and often challenging the transitions in their lives in sometimes unexpected, exceptional, and determined ways. The authors engage with a history that has the potential to expand our understanding of the critical contributions made by Métis women, both during the height of the fur trade and the buffalo hunt and into the transitional period that followed. These stories reveal Métis women's agency and the significant contributions they made throughout different stages of their lives that positioned them as matriarchs in their families and communities, fundamentally establishing them in positions of authority within their family systems. These women were (and are) hard-working women, who played critical roles in their families' and communities' social, economic, and political lives. Their stories promote a positive image of practical Métis women, drawing attention to everyday actions where women saw what needed to be done to support their families and communities and then acted on it.

These women's lives represent stories of strength, detailing their resilience, resistance, refusal, and adaptation in navigating and responding to immense social, political, economic, and environmental change by the male-dominated, patriarchal, and settler colonial Canadian state. These case studies reveal how women such as Victoria Belcourt Callihoo, Marie Rose Delorme Smith, and Josette Lagacé Work faced similar challenges in negotiating multiple identities as Métis, First Nations, farmers, and ranchers as they responded to shifting fur trade economies and the buffalo hunt's decline by looking for opportunities in an emerging agricultural economy. These women very often found themselves "women in between," as described by Sylvia Van Kirk.[4] Delorme Smith and Callihoo became important conduits for preserving and sharing these important Métis histories. Publishing one's memoirs was rare for women during this period, and even rarer for Indigenous women, making their actions extraordinary.

These women, along with Caroline McNabb, Auxile Lepine, and Julia Lamotte, drew upon and maintained family-centred cultural practices to resist government intervention in their everyday lives in a growing settler nation that continued to displace, dispossess, and marginalize Métis people in rural, road allowance, and urban centres in the twentieth century. These stories also reveal how women such as Nora Cummings, Agnes Carriere, Margaret McAuley, and Isabelle Impey have drawn upon the cultural and material inheritances shared with them by their own mothers, grandmothers, and family and community matriarchs throughout their own lives to advance their social and political activism, material culture reproduction, and repatriation efforts and maintain matriarchal social relations, resilience, and strength.

The women profiled in this collection worked hard to provide for and protect their families and often made difficult decisions about resisting racism, sexism, and assimilation. As matriarchs, they held steadfast to their cultural values, traditional skills, kinship networks, and relationships with the land to sustain their families and communities. These women were integral and essential forces in keeping their families strong, yet were not afraid to take a steadfast position or challenge others when they deemed it necessary. Their stories complicate the story of Western Canadian settlement and nation-building and add nuance to Indigenous responses to settler colonialism at a time of increased surveillance of and intervention into Indigenous lives and their subsequent marginalization and removal from the landscape.[5] These women acted as agents of transition because of the myriad roles they played in their extended families—most significantly, their roles as matriarchs.

These life stories demonstrate a breadth of experience and commonality, yielding essential insights into the collective experiences of Métis women as matriarchs of their families and communities.

Indeed, they bring new light to the historical experiences of Métis in the fur trade and development of Western Canada. This collection draws attention to the perhaps surprising roles of Métis, and Métis women in particular, in settlement of the west, as farmers, ranchers, and labourers. Until recently, historical scholarship of the Canadian Prairies has privileged the masculine, making women's work and the multiple roles they filled invisible or added as an afterthought.[6] Yet female homesteaders and other women contributed to almost every area of prairie life. Most recently, historian Sarah Carter has helped to shift this focus away from men by adding a complicated gendered perspective to Western Canadian historiography and to the roles women, including Indigenous women, played in settlement of the west.[7]

The stories profiled extend the historiography of Métis women and their contributions to the fur trade, buffalo hunt, and settlement of Western Canada. Scholarship examining the numerous and varied gendered roles of Indigenous women in the eighteenth- and nineteenth-century fur trade has increased following Sylvia Van Kirk and Jennifer Brown's seminal works on the subject and in response to Brown's explicit call for more detailed studies of Métis communities through a lens of Métis women's kinship.[8] Much of this work has examined Métis women as marriage partners and the economic, political, and social benefits these relationships brought to fur traders. Subsequent scholars such as Lucy Eldersveld Murphy, Tanis Thorne, and Susan Sleeper-Smith have employed a gendered lens in exploring the significance of marriage partners in determining economic, political, and social relationships in the fur trade.[9] Sleeper-Smith argues that Indigenous women who married French men assumed a role as cultural mediators and negotiators of change, helping to establish elaborate trading networks through Roman Catholic kinship connections that paralleled those of Indigenous societies.[10]

It was evident that these women did not "marry out," but rather incorporated their French husbands into a society structured by Indigenous customs and traditions.[11] Thus, these Indigenous women did not reinvent themselves as French but enhanced their distinct identity while expanding their family networks. Van Kirk also argued that, from an Indigenous perspective, the process of women marrying fur traders was never regarded as marrying out.[12] Instead, these marriages were important means of incorporating traders into existing kinship networks where traders often had to abide by Indigenous marital customs, some of which, at times, included the payment of a bride price.[13] Similarly, historian Brenda Macdougall's examination of Métis community formation in northwest Saskatchewan demonstrates the strength of kinship relationships in determining economic, social, and political relations across a broad geography.[14] These scholars were able to demonstrate that Métis women made significant contributions to the fur trade as a result of their complex kinship networks.

Recent scholarship extends the study of Métis women's lives into the transitional period that emerged after the fur trade era.[15] Establishing communities in new geographic areas and creating permanent settlements from Métis buffalo hunting winter camps, Métis women relied on their kinship networks while extending their connections with settlers to develop roles for themselves as matriarchs of expanded networks. Relying on their Métis culture and traditional knowledge, they built new communities within the settler state. Unlike the fur trade era, Métis women's roles expanded to include contributing the necessary labour to ensure survival in a new economy.

Like fur trade scholarship, there has been a focus on Métis women as marriage partners in scholarship focused on nineteenth-century buffalo hunt communities. These studies have focused on the role of female kinship in community formation as Métis hunting brigades shifted according to the hunt.[16] During this period, women's labour was significant; women and men fulfilled somewhat gendered and complementary roles, contributing their labour as necessary. However, it was more important that all the required labour roles were filled. Women were valued for their expertise and knowledge, including their skill in processing buffalo meat into pemmican, preparing robes and hides, making tallow, and sewing various items such as hide coats, pad saddles, and moccasins. The bulk of women's labour was in the preparation of items for sale to the fur trading company, which brought income into their families. In addition, women's knowledge of the environment and labour in harvesting plants and medicines, their work as midwives and healers, and their role in tending to children, the sick, and the elderly were crucial for family survival. These were skills that women first began developing as young girls, learning from their mothers, aunties, and grandmothers. This knowledge continued to grow over their lifetimes so that as they aged, elderly women carried a vast body of knowledge, skills, and expertise for which they garnered respect and were considered family matriarchs.

The decline of the bison herds in the mid-to-late nineteenth century precipitated immeasurable changes for Métis families. It changed how Métis families lived and forced them to shift away from a buffalo hunting, fur trading, and freighting subsistence economy toward small-scale agriculture. This new way of life brought external social, economic, and political stressors to Métis livelihoods, precipitating two armed Métis Resistances as Métis challenged the Canadian state to recognize their rights. Métis communities increasingly found themselves displaced, dispossessed, and at odds with settler society and under increased surveillance from the Canadian state. By the turn of the twentieth century, Métis in Southern Manitoba, Saskatchewan, and, to a lesser extent,

Alberta, found themselves living on marginal land set aside for the creation of roads next to First Nations reserves or on vacant land owned by the provincial or federal governments. These communities became known as road allowance communities.

Families in these road allowance communities continued to organize themselves along extended family kinship networks. They relied upon a subsistence lifestyle of fishing, trapping, and gathering wild foods, but also on small-scale agriculture and seasonal wage labour.[17] Women's labour in harvesting, preparing, and preserving food and medicines for their families was crucial to the survival of the family.[18] While men worked as seasonal or day labourers for local farmers, women sometimes worked alongside, clearing fields and picking rocks or potatoes. Women also worked for settler families and maintained more domestic responsibilities such as caring for children and older people. Scholarship on this period has not until recently begun to examine the significance of women's labour. Instead, it has depicted the Métis in terms of their poverty and health and social problems and as being at odds with the settler society.[19] Despite their marginalization and the racism they experienced at the hands of settlers and the state, Métis women as matriarchs, including and similar to those explored in this collection, continued to pass on knowledge and cultural teachings and fulfill their roles as women, mothers, aunties, and grandmothers to ensure their kinship networks and community structures remained strong.

Throughout these many transitions, Métis women's practical skills afforded them continuity of culture and community and helped their families adjust as fur trade and buffalo hunt economies gave way to an industrialized sedentary economy of the western prairie. When Métis women participated in the shifting economy, such as by providing traditional clothing to newcomers, they assumed roles as cultural brokers, just as they had during the height of the fur trade.[20] The roles of Métis women, their skills, and their elaborate kinship networks that facilitated trade in the earlier period later served to transform the impersonal exchange process characteristic to capitalism into a socially accountable process.[21] Despite their integral roles and contributions, few of these women, who contributed so much unpaid labour vital to the success of both the fur trade and the transitional economies of the Northwest, viewed their roles as significant enough to record their lives with the intention of passing them on to a public archive. Few Métis men left archival records of their experiences during the transitional period. This means that we must often rely on sources created by the state and by men. These essays, however, demonstrate the strength and richness of sources such as family held stories, oral histories, and material culture created within social and cultural contexts in helping better understand the emergence and retention of Métis identity and culture in areas well beyond the Red River area.

The permeable boundaries of identity, established during the fur trade and buffalo hunt eras, remained for many Métis people during the transitional period that followed—and indeed remain in contemporary society, as there is little consensus on the "idea of being Métis in Canada today."[22] Some contemporary narratives by the Métis note that there was a silence about Métis identity in their own lives,[23] just as there was for many Métis near the end of the fur trade as they struggled to maintain their livelihoods with the influx of Euro-Canadian settlers. This makes it challenging to gain a complete understanding of the Métis story as the fur trade transitioned and as many Métis settled in new geographic areas across the Prairies. Yet it is important to remember what many scholars have noted, specifically that Métis identity was never static. Rather, it was (and continues to be) negotiated and renegotiated, attesting to the "diversity, fluidity, resilience and [often] silence of Métis identities."[24] This collection offers lessons on the enduring importance of Métis matriarchs in their families and in shaping current identities. In her story about her great-grandmother Matriarch Caroline Laframboise, not unlike the stories of the Métis women in this collection, Métis scholar Zoe Todd celebrates Caroline's strength, determination, and refusal of settler colonialism, showing how her life and legacy shaped Todd's identity as a Métis woman and scholar and her family's understanding of who they are and how they relate to one another and the world as Métis people.[25]

The matriarchs examined here speak to the diversity, fluidity, and resilience of Métis identity, history, and culture. Their stories have been held and passed down within families and rarely shared beyond the Métis community. Their legacies remain felt today. The authors, many of whom are Métis, and some of whom are relating the stories of their own families, have used a family-centred approach, exploring the archival and oral records and the stories of Métis elders and family, as well as treasured pieces of Métis material culture left behind in families, museums, and private collections. Individually, the authors in this collection draw upon the relationships they have with the matriarchs whose stories they are privileged to share. Jade McDougall, Janice Cindy Gaudet, and Gabrielle Legault each share personal family stories of their own grandmothers and matriarchs, serving as a point of connection to their own identities as Métis women and as scholars. Authors Cheryl Troupe, Allyson Stevenson, and Madalyn Mandziuk utilize their long-standing personal and professional relationships with individual matriarchs and their families and communities to document their life stories. MacKinnon, a settler ally whose research about Marie Rose Delorme Smith has enabled her to build respectful relationships with her family members, was able to support their goal to see Delorme Smith recognized as a person of national historic significance. Vanessa Winn, a public historian who has long researched and written about Josette Work, used this collection to revisit this matriarch's story and to write about her in a new way. Together, the stories of the Métis women in this collection demonstrate the transmission and retention of Métis culture and identity across generations and the significant contributions Métis matriarchs made to their families and communities as they adapted to dramatically changing times. It is hoped that their stories and this methodological approach will inspire others to look within their own families for examples where women acted with strength and agency in their everyday experiences, further stimulating new research with and about Métis women as matriarchs.

Relying on a family-centred approach to write the life histories of these matriarchs, the authors have, to different degrees, each pieced together family genealogies of the women they profile. They rely on family-held stories as well as birth, death, and marriage records to examine Métis kinship relationships and lived experiences. Genealogical reconstruction and analysis of Métis kinship systems has increasingly been employed by scholars of Métis history since historian Jennifer Brown called for a more thorough examination of Métis women's kinship relationships in understanding the emergence and development of Métis in the West.[26] Genealogical reconstruction is useful for tracing individual lineage and identifying where individuals fit within their family structure. However, it tells us little about how these relationships operated and nothing about how individuals experienced such relationships. Combining these sources with oral histories, memoirs, stories, and other sources adds richness to the data and helps us understand the broader family and social relationships. A kinship or family-centred approach is a useful framework for examining the relationships between individuals and members of their extended families and for understanding the social, economic, and political relationships these matriarchs maintained, and the changes brought about by settler colonialism to their lives. Indeed, a family-centred approach is significant for telling Métis stories. It locates individuals and their experiences in specific families, communities, and places and allows for detailed family- and community-level studies from which broader patterns of Métis community formation, organization, and operation can be understood, revealing an underlying and consistent organizational structure with kinship relationships at its core.

While this work spans a broad temporal and geographic scope, we have attempted to organize the case studies thematically and chronologically. The women featured herein lived in what was in the nineteenth century considered the North-West Territory, known since the early twentieth century as the western Canadian provinces. As a result, there is a commonality of experiences for many Métis women, but there is also nuance and diversity in their everyday lives, in how they responded to, resisted, and refused settler colonial intrusion, and in the ways they persisted in the face of the many transitions that infringed on their traditional ways of life. There is also a commonality in how these women assumed authority in providing family and community leadership and made decisions in the best interests of their extended families by drawing on their cultural understandings and experiences.

We begin with case studies of women who played an important role in their families and communities in the mid-to-late nineteenth century, when families grappled with economic, political, and environmental changes, particularly as economies shifted from a subsistence-based buffalo hunting and fur trading economy to sedentary agriculture under pressure from an encroaching settler economy. Within this transition, Métis matriarchs worked hard and held firm to their cultural traditions, helping their families through changing times. Co-editor for this collection Doris Jeanne MacKinnon chronicles the life of Marie Rose Delorme Smith, a woman whose experiences were introduced to readers in 1977 by Smith's granddaughter Jock Carpenter in her book *Fifty Dollar Bride*.[27] MacKinnon's chapter reintroduces Delorme Smith as a child growing up in a buffalo hunting family and later as the wife of buffalo robe and whiskey trader and rancher Charlie Smith. Together they became one of the first families to ranch in the Pincher Creek, Alberta, region. Delorme Smith's life speaks to the retention and resilience of Métis identity as she became an author, publishing her memoirs in the magazine *Canadian Cattleman*, as well as a respected medicine woman, homesteader, and businesswoman known to many as "Buckskin Mary." Next, Madalyn Mandziuk explores the life of Victoria Callihoo, who, like Delorme Smith, grew up following a Plains-based lifestyle of buffalo hunting, trading, and freighting, and who later settled in the Lac Ste. Anne, Alberta, region. Through Callihoo's memoirs and written work, as well as oral histories, genealogies, material culture, and the voices of family members and descendants, Callihoo emerges as a powerful example of how one Métis woman persevered through hardship and upheaval while sustaining and passing on her cultural traditions to emerge as a community leader.

Vanessa Winn traces the life of Josette Lagacé Work, born in the Rocky Mountains plateau. Marrying a Hudson's Bay Company trader, Work accompanied him on many of his long trading trips before settling on a large farming estate in Victoria, British Columbia. Work lived during Victoria's transition from fur trade fort to agricultural community, gold-rush city, and commercial port, as well as British Columbia's transition from a colony into Canadian confederation. While mixing amongst the elites of Victoria society, Work maintained close relationships with her Indigenous relatives, bridging class, racial, and religious differences.

Like Winn, author Jade McDougall explores women's experiences resulting from political upheaval, encroaching settlement, and armed resistance. These experiences often necessitated that women and their families moved across sometimes broad geographies. McDougall explores the experiences of her great-great-grandmother Caroline McNabb, who lived through the 1869–70 Red River Resistance before migrating with other Métis families from Red River to Saskatchewan in the 1870s and 1880s, only to witness a second armed resistance in their new homeland. With such political upheaval, McNabb privileged community stewardship and her roles and responsibilities to her relatives, emerging as a matriarch within a large extended community of Scots-Métis families in the South Saskatchewan River region. McDougall's chapter is a personal story drawing on family reminiscences, like Legault's and Gaudet's chapters that follow.

Gabrielle Legault relates the life experiences of her great-grandmother Julia Lamotte (née Fayant), whose family was interconnected with the former fur trade country and kinship systems in the Red River and Qu'Appelle Valleys. Julia worked in a fishing camp in the Métis settlement at Lac Pelletier in her early years before marrying a settler ranch owner. Legault draws on archival material and the oral history of Fayant family members and Elders to reveal the complex and, at times, paradoxical position of Métis women living in between and among societies on the verge of transiting from the old ways to sedentary farm life. Janice Cindy Gaudet explores the stories of her grandmothers and aunties, including her grandmother Auxile Lepine, to better understand these women's efforts to resist patriarchal and racist attitudes as part of living and being well. Gaudet reflects on these stories in reconnecting with the land where these women lived, helping us better understand how womanhood and matriarchy is constructed within contemporary Métis family kinship systems.

The final two case studies reveal the experiences of more contemporary Métis women and their efforts to preserve, promote, and advocate for Métis culture and pass on traditions. These stories speak to their inspiring persistence, resilience, and resistance that provide teachings for the coming generations. Indeed, these women are matriarchs steadfast in their identity as Métis, grounded in their history and culture. Allyson Stevenson explores artistic production and social relationships between Métis matriarchs of Cumberland House in northeastern Saskatchewan. She argues that the artistic work of several closely related women and the return of rare nineteenth-century beaded and embroidered items back to the community demonstrate the persistence of Métis lifeways, their connection to the land and water, and the significant role women continue to play in the cultural, social, political, and economic life of the Cumberland House community. Last, co-editor of this volume Cheryl Troupe explores the accomplished social and political activism of contemporary Métis Matriarch Nora Cummings and the cultural teachings instilled in her by her mother, grandmother, and other women in her family. Lessons about the significance of visiting and hospitality and the importance of taking care of family drive Cummings's activism as she continues to advocate for social and political change in the lives of Métis and Non-Status women and children in her community and at provincial and national levels.

The women explored in this collection represent real and symbolic examples of the strength, resilience, and agency of Métis matriarchs. They embody resistance to the colonial and patriarchal ideology that has wrought systemic violence perpetrated against Indigenous women and girls. This systemic violence has persisted since the forced displacement of Indigenous peoples and the historical interference in their societal structures. The evidence of strong Métis communities that continues through the generations is constituted by the transmission of cultural knowledge that manifested in the lives of the Métis women explored in this collection and invites us to expand our exploration of Métis history further. These stories challenge and disrupt the narrative of the Canadian state that has long dominated the presentation of the lives of Indigenous women. Their lives and examples invite us to appreciate and to further explore the roles of Métis matriarchs as agents of transition and transmission, both during the fur trade when the Métis developed as a nation and into the present as they continue to serve integral roles as knowledge keepers and leaders of their Métis communities.

NOTES

1. Macdougall and St-Onge, "Rooted in Mobility"; Troupe, "Métis Women"; Macdougall, *One of the Family*; Foster, *We Know Who We Are*; Devine, *The People Who Own Themselves*; Payment, *The Free People*
2. Oral histories and oral history collections that relate to the Prairie Métis experience and reveal the contributions of Métis women in different stages of their lives are held by the Gabriel Dumont Institute of Native Studies and Applied Research (www.metismuseum.ca), the Provincial Archives of Saskatchewan, the Provincial Archives of Manitoba, and other repositories. There is also a growing body of autobiographies, oral stories, memoirs, and community histories based on this oral history that reveals women's roles within their families and communities. See Campbell, *Halfbreed*; Zeileg and Zeileg, *Ste. Madeleine*; Harpelle, *My Children Are My Reward*; Belcourt, *Walking in the Woods*; Riviere, *Washing at the Creek*; St. Pierre, *Remembering My Métis Past*; Moine, *Remembering Will Have to Do*; Oster and Lizee, *Stories of Métis Women*.
3. Anderson, *Life Stages and Native Women*, 134.
4. Van Kirk, *Many Tender Ties*.
5. For discussion of Indigenous removal from the prairie region, see Ray, Miller, and Tough, eds., *Bounty and Benevolence*; Miller, *Compact, Contract, Covenant*; and Daschuk, *Clearing the Plains*.

6   Carter et al., *Unsettled Pasts*, 4.
7   Carter, *Imperial Plots*.
8   Brown, *Strangers in Blood*; Van Kirk, *Many Tender Ties*; Brown, "Woman as Centre and Symbol," 39–46.
9   Murphy, *A Gathering of Rivers*; Thorne, *The Many Hands of My Relations*; Sleeper-Smith, *Indian Women and French Men*.
10 Sleeper-Smith, "Women, Kin, and Catholicism," 423–52.
11 Sleeper-Smith, *Indian Women and French Men*.
12 Carter, *The Importance of Being Monogamous*. As many historians have now concluded, the concept of punishing Indigenous women for "marrying out" was a manifestation of the Indian Act, instituted in 1876, and aimed at saving money and forcing Indigenous people to adopt European Christian standards of patriarchal and monogamous marital unions.
13 Van Kirk, "Toward a Feminist Perspective in Native History," 6.
14 Macdougall, *One of the Family*; Macdougall, "Wahkootowin: Family and Cultural Identity," 431–62.
15 MacKinnon, *Metis Pioneers*; MacKinnon, *The Identities of Marie Rose Delorme Smith*; Troupe, "Mapping Métis Stories"; Payment, *The Free People*; St-Onge, "Memories of Metis Women," 90–111.
16 Troupe, "Métis Women"; Macdougall and St-Onge, "Rooted in Mobility."
17 Troupe, "Mapping Métis Stories."
18 Troupe, "Mapping Métis Stories"; LaVallee, *The Metis of St. Laurent*; Payment, "Batoche after 1885"; Payment, *The Free People*; St-Onge, "Memories of Metis Women."
19 Sealey and Lucier, *The Métis: Canada's Forgotten People*; McLean, *Home from the Hill*; Barron, *Walking in Indian Moccasins*; Barron, "The CCF and the Development of Métis Colonies"; Quiring, *CCF Colonialism in Northern Saskatchewan*.
20 Farrell Racette, "Nimble Fingers and Strong Backs"; Farrell Racette, "Sewing for a Living."
21 Sleeper-Smith, *Indian Women and French Men*.
22 Adams, Dahl, and Peach, *Métis in Canada*, xviii.
23 Kearns, "(Re)claiming Métis Women Identities."
24 Kearns, "(Re)claiming Métis Women Identities," 60.
25 Todd, "Honouring Our Great-Grandmothers."
26 Brown, "Woman as Centre and Symbol." See Payment, *The Free People*; Ens, *Homeland to Hinterland*; Devine, *The People Who Own Themselves*; Foster, *We Know Who We Are*; Troupe, "Métis Women"; Macdougall,

One of the Family; Macdougall and St-Onge, "Rooted in Mobility"; Troupe, "Mapping Métis Stories."

27 Carpenter, *Fifty Dollar Bride*.

One

Marie Rose Delorme Smith
"Buckskin Mary—Queen of the Jughandle" (1861–1960)

by Doris Jeanne MacKinnon

INTRODUCED TO READERS IN 1977 BY HER GRAND-daughter Jock Carpenter in the book *Fifty Dollar Bride: Marie Rose Smith—A Chronicle of Métis Life in the 19th Century*, Marie Rose (Delorme) Smith's life spanned nearly one century. At the age of sixteen, Marie Rose was married to a robe and whiskey trader seventeen years her senior after a transaction negotiated by her mother. Recognizing that Charlie Smith was a trader of some worth, Marie Rose's mother extended her network at a time when the Prairies were transitioning to a sedentary economy. For his part, Charlie appreciated Marie Rose's worth. Conversant in French, English, and Cree, she had traversed the Plains for years with her Métis parents who followed the traditional lifestyle of farming, buffalo hunting, and trading. Together Marie Rose and Charlie, as she put it, "followed the treaties,"[1] amassing enough wealth to travel from present-day Alberta to Montana, and to gather a herd of cattle, which they transported to southern Alberta, becoming among the first settlers in the Pincher Creek area. Soon joined by her mother and many of her Métis family members who settled near her in southern Alberta, Marie Rose managed the ranch and raised seventeen children while her husband maintained a somewhat independent lifestyle by setting off regularly from their home to hunt and trade. Marie Rose was proud of her own independence, referring to herself in her writing as "Queen of the Jughandle."[2] As a widow who lived over forty years after Charlie passed, Marie Rose took a second homestead while also maintaining a boarding house and serving as a midwife. Taking a second homestead was not a common practice for women, and particularly not for Indigenous women.[3] Marie Rose was only able to stake a claim to that homestead due to the fact that she was a widow and by that time considered to be the head of her household.

In a short series of articles published in the periodical *Canadian Cattlemen*, Marie Rose chronicled her experiences, demonstrating her resilience and her ability to adapt to the changing social structure, all while maintaining and expanding her family and community networks.[4] In addition to the published articles, Marie Rose wrote a book-length manuscript[5] in which she recorded her experiences as a Métis woman establishing herself as matriarch of a large family who continued to rely on their Métis culture and identity to survive in a transitioning Prairie economy and society. By the time of her death in 1960 at the age of ninety-nine, Marie Rose was a respected pioneer of southern Alberta. She was a published author, medicine woman, chronicler of the role of Métis women, and homesteader, and was known by many as "Buckskin Mary" in recognition of her skills in traditional Métis leather and beadwork.[6] By virtue of her experiences and her choice to record them, Marie Rose made an important

FIG. 1.01. *(left)* Marie Rose as a young girl, c. 1877. This image appeared on the cover of grand-daughter Jock Carpenter's book *Fifty Dollar Bride*, published in 1977. Given the age of the image, it is difficult to determine any background where it may have been taken. It is the only surviving photo of Marie Rose as she may have looked when she first encountered the man who was to become her husband. FIG. 1.02. *(right)* Donald McCargar, great-grandson of Marie Rose, c. 1965, wearing buckskin clothing made by Marie Rose. Donald would have been approximately three years of age and the photo was likely taken in the city of Edmonton, where Marie Rose lived with her grand-daughter (Donald's mother) when she was in her nineties. According to Donald, this clothing was made by Marie Rose and worn by a number of her grandchildren through the years.

contribution to our knowledge of the roles of Métis women as they adapted to cultural change on the Prairies when the fur trade transitioned to a more sedentary and agricultural economy. Indeed, Marie Rose's presentation of this transition is passive in the sense that there is little to no acknowledgement of the devastating collapse of Métis traditional economies and the large-scale dispossession of the Métis from their communities.

Getting to Know Marie Rose

> I was very excited as any other little girl might be, who, at the early age of ten years, was embarking on a winter trip over the great western plains, from the Great Lakes to the Rocky Mountains. The rising sun was just beginning its morning dance on the grey-white waters of the Assiniboine River, as my father, Urbain Delorme, with all his household sat down to the early morning meal. To-day, October 5th, 1871, father was taking all of us on his annual fur-trading trip into the great North-west, and for the winter months, we must bid "Au revoir" to the farm on White Horse Plains, and until our arrival back in the spring, father would now be known as Trader Delorme.[7]

These were the words of a young Marie Rose Delorme as her father was about to set out with his Métis family on their annual hunting and trading trip over the Plains from their summer home on their small plot of land in the Red River area.[8]

Marie Rose was of the last generation of Métis to live both a traditional seasonal lifestyle following the herds on the western Plains and that of a homesteading pioneer and rancher. Born in St. François Xavier, Red River, on October 18, 1861, she experienced first-hand the Métis transition from their traditional life as buffalo hunters to that of sedentary landholders in a commercialized and industrialized economy. Marie Rose was a descendant of Métis who were active in the political and economic life of Red River. Her grandfather Urbain Delorme Sr., an ally of Cuthbert Grant (now recognized as a person of national historic significance), was widely known as "le chef des Prairies" for his work as a captain of Métis hunting brigades. He had joined other Métis free traders, including Louis Riel Sr., in their opposition to the attempt by the Hudson's Bay Company (HBC) to control trade in the Red River—opposition that in 1849 resulted in victory for the Métis during what has come to be known as the Sayer Trial.[9] The conflict that led to this trial was the result of the HBC attempting to thwart the traditional Métis economy in which they were established as fur traders. Although the HBC had long been reliant on the labour of the Métis, by the mid-1800s, the fur trade company sought and failed in their attempts to isolate the predominantly French-speaking Métis from the fur trade.[10] Urbain Delorme Sr.'s sons Norbert and Joseph Delorme remained active in the Red River economy and leadership, joining Louis Riel in challenging incoming central Canadian government officials and settlers in 1869–70 and 1885.

Marie Rose's father, Urbain, would likely have joined Louis Riel's soldiers had he not died at a young age before the conflict of 1869–70. Shortly after his death, Marie Rose's mother married Cuthbert Gervais, and the family continued engaging in the Métis buffalo hunt economy. Marie Rose's father, however, had left money so his daughters could receive a westernized education. At the age of twelve, Marie Rose began attending the boarding school operated by the Grey Nuns in Saint Boniface, Manitoba, where she learned to read and write in French and English. At the age of sixteen, after having rejoined her mother and stepfather on the trail, Marie Rose was "traded" to Norwegian robe and whiskey trader Charlie Smith, seventeen years her senior, for the sum of fifty dollars paid to her mother. Marie Rose writes that this was an unsettling experience for her, and that she tried desperately to convince her mother to change her mind.

While Marie Rose wrote of her mother's marriage arrangement, we don't know exactly when she recorded her thoughts. Of course, we can reasonably assume that most of Marie Rose's writing was done later in her life. With seventeen children, a ranch and small cottage industry in buckskin items to manage and maintain, and a husband who continued his lifestyle in which he was away from the ranch for extended periods, there was not much time for writing. Given her busy life, it is not clear when Marie Rose recorded her memories of how she came to be Charlie's wife, but it is important to note that she would have recognized that her audience would primarily be non-Indigenous settlers and ranchers.

In her own words, Marie Rose described her first meeting with Charlie:

> As we neared the house, the three of us hurried real fast, and then Charlie caught hold of me, saying something. I was so frightened I knew not what his words were, but just cried out, "Yes, yes, let me go!" Where upon he kissed me and loosed his hold. I ran like a wild antelope trying to catch up with my sister and brother before they entered the house. I was still trembling with fear as we entered the door, for we girls were not allowed alone with men... "Oh, say Mother," I cried, "you know that white man...he grabbed me and began to talk...But first he kissed me." So ended my courting days.[11]

Marie Rose then went on to explain the ensuing transaction between her mother and Charlie, writing:

The next day, this big Norwegian trader, with his flat sleigh and jingling harness, drove up to our house. He was warmly greeted by my mother and step-father. There was much pleasant conversation between the three, and then Smith asked my mother for permission to marry me. As she looked surprised he said, "I asked her yesterday, and she said, 'Yes.'" "But I didn't know what he was saying," I shouted at them. It made no difference. It was settled between my parents and Charlie right then and Charlie gave my mother a present of fifty dollars. Was I not then sold for that sum? After Charlie left mother called me to her, "Come here, Marie Rose, you promised to marry that man"... I tried over and over again to explain, but it was useless... So I, a little girl of sixteen years, was forced into marriage with a man twenty years my senior, and of whom I knew nothing.[12]

In speaking of her adjustment to married life, Marie Rose wrote:

That year was the most unhappy one of all my life. Day after day I went away by myself and cried; surely God would perform some miracle on my behalf. But for the fact that my parents travelled with us all that summer and I could still be with my brothers and sister, I fear I could not have endured my married life, for when night came and I was alone with my stranger husband, alone in a camp of our own, such fear seized me, that I bound my clothes about me with raw hide ropes. "Beat her into submission," was the advice given to my husband. But Charlie was patient and determined to win me through love.[13]

From Marie Rose's writing, it appears that she grew to appreciate Charlie's approach to his marriage to a young girl. It is also clear that Marie Rose grew to cherish her growing independence and her ability to establish an important role for herself, both in her own family, and in the southern Alberta community where she would spend most of her adult life.

After amassing enough money to buy a herd of cattle, Marie Rose and Charlie first settled in the Edmonton area, but as she notes, "my husband did not like Edmonton area."[14] The couple eventually settled in southern Alberta, establishing the Jughandle Ranch in 1880 near present-day Pincher Creek. Eventually many of Marie Rose's Métis family also settled in this area, following the pattern of many Métis families as they left the Red River area.

Marie Rose and Charlie were among the first pioneers in Pincher Creek. In the only known recording of her voice, at the age of ninety-six, Marie Rose reminisced about the "beautiful country" in which she had settled. As she recalled, "there were no white people" when she and Charlie "followed the treaties." On the shores of Pincher Creek, Marie Rose noted that game was plentiful. "We lived very, very nice...we live happy....It was nice country....I talk Cree...I talk three languages...I talk the French...I talk the English...I talk the Cree."[15]

Speaking Cree, the language of the fur trade, remained useful to Marie Rose as she established herself in southern Alberta. She noted that she traded regularly with First Nations people who came to her ranch for items she used in her traditional leather work. Marie Rose gained a reputation for this work, making and selling items to settlers as well as to those who were beginning to promote the southern Prairies as a tourism destination. She was proud to share that she had made the traditional clothing that was worn by staff at the Prince of Wales hotel in Waterton.[16] The Jughandle Ranch remained Marie Rose's home for much of her adult life. Here, she gave birth without medical intervention to her seventeen children. As well as maintaining important trade relations with Indigenous peoples, Marie Rose hosted many well-known southern Albertans over the years, including John George "Kootenai" Brown, Sir Frederick W. Lynch-Staunton, Colonel James Macleod, "Lord" Lionel Brooke, Father Albert Lacombe, William Gladstone, and Billy Walsh (also known in prairie folklore as Billy the Kid). Widowed in 1914, Marie Rose went on to operate a boarding house, serve as a medicine woman and midwife, stake a second homestead, and become a published author. Living almost one century, Marie Rose recorded her experiences as a Métis woman who continued to rely on the skills she learned from her mother, as well as on her experiences as one of the first homesteaders, ranchers, and woman entrepreneurs in southern Alberta. While alive, Marie Rose gained recognition as an

FIG. 1.03. Marie Rose with other pioneers in the Pincher Creek area. Marie Rose is in the front row, third from the right. Standing to her right is Kootenai Brown, first park warden of Waterton Lakes National Park. Standing to the right of Kootenai Brown is Charlie Smith. The photo was taken in front of the Jughandle Ranch in the Pincher Creek area, where Marie Rose and Charlie settled as a married couple and raised their seventeen children. Date unknown.

important pioneer and was sought out by newspapers and local historians to relate her experiences. Her personal papers were referenced by the biographer of John George "Kootenai" Brown, the first park warden of Waterton Lakes National Park.[17]

In addition to publishing some of her lifetime reminiscences in *Canadian Cattlemen*, Marie Rose also wrote short stories that featured a female protagonist who appears to be based upon her creator. Although her fiction remains unpublished, it forms part of the Marie Rose Smith fonds at the Glenbow Library and Archive Western Research Centre at the University of Calgary (formerly the Glenbow Museum),[18] along with an autobiographical chronicle of her life, as well as correspondence, photographs, news clippings, and greeting cards.

While Marie Rose (Delorme) Smith's family recognized the value of her personal papers by donating them to a public archive in the 1960s, it was not until the twenty-first century that scholars engaged with them to share Marie Rose's story with a wider audience. Sherry Farrell Racette, Helen Buss, and Maggie MacKellar each referenced the archival collection in their writing.[19] The first comprehensive studies of Marie Rose were conducted by the author of the present chapter, with subsequent full-length publications in 2012 and 2018.[20] In addition to the Marie Rose Delorme Smith fonds located at the Glenbow, other material about her is located in smaller local archives in Western Canada, and several family members also shared memories of Marie Rose with this author. As a non-Indigenous researcher and author, it was important to the author that her efforts as a settler ally were welcome by Marie Rose's family members. As that relationship was established and grew into one of respectful inquiry and sharing, the story of Marie Rose's life and important contributions to the retention and resilience of Métis identity and culture emerged.

This extensive research and storytelling led to the discovery that Marie Rose had written a detailed manuscript about her life and about prairie history that she had hoped to publish with Macmillan Publishers. There is evidence in Marie Rose's papers held by the Glenbow of some interest in publishing her work: a letter from the MacMillan Company of Canada, dated July 22, 1938, confirms that the company was awaiting delivery of the manuscript for possible publication.[21] This manuscript text was the source of material for the serial articles published in *Canadian Cattlemen*. I also located (and shared with family members) an audio recording of an interview of Marie Rose, conducted by local historian H.G. Baalim in 1957.[22] Marie Rose's writing represents a key reason for her historical significance. She is recognized as an important Métis chronicler of the roles of Métis women during the fur trade and of the transitional life and cultural change on the Prairies. While Marie Rose's published articles long remained available only in the physical archives in Pincher Creek, renewed interest in the early writing of Métis women recently led to those articles being made available to the public on the website of *Canadian Cattlemen*.[23] Interest in the life and historical significance of Marie Rose (Delorme) Smith has continued to grow. Beyond the publications, evidence of this is found in the recent designation by Parks Canada of Marie Rose as a person of "national historic significance."[24]

The Significance of Her Life

While Marie Rose's life story has become more accessible in recent years, she was recognized as a Métis pioneer of some significance even during her lifetime. Emma Lynch-Staunton, a rancher who settled near Marie Rose in the 1890s, also wrote, and published some articles about her in local newspapers.[25] The fact that Marie

Rose, a Métis woman, was featured in these articles is rare and speaks to her networking and survival skills, as well as the resilience of her Métis culture and identity. According to her daughter Mary Hélène Smith Parfitt, the skills that Marie Rose learned "at her Mother's knee," such as "beading, cooking with native roots and herbs, tanning skins, making soap, [and] drying meat," helped to keep the family fed and well looked after.[26] According to an article written by Mary Hélène, her mother worked as a midwife and "spent countless hours making buckskin articles,"[27] a skill which earned her the name "Buckskin Mary."[28]

Marie Rose's storytelling skills were also recognized by readers of the southern Alberta newspapers. In one instance, a woman from Utah wrote a letter to the *Lethbridge Herald* asking to be notified when Marie Rose's full-length book was available for readers. In the letter, Mrs. Hyrum Ririe references a November 14, 1941, article in which Lynch-Staunton referred to the anticipated book.[29]

Like her daughter Mary Hélène's comment above, during an interview that Marie Rose gave to Harry Baalim just a few years before her death in 1960, she was still referred to as "Buckskin Mary." In her own writing, she described her contract work with the Canadian Pacific Railway, payment for which she often exchanged for food. Her contracts involved making tents for the railway construction crews, as well as shirts for the men. Marie Rose felt that this was a tremendous responsibility, doing her "bit for the two great companies." This tremendous responsibility allowed Marie Rose to set up what we might refer to now as a cottage industry, when she hired "two half-breed women" to help her fulfill her contracts. As Marie Rose noted of her many duties, "with my buckskin work of shirts, gloves and all wearing garments; tents for habitation; cooking in my boarding house; and running a homestead, you will think that I never hesitated to lay my hand to any work that called for my attention."[30] It is with pride that

FIG. 1.04. Marie Rose as a young mother. This photo was taken in a studio, likely in the Pincher Creek area. Family members are not clear on which of Marie Rose's seventeen children appear in the photo. Date unknown.

Marie Rose shared with readers her ability to contribute to the household economy. Indeed, this was very much the case given that Charlie continued his journeys across the Plains for much of their married life, at times being away for extended periods. Marie Rose also spoke of contract work, which involved making a beaded buckskin blouse and beaded moccasins for the "checking girl at the hotel in Waterton Lakes Park."[31] She wrote that, when Charlie saw how interested she was in buckskin work, "he gave me a wonderful surprise. On one of his semi-annual trips to Fort Macleod for supplies, he returned at the end of two weeks and brought me—yes—a brand new sewing machine. I thought that the whole wide world was mine."[32] Marie Rose continued that she was "young, full of energy and ambitious," and that she always had pocket money for her children and herself.[33]

Marie Rose was clearly proud of the fact that she was able to provide for her seventeen children. In addition to the small cottage industry that she established in making traditional beadwork, she often managed the ranch to some success while Charlie continued to traverse the Plains. There was a time when Marie Rose and Charlie amassed what some family members believe was a substantial estate. In fact, according to an interview given on his hundredth birthday, J.R. "Bob" Smith claimed that his parents Marie Rose and Charlie "ran a herd of 1,000 head of cattle on the Jughandle."[34] While some family members believe this may have been an exaggeration, the 1906 census does confirm that Charlie and Marie Rose held considerable property in comparison to other Métis people in the Pincher Creek area, and likely in comparison also to many non-Indigenous settlers at the time; specifically, they had two hundred horses, five milk cows, two hundred horned cattle, and four hogs. In comparison, that same year, Marie Rose's mother and stepfather, Cuthbert and Marie Gervais, had nine horses, four milk cows, six horned cattle, and four hogs. Marie Rose's stepsister and her husband, Zilda and Robert Gladstone, were similarly of lesser wealth, with eleven horses, eight milk cows, sixty horned cattle, and no hogs.[35]

Whatever the level of their material wealth, Marie Rose clearly appreciated the bounty of the land, as she described the life of those pioneers who were on the Prairies before what are now viewed as traditional farmers and their fences:

> The early rancher always squatted where he could find a spring and plenty of range with good hay land. They would put shacks and corrals on his holdings and ranged his cattle for miles around. About in November before the cold weather would come, the fall roundup commenced. The rancher and his men then rode the range continuously for about two months so as to have his cattle near the place so that when severe weather set in they would be close to hand to feed...cattle were always in good shape as grass grew abundantly and luxuriously.[36]

Indeed, in some of her writing Marie Rose wrote that "the fur trade really was the pioneer of civilization in the Northwest...my father was a fur trader amongst the Indians of the Plain. In his younger days he was a settler in the White Horse Plain, he took land west of Winnipeg staying on the land farming on a small scale."[37]

As a married woman, and as one of the earliest pioneers of the southern Alberta region, Marie Rose noted that when cowboys travelled to different locations to "ship their surplus stock," both Marie Rose and Charlie often went along as cooks, then carried on to Calgary to invest their earnings.[38] This additional work that Marie Rose and Charlie undertook as a couple speaks to their ability to diversify, and it explains the census records verifying their significant assets at times in their life together. As Marie Rose wrote, "No trip was too hard for us pioneer women to accompany our husbands."³⁹ In fact, Marie Rose undertook some extensive travel without her husband, reflecting her faith in her own abilities and independence. In 1882, when Charlie left in the spring to travel to Winnipeg, spending the whole summer there, Marie Rose was left with her three boys and a hired man to look after the cattle and horses. After carrying on alone for some time, Marie Rose writes, "[I grew] lonesome with only my small children and decided that I would rather suffer hardships of the trail than be subjected to the ugly attentions of this hireling.... Thus I made ready for the trip, heading toward Winnipeg, with a covered democrat, five head of horses, a tent, the necessary clothing and food enough to last until I would meet my husband, some where on his route back."⁴⁰ Marie Rose never did meet up with Charlie as he had very likely returned to the ranch by an alternate route, but she did make it to Winnipeg, some nine hundred miles across country. She was then joined by her mother and stepfather for the journey back to the Jughandle Ranch in Pincher Creek. Upon their arrival back at the ranch, Marie Rose noted that Charlie was beside himself with worry for his wife and children.

While Marie Rose's writing confirms the hard physical labour that she undertook, she also wrote about the socializing that she always enjoyed with her expanded network of family and community members. According to Marie Rose, entertainment for the Métis changed when their lives became more sedentary but still reflected some of the activities from previous days when, along with new activities like polo and gymkhana, many nights were spent dancing, singing, playing games, and racing horses.⁴¹ Indeed, scholar Jennifer Brown, in support of her argument of the need to study the detailed family histories of Métis women, speculated that the economic roles that some of them assumed afforded them the opportunity to maintain a sense of continuity with their past.⁴² This was clearly so for Marie Rose, as Mary

Hélène's testimony demonstrates that her mother's economic role resembled, in many ways, that of her Métis ancestors. Further, Marie Rose's granddaughter Shirley-Mae McCargar and great-grandson Barry McCartney both recalled Marie Rose's role as healer and noted that she had compiled a voluminous book detailing the natural remedies she relied upon when Indigenous people would come to her home for medical help.[43]

The role of healer was one typically reserved for powerful figures in Plains cultures, and, as historian Maureen Lux notes, most women who were healers were also midwives, skills they had learned from their own mothers.[44] Although Marie Rose did not mention her own work as a healer or a midwife, Jock Carpenter recalled that Jock's mother, Mary Hélène Smith Parfitt, related stories of Marie Rose's abilities: "Marie Rose let it be known that she would take in boarders and ladies-in-waiting. Women, feeling that their time to deliver was near, moved into the big house...Marie Rose's midwifery, carried on while she was at the ranch, increased now that she was in town."[45]

While historian Kristen Burnett wrote that Marie Rose's manuscript "contains no specific reference to interactions with Aboriginal women,"[46] Marie Rose actually did write about her relationships with Indigenous women, such as Olive D'Lonais, the Métis wife of her neighbour John George "Kootenai" Brown. Marie Rose also wrote about Brown's second wife, the Cree woman who she and Brown referred to as Ni-ti-mous. However, while Marie Rose's community and her descendants acknowledged her role as healer and midwife, in her own manuscripts she seemed to suggest at times that her knowledge of Indigenous healing was in terms of "their" practices, not hers. For example, she wrote that "for to doctor themselves they used the warth of poplar tree...they have a weed that grows in swamps...they call *ki-ni-ki-nick*."[47] It is important to remember, though, that as noted earlier, Marie Rose wrote her manuscripts in the early part of the twentieth century, a time when her audience was expected to be non-Indigenous settlers who were increasingly intent on establishing and maintaining rigid racial boundaries. Marie Rose astutely identified these new boundaries as she worked to expand her own community network. Her writings in no way suggest that she had abandoned her own Métis identity. In regard to the continuity with her Métis culture, often indicated by the retention of language, Mary Hélène reiterated what her mother herself said when interviewed at the age of ninety-six: that Marie Rose spoke Cree, French, and English. Mary Hélène did not indicate that Marie Rose understood Michif, the dialect developed by Métis people which used a combination of French and Cree.[48] However, it is highly likely that Marie Rose did understand Michif, given her family's roots in the Red River area. It may even be that, though they spoke Michif, the family did not refer to it as such.

It is also likely that Marie Rose continued to speak Michif when she settled in southern Alberta. As she noted herself in the interview she gave to Harry Baalim, when she and Charlie arrived in the Pincher Creek area, their only non-Indigenous neighbours were the North-West Mounted Police. Not long after Marie Rose and Charlie established the Jughandle Ranch in 1880, several of her Métis family members also settled there. Her mother, Marie Gervais, and stepfather, Cuthbert Gervais, settled in the Mountain Mill area, while her sister Madeleine and her husband Ludgar Gareau settled near the Jughandle Ranch. At various times, Marie Rose's brother Urbain Delorme and numerous aunts and uncles also lived near her. This followed the pattern for the Métis of settling as family units as they moved further west and north from the Red River area, displaced by colonial policies. As Diane Payment wrote, those who left Batoche after 1885 left not only for economic reasons but for social reasons. While the West was transitioning and there were new opportunities for work, the Métis who settled in southern Alberta often did so with extended family networks, thus ensuring survival strategies as well as the retention of vibrant Métis communities.[49]

Much of Marie Rose's writing was about the community network that she established in southern Alberta. One of her close neighbours and long-time friends was prairie character John George "Kootenai" Brown, the first park warden of Waterton Lakes National Park. Marie Rose was clearly curious about her new network, particularly those such as Brown who had travelled the world. However, rather than portraying him as a folk hero as some have,[50] Marie Rose saw Kootenai for the rounded character that he was. While recognizing him as a "clever, well-educated man,"[51] she also noted that he was somewhat lazy, and that he luckily had his Cree wife Ni-ti-mous to "rustle his food."[52] Marie Rose also wrote about political figures such as Frederick Haultain, premier of the North-West Territories, who she notes was a frequent visitor to the Jughandle Ranch as he came "up to these reunions as one of the boys."[53] While not really acknowledging the historical significance, Marie Rose also wrote about Annie Saunders, one of the first independent businesswomen in southern Alberta. Descendant of enslaved African-Americans, Saunders had met Mary Drever Macleod on a steamboat travelling the Missouri River from Fort Benton, Montana. Saunders initially came to southern Alberta to serve as housemaid to Colonel Macleod's family before venturing out to operate her own laundry, restaurant, and boarding house in Pincher Creek.[54] While Marie Rose did not explicitly acknowledge the significance of the accomplishments of Annie Saunders, she clearly wanted her readers to know that Annie was a part of her own network, noting on several occasions that she had visited at the Macleod residence. At the same time, Marie Rose seemed to feel a need to identify more closely, at least in her written words, with the non-Indigenous settler community, referring to Saunders as the "colored" housemaid "Auntie."[55]

After Charlie passed away, Marie Rose continued with her entrepreneurial work, managing the ranch and producing buckskin articles for sale. Now, as the head of her family, she demonstrated her resilience and adaptability. She moved her family into the town of Pincher Creek where she operated a boarding house and took a second homestead. According to her daughter Mary Hélène, "the Indians too, came to town as they had done on the ranch, seeking treatment for eye infections. Boiling a herb the way Mother Gervais taught her, Marie Rose bathed the infected eyes with the cooled liquid and soon the redness and draining disappeared.... Marie Rose put in many years of midwifery and the doctors were disgruntled at not being called to deliver the babies. Soon Marie Rose had a letter from officials in Edmonton telling her that she must desist from this practice."[56]

Political Realities

While Marie Rose Delorme Smith was very successful at establishing herself as a Métis matriarch and as an independent businessperson in southern Alberta, it is important to remember that her Métis family were French-speaking Métis who had supported Louis Riel both in 1869–70 and in 1885. Her uncles served as soldiers and eventually fled to points further west or across the border. It is also important to note that French-speaking Métis were increasingly isolated within the HBC culture as the fur trade transitioned. While they had been integral to the fur trade's early success, after the merger of the North West Company and the HBC, the HBC sought to isolate French-speaking Métis. One clear example of this is the conflict known as the Sayer Trial, spoken of in another section of this chapter. Another example is the conflict between the fur trading companies and François Beaulieu, patriarch of the northern Métis. Beaulieu was distrusted by the HBC partly because of his ties to the Oblate missionaries.[57] This meant that Métis connections, while still very important to the survival of Métis families, were sometimes relegated to periods of silence as more and more non-Indigenous settlers arrived in the western Prairies.

For Métis women, there were times on the Prairies when it was key to establish links with non-Indigenous community members and leaders. It is clear that Marie Rose was successful at establishing such connections, no doubt due in part to the fact that she was married to a non-Indigenous settler. When Charlie died without having proven his ownership of all of the

FIG. 1.05. Marie Rose's boarding house in Pincher Creek, where Sir Lionel Brooke was one of her boarders, and where she also served as a midwife. Marie Rose left her daughters to operate the boarding house as she spent time on her new homestead. The house no longer exists. Date unknown.

homestead property as required by policies under the Dominion Lands Act, Marie Rose's network in the business and ranching community came to her aid. While there is no clarity in the documented records or from the oral history shared by family members as to their financial struggles, what is clear is that by this time, when she was widowed, much of the couple's material wealth had been expended. Not only did Marie Rose's network write letters to the government land office, they even provided the funds to ensure a respectable funeral service for Charlie. Helpful to Marie Rose's struggling finances at the time was the fact that an important prairie character, the British remittance man, Sir Lionel Brooke, spent his final years as a boarder in Marie Rose's house in Pincher Creek.

While it is not altogether clear, as noted earlier, exactly when Marie Rose did most of her writing, and even less clear what motivated her to write, she composed a brief fictional piece that provides some insight into how she reconciled the conflicts impacting many of the Métis as the Northwest transitioned from the fur trade to a sedentary industrialized and agricultural economy. As a way to perhaps help her readers understand the setting for the conflicts that involved some of her family members in the Red River in 1869–70 and 1885, Marie Rose wrote in a short fictional essay that, when central Canadian government surveyors came to stake claims on previously occupied Métis land, the Métis protested this was a "deprivation of their rights, in vain they protested that the ties of their little farms were dear to them. Claim-jumpers took advantage of the turmoil." She told the potential readers of her fiction, "It all seems incomprehensible and unimportant now, but to the few half starving Métis then it was a matter of life."[58] In this instance, Marie Rose displayed an understanding of the realities for some classes of Métis as more English-speaking settlers arrived in the West. Marie Rose even identified the hypocrisy of officials, writing, "If a half-breed purloined a pair of stockings from the Hudson's Bay store he was punished quickly enough; but if some body trespassed on his land and cut his timber, he was informed that there was no redress, that he had no property right in the soil or trees."[59]

Indeed, it would only be many years after Marie Rose's death in 1960 that the Métis would obtain redress for their concerns. In fact, there continue to be ongoing political activities and petitions to obtain that redress. For her part, Marie Rose was recognized as an important Métis matriarch upon her death. Her obituary in the *Pincher Creek Echo* on April 7, 1960, described her as one of the area's "most colourful figures," and one of southern Alberta's earliest and oldest pioneers.[60] Indeed, Marie Rose witnessed the transformation of the western Prairies, which she often described as a place of beauty and unfenced freedom, to a land governed by industrialized agriculture. Her association with legendary local personalities, and her desire to record her experiences as one of the earliest pioneers on the Prairies, likely contributed to her reputation as a "colourful figure," and indeed make her an important historical character in her own right.

At the end of the interview that she gave at the age of ninety-six, Marie Rose broke into song, laughing at herself because she struggled to remember all of the words. Yet, nearing the end of her long and eventful life, the song that Marie Rose chose to share was "Red River Valley." As she sang, Marie Rose replaced the more well-known lyric "cowboy that loves you so true" with "half-breed that loves you so true." While the interviewer noted this, as he believed the omitted verse to be the more well-known version, Marie Rose's version was also popular.[61] To this important Métis matriarch, her life as an early pioneer of southern Alberta always harkened back to her roots in the Red River.

NOTES

1 Marie Rose Delorme Smith, "Eighty Years on the Plains," file 4:80. Though Marie Rose and Charlie were not part of the treaty-making process that was underway in the North-Western Territory at that time, they did as many other traders did in trading with First Nations people who had entered into treaty. Marie Rose Smith Fonds, Glenbow Library and Archive Western Research Centre (formerly the Glenbow Alberta Institute Archives; hereafter cited as Glenbow).

2 Marie Rose Delorme Smith, "Tribulations of Mrs. C. Smith of Pincher Creek Alta by Mrs. C. Smith," n.d., transcribed by Ben Montgomery, GAIA, Accession No. 998.121.19, File 6: 2.

3 Carter, *Imperial Plots*. Carter explores the homestead rules as they applied to women on the Prairies, and the goals, aspirations, and challenges for those women who sought land of their own.

4 Canadian Cattlemen, "Eighty Years on the Plains: Part 1," June 1948, *Canadian Cattlemen: The Beef Magazine*, https://www.canadiancattlemen.ca/history/eighty-years-on-the-plains-part-1/. While for many years these articles were only available in the archival material on Marie Rose Delorme Smith held by the Kootenai Brown Pioneer Historical Village in Pincher Creek, interest in Marie Rose's story led the *Canadian Cattlemen* periodical to list all of the articles, in the series entitled *Eighty Years on the Plains*, on their website https://www.canadiancattlemen.ca.

5 Smith, "Eighty Years on the Plains," GAIA, Marie Rose Smith Fonds, File 4.

6 Parks Canada, "Marie Rose (Delorme) Smith National Historic Person (1861-1960)," https://parks.canada.ca/culture/designation/personnage-person/marie-rose-delorme. In January 2023, the Historic Sites and Monuments Board of Canada recognized the national historic significance of Marie Rose Delorme Smith. A public announcement was made confirming this recommendation by Parks Canada's National Program of Historical Commemoration. The location of the permanent marker is to be determined at a later date.

7 Smith, "Eighty Years on the Plains," box 1, file 4.

8 Smith, "Eighty Years on the Plains."

9 Fortier, "Urbain Delorme," Société historique de Saint-Boniface. Centre du patrimoine. https://shsb.mb.ca.

10 John E. Foster, "Sayer Trial," *The Canadian Encyclopedia*. Historica Canada, article published February 7, 2006; last edited February 24, 2015, https://www.thecanadianencyclopedia.ca/en/article/sayer-trial.

See also Devine, *The People Who Own Themselves*, 134–35. Sayer had worked in territories controlled by the North West Company until the merger with the HBC in 1821. After working for the HBC until 1829, Sayer again engaged with a competing fur trade company in North Dakota. When brought to trial, Sayer was supported by Louis Riel Sr. and other Métis who surrounded the courthouse. Under pressure, Justice Adam Thom found Sayer guilty but levied no penalty, leading the Métis to declare that free trade was won. While there were three other Métis arrested and charged with illegally trading furs, Sayer was the first and only brought to trial. As Devine notes, these free traders had succeeded in undermining the HBC monopoly. However, the decline in big game populations forced woodlands people onto the plains, where buffalo herds soon disappeared as well. Thus, free traders from Red River were really not able to capitalize on their victory.

11 Smith, "Eighty Years on the Plains," 69–70.
12 Smith, "Eighty Years on the Plains," 69–70.
13 Smith, "Eighty Years on the Plains," 73.
14 Smith, "Interview by Harry Baalim," late 1950s, Glenbow, Accession No. RAT-2-3.
15 Smith, "Interview by Harry Baalim."
16 Smith, "Tales of Wild West," file 3:71–72, Marie Rose Smith Fonds.
17 Rodney, *Kootenai Brown*.
18 Marie Rose Delorme Smith fonds, Record No. M1154, PA 385, NA 2539, Glenbow.
19 Farrell Racette, "Sewing for a Living"; Buss, "Constructing Female Subjects in the Archive"; MacKellar, *Core of My Heart*.
20 MacKinnon, *Métis Pioneers*; MacKinnon, *The Identities of Marie Rose Delorme Smith*.
21 Marie Rose Delorme Smith fonds, file 2, Glenbow. Archivist Karl Spadoni with the William Ready Special Collection Library at McMaster University, which holds the Macmillan Archives, notes that no further records exist that could confirm whether the manuscript was ever received.
22 Marie Rose Smith, "Interviews with Pioneers: Peigan Pow-Wow Nature Sounds," interview by H.G. Baalim, 1957, Accession No. RAT 2–3, Glenbow. Baalim was a local businessman and civic booster who hosted a local history program on CJLH-TV, *Remember When*, and lived in Calgary in the 1960s. CJLH-TV, established in 1955 as a partnership between CJOC Radio and the *Lethbridge Herald*, was the predecessor of Global TV, but there is no evidence that the interview with Marie Rose was ever broadcast on television.

23 Retrieved from canadiancattlemen.ca.
24 Parks Canada, "Government of Canada Recognizes."
25 Emma Lynch-Staunton, "Eighty Years on the Plains: The Story of Mrs. Charles Smith, Pincher Creek," *Lethbridge Herald*, November 14, 1941, 16.
26 Smith Parfitt, *Prairie Grass to Mountain Pass*, 249.
27 Smith Parfitt, *Prairie Grass to Mountain Pass*, 249.
28 Marie Rose Delorme Smith, interview by Harry Baalim.
29 Mrs. Hyrum Ririe, Lewiston, UT, to Mrs. Charles Smith, November 21, 1941, Marie Rose Delorme Smith fonds, file 2, Glenbow. Archivist Carl Spadoni with the William Ready Special Collections Library at McMaster University, which holds the Macmillan Archives, notes that no further records exist that could confirm whether a manuscript was ever received.
30 Smith, "Eighty Years on the Plains," 174.
31 Smith, "Eighty Years on the Plains," 23.
32 Smith, "Eighty Years on the Plains," 170.
33 Smith, untitled document, file 6, Marie Rose Delorme Smith fonds. In a note in file 6, no page number, Marie Rose wrote that she often exchanged gloves that she made for groceries.
34 Library and Archives Canada (LAC), Census Data, 1906: Reel T18361. Also Robert Byrne and Janet Byrne, interview by Doris J. MacKinnon, Robert Byrne provides a copy of a Sandpoint, Idaho, news article, undated, in which J.R. "Bob" Smith, the son of Marie Rose, was celebrating his hundredth birthday.
35 LAC, Census data, 1906: Reel T18361.
36 Smith, "The Adventures of the Wild West of 1870," box 1, file 3: 74, Marie Rose Delorme Smith fonds.
37 Smith, "The Adventures of the Wild West of 1870," 1.
38 Smith, "The Adventures of the Wild West of 1870," 74.
39 Smith, "Eighty Years on the Plains," 172.
40 Smith, "Eighty Years on the Plains," 73–74.
41 Smith, "Eighty Years on the Plains," 73–74.
42 Brown, "Woman as Centre and Symbol," 41.
43 Shirley-Mae McCargar and Barry McCartney in discussion with author, 2005.
44 Lux, *Medicine that Walks*, 92.
45 Carpenter, *Fifty Dollar Bride*, 119.
46 Burnett, *Taking Medicine*, 61.
47 Marie Rose Smith, untitled, file 6: 93, Marie Rose Delorme Smith fonds.

48 Crawford, "Speaking Michif in Four Métis Communities," 47–55. Crawford explains that Michif is a combination of French and Cree. This, combined with Marie Rose's ancestral history, indicates that she might have understood Michif.
49 Payment, *The Free People*, 200.
50 Rodney, *Kootenai Brown*.
51 Smith, Marie Rose Delorme Smith fonds, file 6: 81.
52 Smith, Marie Rose Delorme Smith fonds, file 6: 84.
53 Smith, "Eighty Years on the Plains," 107.
54 Smith, "Eighty Years on the Plains," 100. Marie Rose wrote that "Old Auntie" was "wont to claim that 'the Colonel's Lady and herself were the first ladies 'ob de land.'" Foggo, "Assembling Auntie," 34–39. Foggo studied the elusive Annie Saunders and believes she likely spent some thirty years enslaved before meeting Mary Macleod and "impulsively" accepting her invitation to come to Canada. Foggo surmises that Annie had a keen sense of humour and was fond of saying, "Me and Mrs. Macleod ... were the first white women in the region." Foggo, "Assembling Auntie," 36.
55 Smith, "Eighty Years on the Plains," 100.
56 Carpenter, *Fifty Dollar Bride*, 149.
57 McCarthy, *From the Great River to the Ends of the Earth*, 114. One example, which again involved William Hardisty, was the situation with Catherine Beaulieu, daughter of François, who married Joseph Bouvier of Red River. In 1878, Catherine, reacting to the anti-Catholicism of the HBC postmaster, John Reid, used her influence with Indigenous peoples in Providence so that they gave their grease and good meat to the Roman Catholic mission. Thereafter, William Hardisty "withdrew his recommendation that a pension be awarded to Mme Bouvier following the death of her husband." McCarthy, *From the Great River to the Ends of the Earth*, 110.
58 Smith, Marie Rose Delorme Smith fonds, "The Twenty Warnings," file 5:7.
59 Smith, "The Twenty Warnings," 7.
60 Pincher Creek Echo, KBPA.
61 Fowke, ed., *The Penguin Book of Canadian Folk Songs*, 204. "Red River Halfbreed," sometimes also referred to as "Red River Valley," was believed by some to be a reworking of a popular American song of 1896 entitled "In the Bright Mohawk Valley." However, research by Fowke suggests that the folk song was known in at least five Canadian provinces before 1896.

Two

Remembering and Retelling the Legacies of Métis Women in Alberta

The Life and Memories of Victoria Belcourt Callihoo[1]

by Madalyn Mandziuk

At the age of seventy-four, a Métis woman named Victoria Callihoo took home the top prize, a buffalo robe, at a Red River Jig competition held in Edmonton, Alberta, in 1936.[2] Known to many as "Granny Callihoo," or "Granny Victoria," Victoria did the jig again at her hundredth birthday party in 1962, a celebration well attended by her family and friends.[3] Born in 1861 at Lac Ste. Anne, a historic Métis community in north Central Alberta, Victoria's remarkable life and memories can be traced through her published stories, her countless descendants, and several written accounts of her life.[4] Indeed, before her passing in 1966, Victoria had witnessed the last of the buffalo hunts on the Prairies as a young girl, and recalled these hunts and her early life fondly in several interviews. Despite an adulthood marked by the rapid changes that characterized the late nineteenth and first half of the twentieth centuries in Alberta, Victoria remained rooted in her Métis community and culture by sharing her experiences.[5] Her memories of the buffalo hunts and life in Lac Ste. Anne have lived on in articles she published in the *Alberta Historical Review* late in her life.[6] Through these articles we gain insight into Métis life on the Prairies from the perspective of a Métis women. Victoria's memories are an invaluable contribution to our understanding of Métis lifeways and experience in nineteenth century Alberta, and when viewed alongside her life story, they become an even more powerful source to understand how such lifeways were created and sustained and how they remained dynamic through a changing landscape and social milieu.

Victoria Callihoo was born Victoria Anne Belcourt on November 9, 1861, to Alexis Belcourt and Nancy Rowan, both of Métis ancestry.[7] Victoria grew up in the Lac Ste. Anne area of Alberta, also known as Manito Sakahigan, a Métis community with close ties to the fur trade.[8] Victoria spent much of her adult life between the Lac Ste. Anne area and the Michel Reserve to the south, raising her children and engaging in a variety of economic activities. Victoria's son Vital shared stories of his mother during this time and wrote:

> My mother loved to go on walks in the woods being a great nature lover. One day while out with my brother Willie who was a teenager at the time, [they] were attracted by her dog's barking. They went to investigate and came across a den with a bear in it. This was in the springtime, about the time when the bears come out of hibernation. She sent my brother home for her gun which was a muzzle-loader while she held the bear at bay with a small hatchet. My brother returned with some

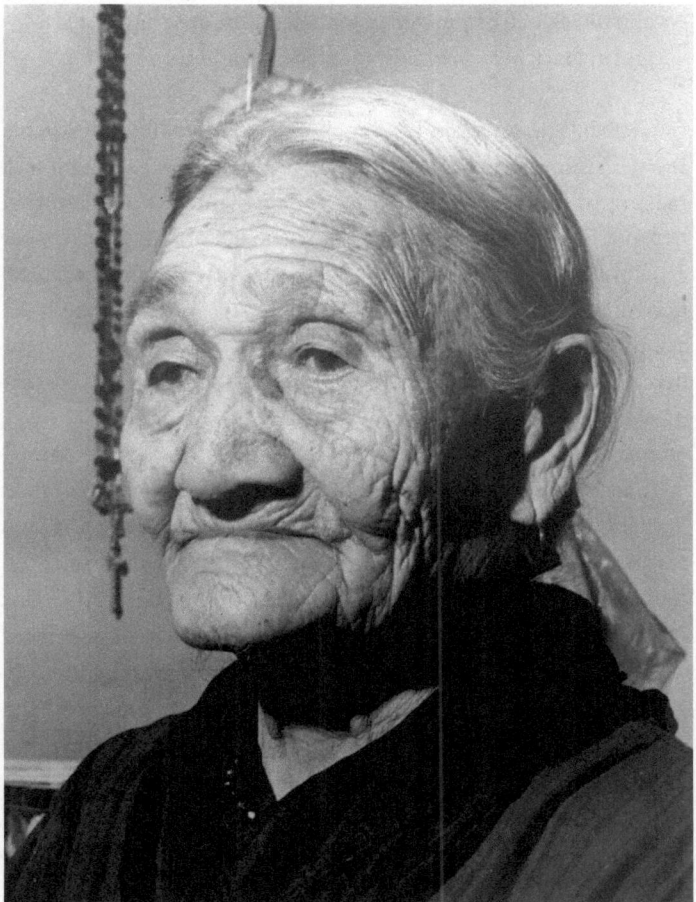

FIG. 2.01. Victoria Callihoo, c. February 18, 1962, at age of 101 years and three months. An original of this photo was found in the Grant MacEwan Fonds, University of Calgary. The inscription on the back of the photo reads, "Mrs. Victoria Callihoo, picture taken February 18, 1962, at age of 101 years and 3 months...Picture given to me by Mr. Vital Callihoo [son]...Dec. 3, 1970."

help as well as the gun, [and] when it was all over mother was amazed as well as frightened to find out the animal was a full-grown black bear weighing about five-hundred pounds.[9]

Victoria was an intrepid woman with an incredible spirit. This story is among many that demonstrate her skill and strength and make clear why her life and stories remain of interest. She recorded her memories late in life and was the subject of many newspaper articles. Most sources, including Victoria's family, indicate that she lived alone in her house into her late nineties, drawing water from a well and chopping her own wood.[10] Victoria was also remembered as "a great medicine woman; [and] many an expectant mother depended on her for the delivery of her children."[11] She was "often called to a dying person's bedside" and known for her knowledge of medicinal herbs; Vital described his mother as "a great herbalist."[12] Even in her late age Victoria continued to sew her own clothes—"every stitch by hand."[13] One of Victoria's handstitched dresses is currently held at the Rochfort Bridge Museum in Lac Ste. Anne—a long flowing dress made of fabric with a pattern of white flowers on a black background.[14] A vest beaded by Victoria is also displayed at the Musée Héritage in nearby St. Albert. The vest shows signs of wear and reflects Victoria's Métis culture and its expression through sewing and beading.[15]

Despite the many sources of information about Victoria and her personal memories, it is challenging to understand her specific motivation when she recorded her memories. The sources have left questions unanswered. Indeed, we learn of Victoria's life from three perspectives: her own, through her published memoirs; those of her family and those who knew her personally; and those of others who knew of her, notably author Grant MacEwan and several reporters.[16] These sources and narratives create complexities; they offer insight into both the challenges of writing about

FIG. 2.02. *(top)* Victoria Calihoo, seated in her own home. Date unknown. FIG. 2.03. *(bottom)* Front of vest handmade by Victoria Callihoo with cotton lining, c. 1950, currently located at the Musée Héritage Museum in St. Albert, Alberta.

the life of an Indigenous woman living within a colonial context and the ways in which Indigenous women were written about and how their lives were captured for a settler audience. What follows remains focused on verifiable information about Victoria's life, her own voice, and the voices of her family and descendants.

Victoria's memories as published in the *Alberta Historical Review* drew my interest in Victoria and her life. As a history student, I was excited to read historical work by an Indigenous woman, something especially uncommon at the time that Victoria's work was published. I am honoured to have talked with some of her descendants, many of whom had known her personally. Her family, and other Métis who shared their knowledge with me, were excited about her story being shared and retold in a new way. As a settler, I am especially humbled to share what I have learned. My goal for this retelling is best described in the words of one family member: "I think that it's nice that all this information is getting put together. So, there's a bigger picture, right? You know, not just little pieces here and there...but you know, it's all being put together, and that's wonderful."[17]

As a matriarch, Victoria is a point of connection for her descendants (numbering in the hundreds) to Métis culture and history. She leaves a legacy for the broader Métis community and for all Canadians. This is in part because of the wealth of information that exists about Victoria's life.[18] Indeed, there is no shortage of information on Victoria, which is not the case for many other Métis matriarchs. In addition to her own written material and the material culture currently on display, she has been featured in many local newspapers and mentioned in several publications for a variety of audiences.[19] However, these works are challenging because they focus on Victoria's own writing less as a source of Métis women's history and persisting culture and more as a reflection of a forgotten past. The problem is exacerbated by her

FIG. 2.04. Victoria Callihoo with family. From top left clockwise: Violet Berube (née Baird), Gloria Jean Henderson holding Calvin William Wait as an infant, Alice Baird (née Callihoo), and Victoria.

portrayal in settler media accounts as an "Indian" woman when Victoria identified herself as Métis.[20] In many of the written fragments about Victoria, especially those in public media, she is presented as a "bridge" to the past. This casts Victoria's unique lived experiences as a Métis woman, and by extension those of Métis people more broadly, solely to the past.[21] Victoria is much more than "a bridge between the buffalo days and modern society," as Grant MacEwan describes her.[22] It is essential to assess the accuracy of information with care given that many accounts of Victoria's life were written by settlers for a public, and thus mainly settler, audience.[23] Despite the problems these sources may pose, they offer insight into how and why Victoria was perceived through the settler gaze at the time these pieces were written.[24]

Looking at the available sources on Victoria's life is also complicated by the inherent issues of researching historical Indigenous women.[25] First, where sources are written by settler men, they often display colonial and patriarchal bias. The loss of an Indigenous woman's voice to that of a settler man is evident in Grant MacEwan's chapter on Victoria in his book *Mighty Women*, which contains no citations for what he writes about Victoria and makes her own voice indistinguishable from his own.[26] A review of MacEwan's personal papers yielded only one find—a letter sent to MacEwan by Victoria's son Vital and his wife, Clothilde, confirming some of the information MacEwan included in his writing and verifying that he did, in fact, have an in-person conversation with Vital and Clothilde in which Victoria was discussed.[27] A second challenge in understanding Victoria's life story is that she is remembered as having only spoken Cree and Michif fluently, but her written memories were published in English.[28] This calls into question who translated Victoria's stories, and under what conditions, ultimately complicating a reading of these sources: What may have been lost in translation?

Dr. Anne Anderson's 1985 book, *The First Metis: A New Nation*, is perhaps an exception in the retelling of Victoria's life story.[29] Anderson's telling is noted as "related by her [Victoria's] daughter Vickie Kildaw."[30] A Métis women, Anderson was a friend to

Victoria and her family and spent considerable time with her, making her work important for piecing together the story of Victoria's life.[31] Anderson was accomplished in her own right, as an educator, author, and advocate for Indigenous people in Alberta.[32] I have also considered sources like Anderson, relying on conversations with family members or Victoria herself, as accurate sources of information. I was able to verify a large amount of information about Victoria's life, but not all information. Many descendants whom I spoke with were unsure about the accuracy of information in much of what is written about Victoria.[33] Based on what they shared with me, I can say with certainty that the words published under Victoria's name are her own, with the necessary caveat that there are subtle (and sometimes not so subtle) differences in meaning that come with a Cree- or Michif-to-English translation.[34]

Centring Victoria Callihoo

Using the books, articles, newspaper features, stories from her descendants, and Victoria's own memories, we can reimagine her life with the richness and complexity known to her family and community, honouring her as a matriarch and centring Métis ways of being and knowing. A closer look at her life also increases our historical understanding of the essential roles and experiences of Métis women socially, economically, and culturally during a time of sustained state and settler oppression of Indigenous people. Thus, multiple histories emerge—a history of Métis women on the Prairies and their role in creating the historical imagination, and a life history of resiliency and cultural continuity amidst tragedy, set against a significant transitional period in Alberta's history.

This chapter adds to the "tradition of Métis historical family and community histories and biographies"[35] and is guided by scholarship addressing the complexities of Indigenous women's life stories and recorded memories, including the work of Sarah Carter on Emma Minesinger and of Judy Iseke-Barnes on Dorothy Chartrand.[36] Their studies place broader histories of Indigenous women's culture and experience within the individual life stories and memories of Emma Minesinger and Dorothy Chartrand; Iseke-Barnes calling this "the ways that their lives are extensions of history."[37] Although Victoria has not been entirely absent from written history, my goal is to capture her legacy as known to her descendants and reaffirm her presence as a matriarch and knowledge keeper. Following the lead of scholars seeking to understand both Métis women's history and the history of individual Métis women's lives, this work situates itself within a larger canon of scholarship working to challenge settler dominated narratives of male-focused histories of Métis life and experience and Indigenous history on the Plains.[38] Indeed, older historical work on Métis communities has often focused on the fur trade, Métis ethnogenesis, and Métis resistance and political movements.[39] This work has also primarily focused on Métis men, and where women are centred, it was only through the relationship between Indigenous women and the fur trade and their connection to Métis ethnogenesis.[40] More recent scholarship has focused on Métis women's experiences beyond the fur trade and in landscapes outside of what is now present-day Manitoba, seeking to centre Métis women's roles in communities beyond the Red River and understand how they were impacted by colonialism in the twentieth century.[41] The recent work by Bailey Oster and Marilyn Lizee, *Stories of Métis Women: Tales My Kookum Told Me*, a collection of oral histories and stories from Métis women, is a community-driven example that adds understanding of Métis women's experiences in the late nineteenth century, into the twentieth, and beyond.[42] As Laura-Lee

Kearns notes in her work on Métis women's stories, "if we cannot recognize the experiences of the Métis in all their complexity and plurality, then we fail to challenge the homogeneity that excludes and silences."[43] Kearns further states that "sharing stories of Métis resistance, resilience, silence, and identities helps open up the public space to legitimize Métis people's diversity, complexity, stories, experiences and understandings."[44] It is this work, along with that of countless others, that has inspired the present work's approach to writing about Victoria's life. With these works as a guide, this chapter draws together the "patchwork of threads" that tell us about Victoria's life and experiences.[45]

FIG. 2.05. Victoria (centre right) with her son Vital (right), his wife, Clothilde Hodgson (centre left), and other family members.

Victoria's Life and Memories

Victoria's family was rooted in the fur trade and the Métis communities of the Lac Ste. Anne region. Her father, Alexis Belcourt, was born in 1827 to Joseph Belcourt and Catherine L'Hyrondelle.[46]

Victoria's mother, Nancy, was born in 1832 at Lesser Slave Lake to Antoine Rowan and Archange Nipissing.[47] Alexis and Nancy married in 1848 and had eight children together before Alexis's death, after which Nancy married Adolphe Taillon in 1884.[48] Antoine, born in 1805 at Lesser Slave Lake, also went by the name Kinnowess, spelled also as Kinaniwis. His parents were Ignace Rowand and Louise Rowand.[49] Antoine has often been linked to John Rowand, the famed Chief Factor of Fort Edmonton; however, interestingly, Ignace, as written on Nancy's 1855 scrip record, is recorded above the first name of John, which is scratched out.[50] Little is known about Louise, Antoine's mother, whose name is written above "Indian woman," which is also scratched out.[51] Notably, Antoine's scrip claim describes his father as being a "white man," which offers some indication that there were fur trade connections, as European men in the Northwest during this period were mainly fur traders working for the Hudson's Bay Company (HBC) or North West Company, and many of them married Indigenous women.[52] Victoria's maternal grandmother, Archange, was born at Lesser Slave Lake in 1817 to Ignace Nipissing and Lizette Sauteuse.[53] Victoria's maternal genealogy indicates deep roots in the Métis community of the Lac Ste. Anne and Lesser Slave Lake region, which by the time Victoria was born had a strong presence tied to the fur trade.[54] Devoutly Catholic, these families were strongly influenced by the missions and missionaries.[55] One source stated that for a "short time [Victoria] was at school at the Lac Ste. Anne mission... and was taught by Father Lacombe's sister Christina."[56] Although it is possible Victoria attended this mission school, her recorded memories from her childhood centre around the buffalo hunts with her mother, Nancy. According to Victoria, her mother "was a medicine woman who set broken bones and knew how to use medicinal herbs."[57] In 1959, she described her mother's work in the *Edmonton Journal*, where she relayed through her daughter Hermine a story about Nancy "amputat[ing] a man's leg when gangrene set in after it had been badly frozen...[but] the man made a good recovery and lived for years after this amputation."[58] In the same interview, Victoria shared that "when she was indisposed she used the medicine of her mother and grandmother."[59]

A 1960 article entitled "Our Buffalo Hunts" describes Victoria's early upbringing and the centrality of buffalo hunting to the Lac Ste. Anne Métis community.[60] Her descriptions mirror those of Métis hunting brigades within the broader historical understanding.[61] These hunts exhibited a clear social structure and required the involvement of an entire family, each member with their own roles and responsibilities.[62] The buffalo hunts yielded the dry meat, pemmican, and hides that were used or traded with the HBC as a means of economic subsistence.[63] The inherent danger in chasing buffalo on horseback across the uneven prairie terrain necessitated knowledge keepers such as Victoria's mother, Nancy, who knew how to tend to the sick and injured.[64] Victoria recalled hunts involving approximately one hundred families, all travelling in carts, and then settling into camps to process the hunt's proceeds.[65] Victoria was tasked with tending the fires because it was necessary to "keep a little smoke going all day to keep the flies away from the meat," while a larger group of women processed the kill.[66] Victoria's description of women's roles in the hunt is consistent with other accounts, specifically that women were essential to the operation of these large scale hunts, making use of the hides and meat and making pemmican.[67] Victoria's memories, published in a local newspaper, the *Wainwright Star*, also describe the militaristic "manner" of the hunts in order to maintain security in the face of conflict between the Métis and their enemies, the Blackfeet.[68]

The detail in which Victoria describes the hunt itself, its leadership structure, and the processing of the kill is indicative of the engaged role women and children had in Métis buffalo hunts.[69] Indeed, Victoria noted that she and her siblings would accompany her mother on the hunt while her "father stayed home, tending the chores and gardening the small crop."[70] Victoria's inclusion of this circumstance in her writing is important, as Nancy's autonomy in attending the hunt without her husband likely resonated strongly with her.

While such hunts formed a large part of Victoria's childhood, by the time she was entering adulthood, buffalo hunting was no longer viable on the Plains. She did, however, share these experiences with her children. In a 1966 interview, her son Vital recounted one of his mother's stories:

> Metis would gather at Lac Ste. Anne, take their Red River Carts (400 or 500 in one group) and they would travel to the river, take their carts apart, and make rafts to get to the prairie where the buffalo lived. They stayed all summer to make pemmican... [Victoria] was 16 when she started skinning buffalo. To make pemmican, they would grind dried meat with rocks, dry Saskatoon berries, mix them with the meat, and mix it all with fat. It was sundried. They also had birch sugar to sweeten the pemmican. They also had fish for the winter.[71]

Victoria's nostalgia for the past is evident in the memories she recalled later in life and may offer some insight into her motivation for recording her memories as well as sharing them with her children. Victoria's writing about the buffalo hunt not only conveys the independence of these Métis communities, it hints at the stress that the imposition of colonization and decimation of the buffalo caused her and her family. In "Our Buffalo Hunts," she remembered that "we, of those days, never could believe the buffalo would ever be killed off, for there were thousands and thousands," and further that "there was no money; no one knew what it was."[72] In describing her memories in this way, these stories become both a sharing of the past and an expression of resistance to colonialism.

Adult Life and Motherhood

After Victoria's marriage to Louis Callihoo in 1879, they remained at Lac Ste. Anne. Of Métis and Iroquois descent, Louis Callihoo was the son of Michel Band Chief Michel Callihoo.[73] Victoria described their life together as being shaped by materials from the land, by human relationships to objects, and the relationships between groups of people that made these objects available.[74] Mud stoves, made from "poles, mud and hay mixed, and more mud and water," provided warmth while the family slept on the floor on bedding made from "duck and goose feather for mattresses and pillows, and buffalo robes and H. B. Co., four-point blankets."[75] Soap, or *la potash*, was made from a mix of "fats or grease with ashes lye," and "moss was a household necessity," used to clean floors and to "raise babies."[76] The HBC sold cloth such as flannelette that was used for clothing. Women made leggings, which men paired with buffalo skin coats and women wore with shawls.[77] These shawls were a staple for Métis women; they were both functional and acted as "deeply feminine symbols."[78] Victoria's articles "The Early Life in Lac Ste. Anne and St. Albert in the 1870s" and "Our Buffalo Hunts" are filled with details of Métis life in the late nineteenth century and give us small glimpses into Victoria's own feelings about the past and present. Her writings contrast events and items of the present with those of the past using analogy. It is clear that the past is always recalled fondly. Indeed, in referring to tables and chairs that were absent in the past, in Victoria's words, "because we didn't have them, we didn't miss them."[79]

Victoria and Louis were not in Lac Ste. Anne for long, and in 1880 settled on the Michel Reserve, northwest of Edmonton.[80] Two years earlier, in 1878, Louis's father Chief Louis Callihoo and other members of the Callihoo family had signed an adhesion to Treaty 6 that effected the formation of the Michel Reserve.[81] When Victoria and Louis married, Victoria gained Indian status under the Indian Act.[82] While Victoria and Louis raised their children on the Michel Reserve, many members of Victoria's family took scrip following amendments to the Dominion Lands Act in 1885.[83] The lack of clear policy on scrip and "Indian status" meant that some Métis had a choice to either take treaty or scrip, and they "had the ability to move back and forth between the two statuses."[84] Many Métis took scrip; for some this was "preferable to a long term relationship with the federal government and small treaty payments on a yearly basis."[85] It seems that at this time, Victoria chose to keep her treaty status rather than take scrip, likely because of her marriage to Louis and their home on the Michel Reserve.

As the turn of the century waned, Louis and Victoria's life shifted, reflecting a need for new sources of subsistence and adaptation to the pressure of settlers, colonization, and government policy. In this new social and political landscape with new pressures, Victoria worked alongside Louis, adapting and adopting creative—and demanding—ways to support their growing family.[86] In a letter to Grant MacEwan, her son Vital described the situation: "Sometime after my mother came to live on the Michel Reserve, she started cooking for a surveying crew.... She had two small children at this time and carried one on her back and had to watch closely over the other one while doing her work."[87] Vital remembered Victoria and Louis "haul[ing] freight from Edmonton to Athabasca Landing for the Hudson's Bay Company" during his childhood.[88] Other sources describe Victoria and

Louis also raising cattle, running a steam-powered threshing outfit, and later buying a sawmill.[89] Victoria and Louis's varied and successful economic ventures on the Michel Reserve were exceptional given the restrictions imposed by the Indian Act on activities undertaken on reserve lands.[90]

Making a living freighting, following the decimation of the buffalo and the expansion of the railway, was increasingly difficult. Some were able to move goods for incoming settlers, but by and large, the economy evaporated.[91] During this period, life on reserve for Louis and Victoria would have been equally challenging. Individual actions were strictly controlled by the Department of Indian Affairs through the Indian Act.[92] For those like Louis and Victoria who tried to make a living by farming and raising livestock, it was particularly difficult because any produce or livestock farmers may have wished to sell required the Indian Agent's approval.[93] Requests by the band in 1903 to be relieved from this provision and thus become "independent" were "apparently denied."[94] The many ways that Victoria and Louis supported their family economically reflect the significant changes at the turn of the century, particularly prompted by the gradual decline of the fur trade and the increasing pressure of prairie settlement.

It isn't known exactly why Louis and Victoria chose to return to Lac Ste. Anne. Most sources cite the death of their son John as a reason;[95] however, growing restrictions on the Michel Reserve may also have been a factor.[96] As the settler population grew during the late nineteenth and early twentieth centuries, the relationship between the Michel Band and the Department of Indian Affairs became contentious and land was increasingly being expropriated to open up homesteads.[97] It is possible these conditions weighed into their decision.

In Lac Ste. Anne, Louis and Victoria continued to raise cattle and also sold dairy products and ran "a hotel with a coffee shop," before returning to the Michel Reserve in 1921.[98] The hotel was described "as a very busy place at that time because it was located on the main route to the mountains."[99] Their engagement in multiple economic activities suggests they likely needed multiple, and flexible, sources of income.

All six of Victoria's sons and one daughter attended St. Joseph's Industrial School, while the other daughters attended the convent in St. Albert.[100] St. Joseph's, also known as Dunbow, was a residential school located south of Calgary.[101] The two oldest children attended there as early as 1885 and several remained there until they were eighteen or nineteen years old.[102] Victoria's descendants shared that attending these institutions brought trauma to Victoria's children.[103] Vital remembered how Louis, who was illiterate, was determined his children would be educated.[104] While Victoria "objected to her children being away from home [at residential schools] as time went on...she got used to the idea."[105] An article written by Victoria's daughter-in-law similarly indicated Victoria's feelings: "It was rather heartbreaking for Victoria to have her children so far from home, but, with her husband, they usually would make a yearly trip to see their sons at the Dunbow School. They travelled down with a team of horses and a wagon, after the spring work was done, leaving someone in charge of the farm."[106] This experience speaks to the interference that government systems had on Victoria's life and the lives of her children and the challenges brought by increasing colonial policies and settlement in Alberta.

Victoria's experiences raising her family at the turn of the century are reflected in her writings and the memories of those who knew her. In "Early Life in Lac Ste. Anne and St. Albert in the 1870s," Victoria described how the loss of buffalo left the Métis turning to beef as the primary source of red meat, which "some of the Métis didn't care for...at first."[107] She noted the introduction of a cash economy to replace the bartering of furs and lamented how she had "heard of some Indians trading a used five-dollar bill for a brand-new dollar bill."[108] From these sentiments and her descendants' retelling of her family's residential school experience, it is clear that Victoria harboured feelings of distrust for the government. Despite the fondness in which she recalls the way of life of the past, it was clearly not without pain for Victoria.

In 1928, two years after Louis's death, Victoria joined several other members of the Callihoo family in surrendering their "Indian" status for enfranchisement.[109] Enfranchisement removed this status she had gained under the Indian Act when she married Louis.[110] Writer Elizabeth Macpherson speculated that members of the band made the decision to enfranchise so they might "have the freedom to prosper from their work" rather than continue to live under the oppressive Indian Act.[111] Victoria's exact motivation for giving up her status is not known, but she may have been incentivized by the offer of land or the rights of citizenship to which enfranchisement entitled her.[112] Her decision could also have been prompted by her desire to stay independent following the death of her husband and to be closer to those she knew from living on the Michel Reserve; or it possibly could have been motivated by the growing Métis political activism in Alberta during that period.[113] Indeed, the year that Victoria gave up her Indian status saw the formation of the Métis Association of Alberta.[114] Victoria, by choosing enfranchisement, may have been asserting her identity and political rights as a Métis woman, reflective of the autonomy shown to her by her mother, Nancy.

Amongst the change and upheaval that characterized much of Victoria's adult life, gatherings, parties, visits, and family connections were continuous. In her recorded memories and in conversations with descendants, social connection was always paramount. In "Early Life" Victoria described visits with "Métis from Lac Ste. Anne and St. Albert" and Battle River, dances with neighbours following the building of a house, and "the ponies used for fast travelling, [such] as going to weddings and dances."[115] When Victoria and Louis's son Vital married, they hosted the wedding on their farm on the Michel Reserve, an event that was well attended by the community: "People came in wagons and democrats over trails full of mud holes to their home to celebrate and dance all night."[116] A Métis Elder whose family was connected with Victoria's recalled that gatherings and visits between families were frequent for him growing up.[117] Similarly, one of Victoria's great-granddaughters shared about the occasions when Victoria came to visit at her grandmother's house, saying: "I knew a week before she was coming because it was like the Queen was coming to visit."[118] Her great-granddaughter also shared about Victoria's visits: "The last time I saw her, she gave me this hanky and it was white with big red roses on it. And she said, 'You're such a pretty little girl. I want you to keep this and always remember me.' I kept that hanky till it just disintegrated. I remember having the utmost respect for her because of what my grandmother had told me about her. She told me about the buffalo hunts this woman went on."[119]

During these visits, Victoria only spoke in Cree or Michif, the languages she spoke in the home when her children were growing up.[120] This is significant given the influx of English- and French-speaking settlers and the pressure on Indigenous people to conform to new languages and cultures. Victoria's connection to Métis culture and language is exemplified in her choice to speak Cree and Michif with her children and further reflected in the many jigs she danced over her lifetime, chronicled in newspaper articles and through her descendants.[121]

Victoria's memories recorded in the *Alberta Historical Review* and other sources can be tied together by a 1959 interview in the

FIG. 2.06. Victoria (left) with family at her hundredth birthday party.

Edmonton Journal. Hermine, Victoria's daughter, shared: "Mother doesn't think in years as we do, she just remembers events."[122] This is evidenced by the distinctive voice that emerges in Victoria's recorded memories, which show an understanding of the past as diverse events rather than on a linear timeline. Victoria's memories flow between past and present, describing things that happened and how things were done, and imagining this past as intertwined with the present. In this way, the practices Victoria describes are not relayed as ways of being and knowing solely confined to the past, but a way of being in and knowing the world that holds true and is continuous. When we think about these stories of Victoria's life outside of the confines of the settler imagination that in many iterations regulated her life and stories to the past, we can then see her stories as a sharing of knowledge and teachings. Although Victoria lived through remarkable hardship and experienced a profoundly different world in her later years than in her adolescence on the Plains, her life and stories challenge the masculine narratives of the prairie settlement period. Victoria's memories reject this presumption and recentre the role that she and other Métis women held as matriarchs and as leaders in their families and communities. The significance of storytelling in Métis identity cannot be understated and offers valuable insight into Victoria's motivation for sharing her memories.[123] The power of stories to "enrich, inform and potentially help to change and shape the public realm" is reflected in Victoria's retellings. The ways in which Victoria articulates many aspects of Métis identity and the changes she witnessed suggest that she was likely motivated by many forces. Perhaps Victoria saw publishing her memories as a means to share Métis culture and history, as an act of resistance, and "to 'create a sense of home.'"[124]

Indeed, the forces of settler colonialism and government intervention on Indigenous peoples such as the Métis were matched with resilience and adaptation, and Victoria exemplified pride for Métis culture and way of life despite colonial forces. By leaving us with her memories and experiences, we gain an understanding of Métis way of life at the turn of the century and how this change was felt and remembered. A voice that is distinctly Victoria's is heard in many of the sources known to have come from her or conversations with her. Understanding these sources of Victoria's voice not as "bridge" to the past but as cultural knowledge more fully respects what her intention might have been in preserving her memories. They are memories that reveal and represent the centrality of women in every sphere of Métis life, and in a space of settler and Indigenous interaction. Under the pressures of colonization, they reflect how Victoria remained firm in her Métis identity. Little has been left behind about the women who negotiated this world and sought to sustain their families within it, but as Victoria's stories and life show us, what does remain unveils women's prominence in resilient Métis communities in Alberta and their centrality to sustaining Métis culture and a distinctly Métis way of life.

NOTES

1 I would like to sincerely thank Victoria Callihoo's descendants and Métis relatives who spoke with me about her and shared their knowledge: Calvin Wait, Gerry Baird, Grace Dudar, Gloria Henderson, Gary Gairdner, and Sharon Morin. I also would like to thank Vino Vipulanantharajah and his colleagues at Musée Héritage St. Albert, all the staff at Spruce Grove Archives and Museum, Stony Plain Multicultural Heritage Centre Library and Archives, and University of Calgary Special Collections for all your assistance and support of this project. Thank you to Sarah Olsen and Dayle Morin for your assistance with research. Thank you to Sarah Carter for your support and for encouraging me from the beginning. This chapter is dedicated to Grace Dudar, who passed away earlier this year. I spoke with Grace about her grandmother Victoria in 2021 and am grateful to have known her and had the opportunity to speak with such an incredible woman.

2 Petten, "Métis Woman Painted Vibrant Picture of the West," 30. This event was held by the Northern Alberta Pioneers and Old Timers Association; see Barkwell and Dorion, eds., *Women of the Métis Nation*, 49.

3 Petten, "Métis Woman Painted Vibrant Picture of the West," 30; "Indian Woman Recalls Buffalo Hunt in 1874," *Medicine Hat News*, November 26, 1960.

4 Some genealogies and accounts place Victoria's year of birth as 1862; however, 1861 seems to appear more frequently in the records. See Taylor, *Victoria Callihoo*, 150; and Belcourt, *Walking in the Woods*, 193. Victoria tells us in "Our Buffalo Hunts" that she and her family were "from Lac Ste. Anne." Callihoo, "Our Buffalo Hunts," 24–25.

5 "Centenarian Dies in St. Albert Home," *Edmonton Journal*, April 22, 1966, courtesy of Musée Héritage St. Albert. Victoria's memories of buffalo hunts from her youth are detailed in Callihoo, "Our Buffalo Hunts," 24–25.

6 See Callihoo, "Our Buffalo Hunts"; Callihoo, "Early Life in Lac Ste. Anne," 21–26; and Callihoo, "The Iroquois in Alberta," 17–18.

7 A short article written in the *Edmonton Journal* also lists Nancy's maiden name as Drun; similarly, in *The First Metis*, a piece on Victoria

states Nancy's maiden name as being Drouin. See Anna A. Walker, "The Third Column: Across the Years," *Edmonton Journal*, December 15, 1959, courtesy of the Spruce Grove Archives; and Anderson, *The First Metis*, 144–45. In scrip records her last name is written as either Rowand or Rowan; thus, this seems to be the correct name. See Northwest Scrip Application of Nancy Rowan, June 11, 1885, LAC RG 15 v. 1332, Metis Nation Historical Online Database, Library and Archives Canada, https://www.metisnationdatabase.ca/ (hereafter cited as MNHOD). Many of Victoria's siblings took scrip and identified their parents as "halfbreed." See, for example, Northwest Scrip Application of Sophie Belcourt, June 11, 1885, LAC RG 15 v. 1325, MNHOD.

8   For more on the history of Lac Ste. Anne, see Wadsworth, "Healing Waters and Buffalo Bones," 13–28.
9   Correspondence between Vital Callihoo and Grant MacEwan, December 6, 1970, MSC 74.7, University of Calgary Special Collections (hereafter cited as Correspondence between Callihoo and MacEwan).
10 Walker, "The Third Column." Gerry Baird in discussion with author, August 2021.
11 Anderson, *The First Metis*, 62.
12 Anderson, *The First Metis*, 145; Vital (Victor) Callihoo, interview by Allen Shenfield, transcript, Stony Plain Archives, 1966, at 29:54.
13 Callihoo, "History of the Louis Callihoo Family," 308; and Walker, "The Third Column."
14 Photos courtesy of Sara Olsen. It is labelled in the museum: "Handsewn Dress made by Mrs Victoria Callihoo."
15 For more on the importance of material culture to Métis culture and identity, see Farrell Racette, "My Grandmothers Loved to Trade," 69–81.
16 Victoria is featured in MacEwan, *Mighty Women*, 191–99.
17 Calvin Wait in discussion with author, August 2021.
18 At the time of her death, seven of her children were alive and "she had 57 grandchildren, 165 great grandchildren, and 46 great-great grandchildren, and 8 great-great-great grandchildren." Calahoo Women's Institute, *Calahoo Trails*, 19.
19 For examples of publications that discuss Victoria, see Taylor, *Victoria Callihoo*; Macpherson, *The Sun Traveller*, 79–85; and Goyette and Roemmich, *Edmonton in Our Own Words*, 80–82, 113–114.
20 Several short biographies on Victoria and newspapers describe her as "Indian." See for example Calahoo Women's Institute, *Calahoo Trails*, 19; and Jack Deakin, "Indian Woman Dances on 100th Birthday," *Edmonton Journal*, November 1962, courtesy of Musée Héritage St.

Albert. Victoria described herself as Métis in both publications of her memories. Publications such as Cora Taylor's *Victoria Callihoo* follow Victoria's self-identification, Taylor having spoken to many of her descendants at the time of writing.

21 For example, in the chapter on Victoria in *Mighty Women*, Grant MacEwan writes: "Her life, in a most striking way, was like a bridge between buffalo days and modern society; between the travois as a means of transportation, when she knew when she lived for a time on the Michael Reservation, and the unbelievably fast travel she lived to see; between the times when Indians and Métis were numerous enough and strong enough to have annihilated members of the newcomer race and the later years when those native people represented a relatively weak minority." Manuscript of chapter on Victoria Callihoo with edits written by Grant MacEwan, Grant MacEwan Fonds, M7144, box 27, University of Calgary Special Collections, 28.

22 Manuscript of chapter on Victoria Callihoo, 28.

23 I am referring here to the many articles written about Victoria in newspapers. See, for example, Deakin, "Indian Woman Dances on 100th Birthday," *Edmonton Journal*, November 1962; Petten, "Métis Woman Painted Vibrant Picture of the West," 30; "Indian Woman Recalls Buffalo Hunt in 1874," *Medicine Hat News*, November 26, 1960.

24 For more on Indigenous people as written in newspaper sources see Cronlund Anderson and Robertson, *Seeing Red*. An interesting detail often mentioned in articles is that Victoria lived free of alcohol or tobacco. In discussions with her descendants, one shared that this was not true, and Victoria was known to enjoy gin. Gerry Baird in discussion with author, August 2021. Why this became an oft-mentioned claim is not within the scope of this paper, but it may be linked to perceived social values and acceptability of the time period—or perhaps as a way that journalists sold certain social ideals or made an article more acceptable or palatable to a white settler audience.

25 For a discussion of some of the challenges posed by doing historical work on Indigenous women, see Carter and McCormack, "Lifelines: Searching for Aboriginal Women." Writing about Indigenous people by settlers requires a critical eye. As a settler myself writing about an Indigenous woman, I have had to tread carefully to avoid imparting similar problems in this work, and I have endeavoured to involve many members of the Métis community throughout the research and writing process to avoid this.

26 Grant MacEwan, *Mighty Women*. Some of the more interesting stories in MacEwan's chapter were verified by the letter found in the archives. MacEwan described Victoria as "handy with a gun," and went on to describe an occasion in which she shot a bear. See chapter on Victoria Callihoo, 26. See also Correspondence between Callihoo and MacEwan. Similar writing, said to be entirely Victoria's voice but in fact authored by a man, making it unclear what editing was done and what is or isn't Victoria's voice, is copied in Goyette and Roemmich's *Edmonton in Our Own Words*; the article is written as Victoria's voice but authored by Colonel Frederick C. Jamieson, titled "The Edmonton Hunt," and published in the *Alberta Historical Review* in 1953. See Goyette and Roemmich, *Edmonton in Our Own Words*, 113–14. Interestingly, the information about Victoria offered on page 113 of Goyette and Roemmich states that she accompanied her "parents" when she went on the buffalo hunts; Victoria's own words tell us it was only her mother that took her and her siblings on the hunts.

27 Correspondence between Callihoo and MacEwan. Vital (Victor) Callihoo was born June 18, 1888, and married Clothilde Hodgson in Villeneuve on July 7, 1914. They went on to have twelve children. Biographical document, unknown author, courtesy of the Stony Plain Archives.

28 Gloria Henderson in discussion with author, August 2021; Gerry Baird in discussion with author, August 2021. Victoria's descendants confirmed that Victoria spoke only Cree and Michif. See also Walker, "The Third Column." In one biographical article of Victoria in *Calahoo Trails* she is said to have "spoke mostly Cree, learning some English after she was seventy-five years of age." Calahoo Women's Institute, *Calahoo Trails*, 19. Another newspaper article states: "Mrs. Callihoo speaks Cree and only a few words in English, although she says 'in my old age I'm learning to speak the language.'" "Picking up English at Ninety-Nine," unknown publication, 1960, courtesy of Sara Olsen and the Rochfort Bridge Museum.

29 Anderson, *The First Metis*.

30 Anderson, *The First Metis*, 144.

31 Gerry Baird in discussion with author, August 2021; Grace Dudar in discussion with author, August 2021; Gloria Henderson in discussion with author, August 2021; and Calvin Wait in discussion with author, August 2021.

32 For more on Dr. Anderson, see for example Bruce Cinnamon, "The 'Grand Lady of the Métis': Dr. Anne Anderson's Mission to Preserve the Cree Language," Edmonton City as a Museum Project, November 10,

2020, https://citymuseumedmonton.ca/2020/11/10/the-grand-lady-of-the-metis-dr-anne-andersons-mission-to-preserve-the-cree-language/

33 Gerry Baird in discussion with author, August 2021; Grace Dudar in discussion with author, August 2021; Gloria Henderson in discussion with author, August 2021; and Calvin Wait in discussion with author, August 2021. Specifically, the family members I spoke with were unsure of the circumstances around the works that appeared in the *Alberta Historical Review* or much of the information relayed by Grant MacEwan.

34 It is my suspicion that it was either Victoria's daughter Hermine "Lizzie" Vandelle, based on an *Edmonton Journal* article, or Dr. Anne Anderson who were involved in the publication of Victoria's memories. The author of the article, Anna M. Walker, describes going to talk with Victoria with her daughter Mrs. Vandelle present to translate. See Walker, "The Third Column." Anne Anderson, as identified by the family, was fluent in Cree, and was close with Victoria. In Anderson's book, information about Victoria is noted as having come from Lizzie. Victoria's family shared that in her later years, Lizzie lived with Victoria until she went to live in the Youville home.

35 Iseke-Barnes, "Grandmothers of the Métis Nation," 70.

36 See Carter, "The Montana Memories of Emma Minesinger"; and Iseke-Barnes, "Grandmothers of the Métis Nation."

37 Iseke-Barnes, "Grandmothers of the Métis Nation," 69.

38 See, for example, Brown, "Woman as Centre and Symbol," 39–46, and Iseke-Barnes, "Grandmothers of the Métis Nation," 71–75.

39 See Macdougall and St-Onge, "Rooted in Mobility," 1. Macdougall and St-Onge note how most historical work on Métis societies concentrates on the Red River region and how scholarship has had a "singular fixation on political and military traditions" in studies of Métis communities.

40 Work by historians such as Nicole St-Onge, Brenda Macdougall, Doris MacKinnon, and others have all taken different approaches to broaden our understanding of Métis women's lives and experiences in the nineteenth and into the early twentieth centuries. For a discussion of the work by historians on the end of the buffalo hunt's impact on women, see St-Onge, "Of Métis Women and Hunting Brigades," 53.

41 See Farrell Racette, "Nimble Fingers and Strong Backs."

42 See Oster and Lizee, *Stories of Métis Women*.

43 Kearns, "(Re)claiming Métis Women Identities," 86.

44 Kearns, "(Re)claiming Métis Women Identities," 85.

45 Carter and McCormack, "Lifelines: Searching for Aboriginal Women," 13.
46 Anderson, *The First Metis*, 108–9. A scrip record for Catherine exists; however, it is inconsistent with other genealogical accounts such as Anderson's in *The First Metis*. See Northwest Scrip Application of Catherine L'Hyrondelle, June 10, 1885, LAC RG 15 v. 1325. According to the scrip record, Catherine was born in 1793 to Jacque L'Hyrondelle, who is listed as "Canadian," and Josephte Pilon, listed as "halfbreed." This record further indicates that Alexis, Victoria's father, died in 1881, which is close to Anderson's account that he died in 1880. Some of the names that Anderson lists as Alexis's siblings are inconsistent with the scrip record; however, it is possible that individuals may be listed by middle names or that names may have been misspelled, misunderstood, or misread because the documents were handwritten. Anderson's book also offers more on Joseph, who is noted as being a voyageur who worked for the North West Company; however, I was unable to find more information on Joseph or Catherine or their parents.
47 Northwest Scrip Application of Nancy Rowan.
48 Northwest Scrip Application of Nancy Rowan. Victoria's siblings were Sophie (b. 1849), Benjamin (b. 1855), Louise (b. 1858), Virginia (b. 1867), Alexis Jr. (b. 1869), and John (b. 1871). See Anderson, *The First Metis*, 108.
49 Northwest Scrip Application of Nancy Rowan for Antoine Rowan, June 13, 1885, LAC RG 15 v. 1331, MNHOD. The name of Kinnowess is spelled differently in *The First Metis* as "Kininawis," and noted as meaning "one of tall stature." Anderson further notes that this Nancy went by this name. See Anderson, *The First Metis*, 108–9. It is noted as an alias on this scrip application; however, on the application Nancy made for herself it is not listed as an alias. See Northwest Scrip Application of Nancy Rowan. Antoine died in 1875, according to the death certificate attached to Nancy's scrip claim on his behalf.
50 Northwest Scrip Application of Nancy Rowan for Antoine Rowan. Although the John Rowand connection is frequently mentioned as an anecdote about Victoria's family heritage, neither side can be verified. Cora Taylor, in her book about Victoria Callihoo, wrote a long afterword on this issue, stating that "once a mistake becomes family lore, it is sometimes repeated so often it is considered fact." Taylor addresses the possibilities of Victoria's mother's heritage, which, according to Oblate records, does include the Rowand name; but Taylor finds that other Rowand families were also in the same area. See Taylor, *Victoria Callihoo*, 94–106.

51 Northwest Scrip Application of Nancy Rowan for Antoine Rowan.
52 These marriages were known as country marriages or mariages à la façon du pays (by the custom of the country). These marriages are linked to Métis ethnogenesis and were both formed by and formed the social, cultural, and political landscape of the fur trade. For more on women in the fur trade and marriages between European traders and Indigenous women, see Van Kirk, *Many Tender Ties*; Brown, *Strangers in Blood*; and Rollason Driscoll, "'A Most Important Chain of Connection,'" 81–107.
53 Northwest Scrip Application of Archange Nipissing, July 31, 1886, LAC RG 15 V. 1361, MNHOD. This document also tells us that Archange was a member of the "Alexander Band of Indians."
54 Ens and Sawchuk, *From New Peoples to New Nations*, 53.
55 Wadsworth, "Healing Waters and Buffalo Bones," 23–24.
56 "Picking up English at Ninety-Nine."
57 Callihoo, "Our Buffalo Hunts," 24.
58 Walker, "The Third Column."
59 Walker, "The Third Column."
60 Callihoo, "Our Buffalo Hunts," 25.
61 Callihoo, "Our Buffalo Hunts," 25; St-Onge, "Of Métis Women and Hunting Brigades," 49–54.
62 See Macdougall and St-Onge, "Rooted in Mobility," 21–32; St-Onge, "Of Métis Women and Hunting Brigades," 49–54.
63 "Stories of the Days of the Edmonton Buffalo Hunt," *Wainwright Star*, December 7, 1960.
64 Callihoo, "Our Buffalo Hunts," 24.
65 Callihoo, "Our Buffalo Hunts," 24–25.
66 Callihoo, "Our Buffalo Hunts," 25.
67 St-Onge, "Of Métis Women and Hunting Brigades," 52.
68 "Stories of the Days of the Edmonton Buffalo Hunt."
69 The centrality of women in Métis buffalo hunting is also described by Métis Knowledge Holder Norma Spicer. See Oster and Lizee, *Stories of Métis Women*, 24–30. See also Troupe, "Mapping Métis Stories."
70 Goyette and Roemmich, *Edmonton in Our Own Words*, 113. This was identified as a smallpox epidemic at Tall Creek; Victoria accompanied her mother, Nancy, who "nursed the victims" and "helped to bury decently many who died there." See Walker, "The Third Column."
71 Vital (Victor) Callihoo, interview by Allen Shenfield, at 34:10.
72 Callihoo, "Our Buffalo Hunts," 25.
73 Macpherson, *The Sun Traveller*, 25–26.

74 Callihoo, "Early Life in Lac Ste. Anne," 22. For more on the economy in the Northwest during this period, see Colpitts, *Pemmican Empire*.
75 Callihoo, "Early Life in Lac Ste. Anne," 22.
76 Callihoo, "Early Life in Lac Ste. Anne," 24; Callihoo, "The Early Life."
77 Callihoo, "Early Life in Lac Ste. Anne," 24.
78 Farrell Racette, "My Grandmothers Loved to Trade," 76.
79 Callihoo, "Early Life in Lac Ste. Anne," 22.
80 Macpherson, *The Sun Traveller*, 57; Callihoo, "History of the Louis Callihoo Family," 308.
81 Macpherson, *The Sun Traveller*, 46.
82 See Indian Act, 1876, SC 1876, c. 18 (39 Vict.), s. 3(3) states that: "The term 'Indian' means, First. Any male person of Indian blood reputed to belong to a particular band; Secondly. Any child of such person; Thirdly. Any woman who is lawfully married to such person."
83 The Dominion Lands Act is the legislation that outlined the process of land survey and distribution for settlement of the west. It included provisions for how Métis scrip was to be distributed. See Jack Carter, "Dominion Lands Act, 1872," *Salem Press Encyclopedia*, 2021. Amendments in 1879 allowed scrip to extend from Manitoba (where it was provided as part of the Manitoba Act) and was followed by a commission beginning in 1885 in the North-West Territories, which included Alberta. For more on the history of scrip and policies that impacted Métis peoples, see Augustus, "Métis Scrip."
84 Ens and Sawchuk, *From New People to New Nations*, 191. For more on the complexity surrounding the decision to take scrip or treaty status see Niemi-Bohun, "Colonial Categories and Familial Responses."
85 Ens and Sawchuk, *From New People to New Nations*, 191.
86 Victoria had a total of thirteen children, two dying in infancy. The following information about Victoria's children is being referenced from *The Sun Traveller*, at 84; however, several other genealogy accounts from Musée Héritage St. Albert Archives, Stony Plain Archives, Spruce Grove Archives, and the University of Calgary Special Collections Charles Denney Fonds were all referenced for confirmation. Victoria and Louis's children: Anne (1879–1969), Dio Leon (1880–1944), Hermine "Lizzie" (1881–unknown), William (1883–1954), Adolphus (1885–1967), Vital Victor (1888–1972), Henry (1879–1939), Alice (1895–1975), Caroline (1897–1897), Melvina (1897–1898), John (1898–1915), Julia Mary (1901–unknown), Bertha Victoire (1903–unknown).
87 Correspondence between Callihoo and MacEwan.

VICTORIA BELCOURT CALLIHOO • 59

88 Correspondence between Callihoo and MacEwan.
89 Macpherson, *The Sun Traveller*, 83. This sawmill was the site of a significant tragedy in Victoria's life, an accident resulting in the death of her youngest son, John, in 1915. See Correspondence between Callihoo and MacEwan.
90 The Indian Act strictly regulated activities on reserve lands and required that Indigenous people report activities to government agents. During the time when Louis and Victoria were undertaking various economic activities on reserve, several reports of the Department of Indian Affairs name Louis specifically, and Victoria is often mentioned as his "wife." These reports depict Louis as highly successful. In the 1905 report, Victoria is referred to as "Mrs. Callihoo," seen "at St. Albert delivering butter and eggs to her customers." See: "Dominion of Canada Annual Report of the Department of Indian Affairs for the Year Ended 30th June 1894," 1894, item 9418, Indian Affairs Annual Reports 1864 to 1990, Library and Archives Canada, 137; "Dominion of Canada Annual Report of the Department of Indian Affairs for the Year Ended 30th June 1896," 1896, item 10737, Indian Affairs Annual Reports 1864 to 1990, Library and Archives Canada, 323; "Dominion of Canada Annual Report of the Department of Indian Affairs for the Year Ended 30th June 1897," 1894, item 11225, Indian Affairs Annual Reports 1864 to 1990, Library and Archives Canada, 186; "Dominion of Canada Annual Report of the Department of Indian Affairs for the Year Ended 30th June 1899," 1899, item 12698, Indian Affairs Annual Reports 1864 to 1990, Library and Archives Canada, 251; "Dominion of Canada Annual Report of the Department of Indian Affairs for the Year Ended 30th June 1900," 1900, item 13553, Indian Affairs Annual Reports 1864 to 1990, Library and Archives Canada, 266; "Dominion of Canada Annual Report of the Department of Indian Affairs for the Year Ended 30th June 1905," 1905, item 17995, Indian Affairs Annual Reports 1864 to 1990, Library and Archives Canada, 208.
91 Racette, *Métis Development in the Canadian West*, 5.
92 For an overview of some of the policies enacted by the Indian Act, see Joseph, *21 Things You May Not Know about the Indian Act*.
93 Macpherson, *The Sun Traveller*, 67.
94 Macpherson, *The Sun Traveller*, 67.
95 Macpherson, *The Sun Traveller*, 67.
96 Macpherson, *The Sun Traveller*, 70.
97 Macpherson, *The Sun Traveller*, 67–70.
98 Macpherson, *The Sun Traveller*, 84; Anderson, *The First Metis*, 145.

99 Anderson, *The First Metis*, 145.
100 Callihoo, "History of the Louis Callihoo Family," 308–9, and Calahoo Women's Institute, *Calahoo Trails*, 19, discuss Victoria's daughters attending the convent; Grace Dudar, Victoria's granddaughter (daughter of Alice), shared that her mother had spoken about being in the convent. Grace Dudar in discussion with author, August 2021.
101 Macpherson, *The Sun Traveller*, 84.
102 Macpherson, *The Sun Traveller*, 84.
103 For more on the Métis experience of residential schools, see Daniels, ed., *Métis Memories of Residential Schools*. See also Truth and Reconciliation Commission of Canada, *Honouring the Truth, Reconciling for the Future*; Truth and Reconciliation Commission of Canada, *Canada's Residential Schools: The History, Part 1, Origins to 1939*, vol. 1 of *The Final Report of the Truth and Reconciliation Commission of Canada*; Truth and Reconciliation Commission of Canada, *The Survivors Speak*; and Truth and Reconciliation Commission of Canada, *The Métis Experience*.
104 Correspondence between Callihoo and MacEwan.
105 Correspondence between Callihoo and MacEwan.
106 Callihoo, "History of the Louis Callihoo Family," 308–9. Adolphus wrote to his mother, Victoria, from the Dunbow school in 1902 when he would have been seventeen. The letter described playing hockey and the work he was doing at the school. He also expressed his hope to hear from his mother soon. Letter from Adolphus B. Callihoo to Victoria Callihoo, December 17, 1902, Musée Héritage Museum collection, St. Albert, AB.
107 Callihoo, "Early Life in Lac Ste. Anne," 23.
108 Callihoo, "Early Life in Lac Ste. Anne," 25; and Callihoo, "The Early Life."
109 See "Memorandum for Enfranchisement of the Callihoo Band," Department of Indian Affairs, courtesy of Dayle Callihoo; and Macpherson, *The Sun Traveller*, 75.
110 For more on the Indian Act and how it impacted women like Victoria, see Kelm and Smith, *Talking Back to the Indian Act*.
111 Macpherson, *The Sun Traveller*, 75.
112 Macpherson, *The Sun Traveller*, 75. Victoria received a land grant when she was enfranchised. See "Patent no. 21256, sale no. 88: Patent granting Victoria Callihoo southwest 1/4, section 36 township 53 range 27 W4M in Alberta," June 30, 1928, RG10-D-11-a, vol. 10981, item 5418984, Library and Archives Canada.
113 Macpherson, *The Sun Traveller*, 99–100.

114 Macpherson, *The Sun Traveller*, 99–100. Felix Callihoo, a brother-in-law of Victoria, was one of the founding members of the Métis Association of Alberta.
115 Callihoo, "Early Life," 24.
116 Vital (Victor) Callihoo, interview by Allen Shenfield, at 39:58.
117 Gary Gairdner in discussion with author, August 2022.
118 Gloria Henderson in discussion with author, August 2021.
119 Gloria Henderson in discussion with author, August 2021.
120 Vital (Victor) Callihoo, interview by Allen Shenfield, at 39:58.
121 Many sources have discussed Victoria dancing the Red River Jig. See Deakin, "Indian Woman Dances on 100th Birthday"; and "Stories of the Days of the Edmonton Buffalo Hunt." Richard Callihoo, Victoria's nephew, was interviewed in 2001 and shared this about Victoria: "They used have that in the old timers' banquet in the McDonald's hotel years ago eh? One of my aunts there she lived until she was 105, but that's where she took lots of her first prizes and stuff ... She was one of the top old time Red River jiggers." Richard Callihoo interview, 2001, transcript courtesy of Musée Héritage St. Albert.
122 Walker, "The Third Column"; and Gerry Baird in discussion with author, August 2021.
123 Kearns, "(Re)claiming Métis Women Identities," 59–86.
124 Kearns, "(Re)claiming Métis Women Identities," 86.

Three

Josette Lagacé Work
Strong and Elastic as Steel

by Vanessa Winn

THE LIFE OF JOSETTE LAGACÉ WORK SPANNED A large part of the nineteenth century and across the Pacific Northwest. Born to uncertain paternity in approximately 1809, during the first-contact era in the Rocky Mountains plateau, she proved to be remarkably resilient. Despite having limited contact with her fur trade father, she married into the officer class of the Hudson's Bay Company (HBC) and adapted to brigade journeys, to life in a remote northern coastal fort far from her traditional home, and finally to farming the largest estate in colonial Victoria, British Columbia (BC), settling among other fur trade founding families. Despite his glaring racism toward fur trade families, historian Hubert Howe Bancroft, meeting Josette in 1878, was impressed: "The Indian wife, in body and mind, was strong and elastic as steel."[1]

Josette Lagacé's early familial relationships did not follow the common pattern within the fur trade hierarchy in its more established regions, particularly within the HBC. In those regions, as explored in the seminal works of Sylvia Van Kirk and Jennifer

S.H. Brown, clerks often married daughters of their superior officers, who had the potential to support career advancement while maintaining a place in fur trade society for their daughters.[2] The alliance of HBC clerk John Work with Josette did not follow this path. Yet a network of ties supported her upbringing, and she rose in position until, as a matriarch, she was able to support a large extended family and beyond. Transcending parental separation, geographic displacement, and political change, she integrated into a community founded by mostly unrelated elite Métis matriarchs in the Far West, while reuniting with her mother, Emme and her Interior Salish family. Despite a decades-long separation from her mother, Josette passed her maternal culture and language to her children, and regardless of paternal absence, she demonstrated the importance of kinship to following generations. Inhabiting the middle ground between fur traders and Indigenous Peoples, she is recognized by Métis Nation British Columbia as part of the early political and economic power of the colony and province.

Josette's father is reputed to have been Charles Lagacé, a French-Canadian voyageur with the North West Company (NWC).[3] Although he was entrusted with significant responsibilities in the Columbia region, his socio-economic status and illiteracy limited him to the working class of the fur trade. His illiteracy also makes his life and family difficult to trace. Not unlike many Métis women, Josette's story is accessed from multiple perspectives, and in Josette's case they are often inconsistent with one another. Her father's absence and her apparently shifting care and support among fur trade officers encouraged her adaptability.

The fur trade archive's limited references to women, despite their presence, produces a fragmented and oblique history, gleaned from its predominantly male-focused and -created records. Paradoxically, the striking silences call out for "reading conventional archives in unconventional ways," as Adele Perry

FIG. 3.01. Josette Work, wife of John Work, Hudson's Bay Company, c. 1880.

describes.⁴ By reinterpreting extensive masculine collections with Josette foremost in view, her story can be pieced together. To learn more about the role of fur trade women it is necessary to consult other records, such as personal letters, as noted by Sylvia Van Kirk in *Many Tender Ties*.⁵ Furthermore, comparing early public histories as sources of oral family history, and particularly the rare records left by women, aids in extrapolating a fuller portrayal of Josette. Given kinship's importance to Métis history, following her father's intertwining fur trade path is a starting point to glimpsing Josette's early life.

Josette's father, Charles Lagacé, was one of the first non-Indigenous men to traverse the Rockies into the Kootenay region of what would become BC. From Rocky Mountain House at the eastern base, in 1800, NWC trader David Thompson sent La Gassé (Lagacé) and another man named Le Blanc back across the mountains with the "Kootanaes" (Ktunaxa). They had travelled to trade, despite threats from the eastern "Pekenows" (Piikani). To ensure the safe return of the Ktunaxa, Thompson sent Lagacé and Le Blanc to overwinter with them while exploring trapping west of the mountains. Thompson induced the Ktunaxa to return in the spring to guide him to their country.⁶ It would be another seven years, however, before he made the crossing himself.

Ktunaxa oral history suggests that Lagacé and Le Blanc spent multiple winters with them, that one had a child with a chief's daughter, and that they were killed for betraying a Ktunaxa mountain camp to the Stony (Assiniboine).⁷ The child born to the chief's daughter may have been an older half-sibling to Josette. The oral history of the trappers' deaths conflicts, however, with later fur trade records. Thompson's HBC competitor Peter Fidler noted the men's 1801 return, and their illiteracy, in a journal postscript: "2 Canadians... could neither read nor write, what remarks they made was merely verbal."⁸

Curiously, Lagacé does not reappear in fur trade records until Thompson crossed the mountains with him in 1808. Lagacé then served in the Columbia region until May 1810, when Thompson was about to take his winter furs east. Lagacé deserted, declaring he was "unable to do his Duty."⁹ This was close to Josette's birth year. Whether Lagacé was truly unfit or had qualms about leaving a new family behind in the west is unknown. As Jennifer S.H. Brown has shown, voyageurs sometimes attained or kept women by threatening their bourgeois (wintering partner) with desertion, particularly during long explorations.¹⁰

In 1811, apparently in good health, Lagacé resurfaced in the Columbia District with Thompson, who noted the voyageur's abbreviated first name: Chas La Gassé. The voyageur re-engaged in 1812 for two years before returning to Montreal. Since engagés were usually not permitted to bring women to Montreal,¹¹ Josette was presumably left behind with her mother. Lagacé's contract was transferred to the HBC in 1821, when he re-emerged in the Columbia, but by the next year his contract expired and he was a "freeman."¹² Some voyageurs chose to remain in the west with their Indigenous families, trapping and trading independently. No primary fur trade sources confirm how long Lagacé remained, however.

It is difficult to ascertain if the Charles Lagacé who crossed the mountains in 1800 is the same man who accompanied Thompson in 1808. To confuse Lagacé's identity further, family history persists among Lagacé-Work descendants that Josette's father was Pierre Lagacé, a brother to Charles. While Josette's brother was named Pierre, fur trade records do not confirm an elder Pierre in the Columbia. However, the NWC ledger of 1811–13 records a "Pierre LaGaçé" in Saskatchewan, where he drowned.¹³

Almost a century would pass before a direct reference to Charles Lagacé as Josette's father would emerge. HBC clerk Edward Huggins, who married Josette's third daughter Letitia Work, provided editorial feedback to American historian Eva Emery Dye. The Huggins family were among the fur trade descendants Dye interviewed for her research, which represents a significant record of oral history, albeit dramatized. Critiquing one of Dye's depictions, titled "Mr. Work meets Charles Lagacé, the father of Suzette [Josette]," Huggins wrote that his wife "says that her father never saw Mr. Charles Lagacé. He died when the children were quite young, and their aunt and her husband (the latter a white man) brought them up."[14] Charles Lagacé did not, however, die when Josette and her brother were young, but returned to Montreal. Huggins's reference to an aunt suggests that the sibling relation was on the maternal side, rather than a brother of Lagacé. If that is true, he implies the "white man" was unrelated to Lagacé, except by marriage. The discrepancies between primary sources and family history of an uncle could suggest that Josette's mother was "turned off" by her father to the protection of a subordinate, a common practice among fur traders wishing to provide for women and families they were leaving behind.[15]

Dye evidently ignored Huggins's correction. Her 1906 romanticized portrayal of the Pacific Northwest dramatized John Work meeting Josette and Lagacé. Changing the spelling, she designated him Josette's uncle. According to Dye, Work "was led to the lodge of her uncle, deep in the Coeur d'Alêne hills. There he found Charles Legacie, a Frenchman...With him and the Ogdens and John McDonald the Grand, Josette Legacie and her brother Pierre had spent a wonderful childhood."[16] Ogden's older wife, Julia Rivet, who has been identified variously as Interior Salish and Nez Perce, was likely another strong maternal figure for Josette. Despite its inaccuracies, Dye's popular history conveys a sense of Josette's community upbringing.

Dye may have confused McDonalds. It is more likely that Josette spent her childhood near Finan McDonald, who was linked to Charles Lagacé in career and possibly in family ties. Accompanying David Thompson over the Rocky Mountains in 1807, McDonald was his second in command. A towering

Scottish Highlander with shaggy red hair and beard, he was dubbed "McDonald of the Buffalo" for wrestling one to the ground during a hunt. Among fur traders, his participation in Salish buffalo hunting and war excursions was unique, strengthening his ties to his wife's family, possibly including Josette. Early in his nearly twenty years in the Columbia District, he took as his wife Margaret, daughter of Chin-Chay-Nay-Whey, a Kalispel chief.[17] Like Josette's mother, Margaret is sometimes identified as Spokane, and McDonald was later based in Spokane territory, but evidence points to her Kalispel roots.

Another popular history suggests McDonald was linked to Lagacé by marriage. A Canadian account of *The Thompson Country* indicates that "Finan Macdonald and Legace" met a Colville chief in Montana and "ultimately married two of his daughters."[18] The reference to the men marrying sisters would support Huggins's claim that Josette was raised by her aunt. From these early-twentieth-century sources stems the Legacé spelling variant, obscuring Josette's origins. It is noteworthy that these sisters' marriages crossed ranks, with one sister marrying a clerk, and the other a voyageur. In earlier periods, the NWC allowed their men to form alliances with Indigenous women to strengthen trading ties with Indigenous Peoples.[19]

A few years before Josette's birth, however, the NWC proprietors discussed that "the number of women and Children in the country was a heavy burthen to the Concern & that some remedy ought to be applied to check so great an evil." The company resolved that no man, regardless of rank, could "live with [an Indigenous] woman after the fashion of the North West." Proprietors, responsible for their men, would be fined one hundred pounds sterling for a transgression. Thompson signed the resolution. In 1809, two agents were fined for violating it, east of the Rockies.[20]

This resolution proved impractical in the Columbia District. Both Finan McDonald and Lagacé apparently escaped penalty for their relationships with Indigenous women. It might explain, however, Thompson's later claim that he and his men were "too much fatigued to think of women."[21] Despite her parents' forbidden relationship, Josette likely benefited from the support of McDonald, a clerk, while adding to her social mobility. Astorian-turned-NWC clerk Ross Cox noted that McDonald was often accompanied by his wife's relations.[22] As this period overlapped Lagacé's absence in Montreal, Josette and her mother may well have been among these unnamed relations.

Blurring Josette's parentage further, her Indigenous mother has been identified variously as Flathead, Kalispel, Spokane, and Nez Perce. These allied nations engaged in buffalo hunting together for protection against their common eastern enemy, the Blackfeet. The repeated reference to Josette's Spokane origin may have arisen from the location of her marriage, rather than her mother's identity, giving the unfortunate impression that her life began with marriage. Construction on Spokane House (Washington) began in 1810, close to Josette's approximate birth year. Yet, that spring at Saleesh House (Montana), David Thompson paid Lagacé for the loan of three horses and sent him ahead to Lake Pend Oreille (Idaho) with supplies.[23] A month later, Lagacé would desert, refusing to cross the mountains.

Huggins maintained that Josette and Pierre were "half breed Canadian and Kalispel," an Interior Salish nation living around the Pend Oreille Lake and River, a tributary of the Columbia.[24] To Dye, he emphasized that Pierre was a full brother to Josette, perhaps to counter assumptions about the temporary nature of some fur trade relationships.[25]

Curiously, in 1941 Edward Huggins's youngest son conversely claimed that his grandmother descended from the Nez Perce, a different linguistic group from the Salish.[26] Josette may have spoken this language, as Huggins noted that Nez Perce was among the many languages that Pierre Lagacé understood. Huggins's wife Letitia, could speak Kalispel "glibly."[27] She was too young to remember the territory herself, suggesting that Josette taught her maternal language to her daughter.

A distant relation of Finan McDonald and a rare female source, Christina McDonald Williams identified Josette as Pend d'Oreille, a fur trade name used synonymously for Kalispel. Identifying her own Nez Perce lineage, Williams did not indicate sharing this with Josette. Instead, she stated suggestively: "Mrs. John Work was a half breed Pend d'Oreille woman.... David Thompson had a daughter by a Pend d'Oreille woman."[28]

The existence of this daughter by Thompson is unconfirmed, except by Christina's brother Duncan McDonald, who in 1934 asserted that David Thompson "lived among my people.... He had a woman among the Selish. His descendants still live on the reservation."[29] Although unable to identify them, McDonald did locate the chimney remnants of Kullyspel House, one of Thompson's earliest western trading posts. Built in 1809 on Lake Pend Oreille by Finan McDonald, this short-lived post is a possible birthplace of Josette. If Thompson had a daughter with a Salish woman, her age would align with Josette's, putting Josette at the fitting time and place to be this claimed child.

By the time Josette married HBC clerk John Work in the fashion or custom of the country (without consecration by the church, which had not arrived), she was living at Spokane House, where Finan McDonald and his family were based. A first class clerk in the Hudson Bay region, Work arrived in the Columbia District in 1823 with Peter Skene Ogden, a chief trader whose career Work shadowed. As told by Dye, this is the Ogden with whom Josette had spent her childhood. Ogden probably knew Josette earlier, when the NWC sent him to the Columbia District in 1818 to avoid a murder charge by the HBC. He was reluctantly taken on after the companies amalgamated.

After wintering at Spokane House, the next year Work assisted Finan McDonald trading in the Flathead region. It is unknown when Work first met Josette. She may have been too young to attract his notice initially, and he was often absent on the coast until 1825.

Josette was not Work's first partner. In an 1826 letter, fellow clerk Francis Ermatinger described Work's union with Josette. "Just after I left Spokan [sic] last fall he purchased a fine young milcher, which with the fees to the relations requisite cost him about 10-10—and he took her on with him to the Flathead post.... But upon his arrival at Spokan, to spend the holydays, he was smitten with the charm of Madamoselle [sic] Laguin, a ward of Mr. Ogden's, and fancying that he would get some credit by carrying off the prize from two rivals (Messrs Black and Manson) who had been treating for *empassant*, he fairly agreed to sign and seal, and is now safely moored with her for life."[30]

Marriages with Indigenous women traditionally involved gifts to her parents—the "fees" Ermatinger callously described. His uncertainty of Josette's surname implies that Charles Lagacé was uninvolved. That Josette was a ward of Work's superior provided her some security. At that time, the HBC forbade its employees from taking a woman without binding himself to the maintenance of her and their children.[31] Although this did not transpire with the first woman, it is significant that Work apparently formalized his marriage to Josette by signing a contract. In doing so, Work defied the recommendation of Governor Sir George Simpson that he marry a Cayuse woman to improve trade relations with the tribe.

The letters of Francis Ermatinger to his brother Edward (Ned) are a valuable insight into Work's family life. Work was particularly close to Edward, whose departure from the fur trade created a lifelong correspondence with former colleagues. Francis Ermatinger's gossip roughly aligns with Work's unusually sparse journal of this trip. Chief Trader John Warren Dease at Spokane House requested a visit, and Work left Flathead in early January 1826 for the five-day journey. Demonstrating women's invisibility in fur trade journals, he did not mention Josette during his five days at Spokane, only that Mr. Dease "with his people were found well."[32]

Ermatinger's description of Josette as "a ward of Mr. Ogden's" implies she ultimately came under his authority as a chief trader, although they were otherwise unrelated. Ogden was frequently absent from Spokane, leading the gruelling Snake River brigade for six years. Josette's ward status suggests that her father was either dead or had abandoned her. While posts sometimes supported abandoned families of traders, children of departed voyageurs were more often absorbed by their mother's Indigenous family.[33] It is curious that Ogden would provide for a daughter of a freeman trapper, who likely left behind no means to support her.

With multiple suitors, it is intriguing to consider Josette's agency in her partner choice, apparently made without her father's presence. Both of Work's "rivals" were officers. Senior to Work in both age and rank, Samuel Black, like Ogden, was a former Nor-Wester with a violent reputation. Donald Manson would later become known for rough treatment of subordinates and his wife. With Ogden frequently away, it is possible that Finan McDonald and his wife, who were about to move east with their family, maintained some parting protection and influence in Josette's future. About to lose their long-time presence, she may have been seeking stability in a relationship.

With McDonald's retirement, Governor Simpson placed Work in charge of Spokane House, directing him to build a new post at Kettle Falls on the Columbia. Josette transitioned from being a ward of the fort to wife of its manager. Although formerly NWC bourgeois had married their voyageurs' daughters, this class-crossing practice was less common in the HBC,[34] making Josette's rise in rank more exceptional. Work also spent this first winter with Josette trading into the Flathead territory, where her interpretation skills were of value among the Interior Salish, although this detail is missing from his journals. It is of note also that the eight men who accompanied Work to Spokane were "Iroquoy" (Iroquois), illustrating the fur trade's diverse linguistic and cultural demographic which Josette, married at about sixteen years old, navigated.

As business records, fur trade journals accounted for men. Work's first journal reference to his wife was in February 1826 at Flathead House. "I gave one of the men, Togonche, a boxing for making too free with my wife." Three days later Togonche stole back into the fort in the night to get his things and vanished.[35] While explaining the desertion of one of his men, Work's note reveals the vulnerable situation of wives, even among the fur trade's officer class. He did not assign any blame to Josette for the incident, despite previously "divorcing one of his women" for infidelity.[36]

In Josette's favour against attitudes toward Indigenous women, Interior Salish women were renowned by fur traders for their chastity, making them attractive to British men looking for Victorian ideals in a potential wife and mother to their children. David Thompson recalled a winter spent with them: "The Saleesh Indians were a fine race of moral Indians, the finest I had seen, and set a high value on the chastity of their women; adultery is death to both parties."[37] Despite the value fur traders placed on Salish women, this had not protected Josette's mother from apparent abandonment, a circumstance no doubt impressed upon Josette.

Two months after the incident where Togonche "made free" with Josette, she and John Work closed Spokane House, moving its goods north through deep snow to the new Fort Colvile (Colville, Washington). Between trading expeditions, the couple spent the next three years based at Colvile, developing a farm to reduce dependence on imported provisions. This farm foretold Josette's later life. Her obituary would state that she was born in Colville, Washington.[38] This is questionable, given the earlier discussion and that her husband supervised building the fort when Josette was soon to become a mother herself.

While at Colvile, the first and second of their daughters, Jane and Sarah, were born. In March 1829, Work wrote of the second birth to his close friend Ned Ermatinger: "My little partner presented me with another daughter in the beginning of the winter, which cannot be considered a fortunate occurrence in this part of the world." Despite this, Work's letters show much affection for Josette, who he is also called "my little rib." He also asked Ned, who had left the fur trade to settle in Ontario, to purchase gifts for her.[39]

Raised on a farm near Londonderry, Ireland, Work was a natural choice to oversee the agricultural development of the Colvile farm, the first in the region.[40] Josette's assistance in operating the farm can be inferred, particularly as, by 1829, Work was stricken with lifelong eye trouble. At one point, recovering from quinsy (tonsillitis), he was "fiercely encountered by a young bull, the effects of whose blows, he is never likely to get the better."[41] Demonstrating his hallmark endurance, Work recovered. Left unsaid was Josette's skill as a nurse, only later acknowledged. With Chief Trader Dease's fatal illness, Work took charge of the region and the family moved to the Flathead post to the southeast.

In 1830, Work succeeded Ogden in charge of the Snake country brigade, HBC trapping expeditions designed to deplete beaver in the disputed Oregon territory to discourage American encroachment there. The brigades extended far beyond the Snake River into Utah and Nevada, probably marking Josette's lengthy separation from her mother, if not earlier. Like Ogden, Work did not often specifically mention his wife in these journals, but his letters indicate Josette accompanied him. For nearly a year he travelled with his wife and young family in a region already competitively trapped, speaking to the survival strategies and skillsets of both John and Josette, prepared by earlier journeys. Although disappointed by the brigade's lower profits, Work returned to Colvile to news of his promotion to chief trader.

A third daughter, Letitia, was born in Idaho on brigade the following year. Letitia Huggins later related some of her childhood stories to her daughter-in-law Annie. Like Edward Huggins, Annie also exchanged numerous letters with public historian Eva Emery Dye, providing a rich source of maternal oral history. Annie relayed a memory shared by Letitia of Josette when the brigade set up camp, revealing its community of women: "One of the women took mother [Letitia] who was then a wee baby from Mrs. Work and laid her sleeping on the grass." After Josette had dismounted and the camp made, they found Letitia covered with ducklings, having been laid near a nest. Some of the women said "they would bring her good luck and for a long time the Indians called her tous-esh or tawees," meaning duckling.[42] Of the same expedition, Edward Huggins imparted its harsher aspect: "I have often heard Mrs. Work, a brave intelligent woman, tell of the dangers they experienced.... They were amongst a lot of hostile Blackfeet, and one night they were attacked, and in the morning they found many arrows sticking in the walls of their tent, which was made of thick buffalo skins."[43]

In 1832, just returned from the Snake country, John Work described the perilous conditions for the family and the brigade: "Fever attacked the people and they fell off so fast that every boat was like an hospital." Bordering Blackfoot country, the brigade lost six men in a battle, with more wounded. Work received a wound in the arm, grazed by a musket ball. Despite this, he related that Josette and their three little girls were well.[44]

Expecting worse misery, Work did not intend to take his family on his next brigade, to the Rio Sacramento (California): "I shall be very lonely without them, but the cursed trip exposes them to too much hardship." Perhaps influenced by her mother's experience, and no doubt by confidence in her own abilities, Josette evidently determined not to be left behind and Work relented. Writing again to Ned Ermatinger after the fourteen-month journey through rugged terrain amid hostile tribes, he conveyed that "worst of all the fever broke out among my people (near 100 in number) and spread so rapidly among them that...more than three fourths of the party, myself, the three little ones and their mother among the number, were attacked by it."[45] With medication soon exhausted and reduced to a skeleton, Work led the months-overdue, wretched brigade to Fort Vancouver (Washington) in October of 1833. It is clear now that the intermittent fever, the "ague," was malaria.

Work spent the next year recuperating at Fort Vancouver and was impressed by its agricultural development since he had helped move the HBC's western headquarters there, upriver from the Columbia's mouth. As Work was treated by a London physician, Josette benefited from female company of her own social station. A few days after the arrival of the Works, Amelia Douglas, the Métis wife of James Douglas, bore a son who died at birth. She needed support, particularly in her husband's frequent absences.[46] Close in age, Josette and Amelia had both experienced separation from their maternal families and married in their mid-teens. They formed a lifelong friendship with each other that continued into subsequent generations.

While at Fort Vancouver Josette bore her fourth daughter, Margaret, named after Marguerite, the Métis wife of Chief Factor John McLoughlin, head of the department.[47] Possibly Josette was also remembering Finan McDonald's wife, Margaret. Similarly, Marguerite, in her mid-fifties, became the godmother to two of Douglas's daughters born at Vancouver.[48] Recognizing one another with namesakes and godmother relationships demonstrates the women's close-knit community, regardless of their different origins.

At the end of 1834, Work was assigned to the coastal shipping trade and Josette was forced to remain at Vancouver with their four daughters. Dr. McLoughlin forbade women aboard ships, expecting they would lead to trouble among the men. While Josette may have had mixed feelings about not accompanying her husband north, at Vancouver she enjoyed the community of other Métis wives of officers. Amelia was of British-Cree origin. Although their Indigenous maternal languages differed, the wives communicated in French, English, the Chinook trading patois, and probably their own languages.

Instructed to rebuild the recently moved Fort Simpson (Port Simpson/Lax Kw'alaams, BC) while trading along the northern coast, Work was away for much of the year. Whether due to the power of the newly arrived steamer *Beaver* or of her own will, Josette joined her husband at Fort Simpson in December 1836, steaming north with five-year-old Letitia and two-year-old Margaret. Her brother Pierre accompanied them.[49] Josette's heart-wrench at leaving Jane and Sarah behind at Fort Vancouver to attend school can be imagined, and perhaps may have been assuaged by the continued presence of Marguerite McLoughlin and Amelia Douglas at the fort.

Work had wanted to place his two eldest daughters with the aptly named Reverend Beaver and his wife, but he did not wish to aggravate Chief Factor McLoughlin, who furiously caned the chaplain for insulting his wife while condemning country marriages. Instead, another kind of abuse awaited at Fort Vancouver's school, "The school master...from discoveries that were made by Mr. Douglas, was this year flogged in the most public manner twice, yet not half severe enough for the villain.... [He] has been in the habit of taking advantage of the female part of his pupils and our friend Work's daughter has had her share of the odium, altho' a mere child yet."[50] Jane and Sarah were then about eleven and ten years old. Rather than disclosing the teacher's sexual abuse directly to Douglas, temporarily in charge during McLoughlin's absence, the girls may have confided in Mrs. Douglas. Given Josette was raised by an aunt, it is plausible she had encouraged her daughters to turn to a close surrogate in her own absence, thereby replicating kinship ties with unrelated Métis women. These ties are shown by a young teenage daughter of the Ogdens, Sarah Julia, receiving advice from her godmother, Amelia Douglas, about delaying her arranged marriage to her father's clerk.[51]

Meanwhile Work engaged the assistance of Dr. William Fraser Tolmie, an HBC surgeon at Vancouver, to place his daughters with Reverend Leslie and his wife, Methodist missionaries in the nearby Willamette River valley settlement. A studious young Scot from Inverness, Tolmie took "a peculiar interest" in Jane's education and would later marry her.[52] Tolmie's interest has been interpreted as a betrothal, but they did not marry for another decade, when Jane was twenty-two. Josette may have been more successful at delaying Jane's marriage than Sarah Julia Ogden's mother had been. Most of Josette's eight daughters would marry in their twenties.

Aside from her absent eldest daughters, Josette faced other stresses at Fort Simpson. Letitia recalled arriving at Fort Simpson to smallpox. She and Margaret played with the children of Work's clerk, Dr. John Frederick Kennedy, outside the men's quarters until chased away by the doctor, scolding them with threats of smallpox. Neither Letitia nor her sister got the disease, but their uncle Pierre did.[53] His lower-class disadvantage emerged here, requiring him to live in closer men's quarters than Josette's family in the officer's freshly roofed "Big House."

The fort's 1836 journal confirms the disease striking in the fall. Several "cow inoculations" given were ineffective, but in the spring Dr. Kennedy's Coast Tsimshian wife Fanny, and one of their children were recovering.[54] The Works fared better. Almost predictably, their fifth daughter, Mary, was born at Fort Simpson in 1837.

As he had done at Colvile to make the fort self-sufficient, Work hacked a garden out of the rainforest. Clearing the land was strenuous, and in 1840 he ruptured his abdomen falling onto a tree stump. Weeks later he aggravated it jumping from a fallen tree. With Dr. Kennedy at another post, Work tried "to return the rupture" himself and injured his intestines. With the ensuing inflammation he "was for four days at the point of death" and bedridden for two months, with Josette as his primary caregiver.[55] The previous year Josette had probably treated Dr. Kennedy's two accidental gunshot wounds. Given her sewing skills, it is more likely she who stitched up the doctor's profusely bleeding headwound than Work, who recorded "the wound was sewed up" without indicating by whose hand.[56]

When he thought he was dying, Work agonized over his family's fate. He wished he was settled near his brother David or friend Ned in the east. While he had regrets of his duty to God, he lamented, "Yet the thought of leaving my helpless wife and children in this cursed country which I detest rendered the near approach of death more unpleasant than anything else."[57] Though clearly concerned for Josette, his view tended to be patronizing compared to others' acknowledgement of her intelligence: "She is to me an affectionate partner simple and uninstructed as she is and takes good care of my children & myself." When Work believed his family, "being natives of this country, would not be fit for society,"[58] he underestimated their ability to adapt.

However, the "good wife" was not so helpless, and the previous winter Josette had presented him with a boy. Typical of a Victorian father, "like most old fogies [he was] quite proud of the little fellow." Though friends informed him that his eldest daughters were improving in Willamette, he had not seen them in two years. Josette had not seen them in over four years. While ill, Work delayed letting her go, implying she was needed as his nurse.[59]

Jane and Sarah had more to endure in Willamette, where the Reverend Leslie's wife developed a fatal illness. She gave her bible as a parting gift to Jane, who nursed her, showing similar aptitudes to her mother. Josette was at last able to retrieve her eldest daughters in 1841. Although happy to be reunited, Work continued to wish he could settle his family in the east to have them educated. Despite finding Jane and Sarah "greatly improved," their progress was less than he expected. At most they had a "tolerable command of the English language and much pain seems to have been taken with their religious instruction."[60]

To her daughter-in-law, Letitia later described her sisters' social introduction to the north. She and Margaret remained at Fort Simpson with their father, while Josette took the two youngest children with her, accompanied again by her brother Pierre, regardless of the siblings' class barriers. Returning on the schooner *Cadboro* during a storm, the captain, keeping far offshore, refused to risk letting them disembark. The Tsimshian, however, came out in their canoes, and Pierre returned with them to give Work the news. The ship continued to Sitka, where Josette and her children were entertained by the Russian governor. Since their

1839 agreement with the Russian American Company, the HBC had trading rights on a strip of the Alaskan coast in exchange for agricultural products.[61] During her visit, Josette apparently navigated the delicacy of diplomacy, probably aware that several years before the agreement the Russians had blocked Ogden and Tolmie from entering the Stikine River to establish a fort. This journey no doubt impressed Jane and Sarah with the cultural adjustment they faced in the north.[62]

Work's illness would have dramatic repercussions for himself and his family. Touring the coast that autumn, Sir George Simpson transferred clerk Roderick Finlayson from Fort Stikine to assist Work while recuperating, since Fort Simpson was the most valuable northern post. This transfer left Chief Factor McLoughlin's son John Jr. in charge of Stikine without assistance from another officer. The next spring, his men murdered him, angry at being denied free access to their Indigenous wives. Governor Simpson blamed the victim, citing abuse while drinking.[63]

Grief-stricken and outraged, McLoughlin embarked on a vendetta to clear his son's name. Defying Simpson's hasty verdict, he blamed Finlayson's transfer, claiming that Work needed less aid, with "three first Rate common men," including Pierre Lagacé.[64] Work, the deceased's immediate supervisor, had, however, previously warned Sir George that he heard from the "Natives" of attempts on McLoughlin's life. Indigenous wives communicated between the forts, and McLoughlin Jr.'s widow came to Fort Simpson, where Work questioned her regarding depositions taken by Governor Simpson. Josette conceivably participated in this communication network,[65] particularly since her brother had married a Tsimshian woman, Lisette.

McLoughlin sent Kanaquassé, an Iroquois who admitted attempting murder and "one of the Greatest villains in the country," to be detained at Fort Simpson.[66] With a newborn, her seventh child Catherine (Kate), Josette was doubtless relieved when Kanaquassé was sent to Sitka for possible Russian prosecution, as Fort Stikine was on Russian territory. Both Russia and the Canadian colonial government declined to prosecute due to the complicated jurisdictional questions. Other than detainments and discharges, the murderers were not punished, heightening the danger at the northern posts.

The investigation revealed plots against both McLoughlin Jr. and Finlayson. After his narrow escape, young Finlayson enjoyed life at Fort Simpson, where he was "blessed with the kindest of masters (Mr. Work, C. T.)."[67] Finlayson had a severe fall from the stairs to the storage attic and was treated by Dr. Kennedy, and probably nursed by the women in the Big House. Here he met Sarah Work, whom he would later marry. Accidents were common and dangerous. Josette, during her last years at the fort, would seriously injure herself falling from the ladder that accessed the gallery running around the pickets, giving her a rare appearance in the fort journal.

Work's sickbed fear for his wife and family was destitution. In other respects, Josette was far from "helpless." Letitia, describing her mother's room, recalled, in addition to the chintz curtains around the bed, a pair of loaded pistols hanging on the wall. Aside from taking care of her growing family, Josette was later credited with doing "a great deal towards civilizing the Indians, and...at Fort Simpson helped very materially to put a stop to the barbarous system of slavery formerly practised by the tribes. Mrs. Work also devoted a great deal of time towards teaching the Indian women useful things, such as sewing and cooking."[68]

This reference raises questions of the women's agency in learning. If Josette taught Indigenous women cooking, these were skills she herself no longer needed, since forts employed male cooks for the officers and their families. She also facilitated the use of cookware trade items, by loaning the pans in which she served molasses-soaked biscuits to visiting chiefs' wives, who she received "courteously." They returned them afterwards, suggesting a respectful and ongoing relationship. Letitia recalled that she and her sisters baked, assisted by their cook, Cantal, for amusement.[69] However, Letitia was later paid to cook at Fort Nisqually, implying she had learned considerable skills, plausibly from her mother. Since Huggins remained a clerk, Letitia's employment supplemented income for her growing family.

In advocating to enhance the lives of women, Josette may have been assisted by Fanny Kennedy, who Letitia remembered as having great influence over the Tsimshian. However, Fanny had a slave taking care of her family, a hindrance to Josette's initial efforts toward abolition. Indigenous slavery on the Northwest Coast was a pre-contact hereditary system, unusual in North America. Supplied primarily by warfare, raiding, and intergroup trading, slavery had deep economic and cultural ties, making it difficult to dislodge.[70] This system differed substantially from Josette's Plateau origins, where temporary war captivity typically ended in death or adoption.[71]

While the company generally did not interfere in Indigenous affairs outside of trade, Work was often moved to intervene by paying for slave women and returning them to their own nations. His fort journal described a quarrel between two Kygarnie (Kaigani Haida) women who proposed killing slaves to demonstrate their wealth, in which, he wrote, "we interfered and pointed out to [them] the sin, inhumanity and uselessness of such a step and used every means in our power to dissuade them from such an atrocious act." While "we" might include Dr. Kennedy, it apparently also included Josette, so often unmentioned in the journals.[72]

Although deterring slavery on the coast is often attributed to missionary influences, the Works' tenure at Fort Simpson predated the arrival of protestant missionary William Duncan by over twenty years. In 1857 Duncan developed a Tsimshian following who would build a lauded mission at the nearby village of Metlakatla. It is plausible that Josette, as a forerunner, was influenced by American missionary Narcissa Whitman, who arrived at Fort Vancouver in the fall of 1836, a few months before Josette left for the north. Whitman spent time with the elite women of Vancouver and taught McLoughlin's daughter, Amelia Douglas, and probably others.[73]

Corroborating Josette's efforts to abolish slavery, inspired by pity and "warmest indignation," a 1928 popular history claimed it was due to Josette's influence that the Tsimshian became "amenable to Christian teaching." Even during Work's absences, "her efforts never slackened. By precept and example, by earnest teaching and loving care, she began to make her influence felt." Like Dye's work, *Pioneer Women of Vancouver Island* drew on interviews with descendants, including a granddaughter of Josette, and focused a chapter on the Work women.[74]

Josette's influence is remarkable considering the language and cultural barriers she faced on the northern coast. Despite geographic displacement, she taught skills to the community and shared elements of her own culture with her daughters. Letitia recalled embroidering moccasins, showing the patterns, leather cut outs, and beads she had kept and shared with her daughter-in-law, over fifty years later.[75] Evidently missing the community at Fort Vancouver, Josette wished her husband to settle in the Willamette valley, which was becoming popular with retiring fur traders and their families.[76]

At Fort Simpson, Josette's female company of her own station was initially limited to Dr. Kennedy's wife Fanny, who understood her rank was second to Mrs. Work. The women and children usually dined separately from the officers, although Letitia recalled her father teaching her and her sisters to carve when others were absent. In the mid-1840s, a conflict apparently arose between Josette and Captain McNeill's wife, Mathilda, a Kaigani Haida chief. While its cause is unknown, Work denied McNeill's family lodgings in the spare rooms of the "Large House." He later relented, but only temporarily during the *Beaver*'s stay. McNeill reported to Governor Simpson that after the ship's departure, "the family must go into the Indian hall but to be brief this is all about the women."[77] He also complained to Work that women were arranging the HBC's affairs. It is plausible that Josette was protecting her top status within the fort hierarchy from a woman who enjoyed her own authority and autonomy among the local Indigenous population, who were equally class-conscious. Possibly Josette's sense of social vulnerability was exacerbated when a Tongass chief taunted her engagé brother Pierre with the insult "slave" a few years earlier. Pierre responded with a cutting blow to his head that knocked him down, risking a revenge killing.[78] Social exclusions were an authority measure available to Josette's position.

Bridging cultures while distinguishing herself, Josette was resourceful. Blending traditional practices of curing animal pelts with British culture, at Fort Simpson Josette developed the Victorian penchant for taxidermy. Birds were her expert specialty, and a diverse assortment decorated the walls of the living area. Letitia recalled the birds were later sent to England, conceivably at the urging of Dr. Tolmie, Josette's future son-in-law, who was a keen naturalist and sent specimens to Kew Gardens, London.[79] British acquisition of the birds separated Josette from her material culture. It appears Josette learned taxidermy, an unusual pastime among Métis women, earlier. In 1826, renowned botanist David Douglas met his "old friend Mr. John Work," who "kindly preserved for me a large female grouse and a male black rock-grouse, both very well done."[80] Newly married, Josette adapted her skills to her husband's culture, increasing her value outside the fur trade to science. The stuffed birds in the Fort Vancouver Heritage Site's collection, although twentieth-century additions, reflect Victorian interest in naturalism due to exploration.

Other than individuals such as Fanny, Josette was wary of the coastal Indigenous population. Letitia remembered the Haida informing the fort that a band of "marauders" watched the children on a fishing outing, implying they could have taken them captive, and her "parents were more careful than ever."[81] Josette also feared that Work's pipe would make him a target when touring the fort's gallery at night. His frequent smoking created other worries, and he developed a tumour on his lip. When carrot poultices failed, two Royal Navy surgeons removed it with Dr. Kennedy's assistance, along with part of his lip in several operations.[82]

These were bitter years for Work, already known as the "Old Gentleman"; his career stagnated during his decade at Fort Simpson, regardless of its substantial gains. Despite eventually clearing his son's name, McLoughlin's clashes with Simpson cost him his sole rule of the Western Department. Work replaced McLoughlin on the new three-man governing board and was promoted to chief factor in 1846, which would lead to more social opportunities for Josette.

Resuming responsibility for the coastal trade and the steamer *Beaver*, Work travelled more often. He had been teaching his children, now ten in number, at Fort Simpson. But in 1849 when a school opened at Fort Victoria, the company's new western depot, he and Josette took their family south. With the arrival of schoolmaster Reverend John Staines and his wife, Work took the opportunity to have the Anglican Church solemnize his marriage to Josette. As well as finally giving Josette legal and social security, this marriage removed any questions of illegitimacy for their children in

British society, particularly as Vancouver Island became a colony this year. A month later Sarah married Roderick Finlayson, who had overseen the building of Fort Victoria and was Douglas's second in command. Another marriage soon followed between Jane and Dr. Tolmie, now a chief trader in charge of Fort Nisqually and its farm, part of the Puget Sound Agriculture Company, a subsidiary of the HBC. Like her parents, Jane transitioned into farming. As Sylvia Van Kirk has amply shown, fur trade daughters frequently married their father's junior officers.[83] By 1860, Letitia and Mary would follow the example of their eldest sisters.

At Fort Victoria, Josette was reunited with Amelia Douglas. The residence of both her long-time friend and Sarah at the fort may have eased Josette's apprehension of leaving five of her children at the Staines' boarding school, as well as the Kennedys' daughter Eliza. Among their classmates were four Douglas children and three McNeills,[84] the latter whom they knew from Fort Simpson. With the older children settled, the Works returned to Fort Simpson with their three youngest children, accompanied yet again by Pierre Lagacé.

For their last two years based at Fort Simpson, Josette was often without her husband. He established Fort Rupert and a coal mine on northern Vancouver Island, where a miners' strike in 1850 compelled him to make a canoe trek south to Victoria. Work also brought gold specimens from Haida Gwaii, foreshadowing events that would dramatically alter the family's future. He dispatched his brother-in-law Pierre Lagacé by canoe from Fort Simpson to investigate, but "the jealousy of two influential Chiefs" prevented him from reaching the gold area. However, Lagacé discovered a navigable passage through Haida Gwaii, revealing that it was two large islands. Work then journeyed with Lagacé to the rock-embedded gold vein, made more frustrating by the protection of competing Indigenous tribes.[85]

After repeated stretches alone, in 1851 Josette was able to voyage south with her husband on the *Beaver*, taking supplies to Fort Nisqually, Puget Sound, with the *Mary Dare* in tow. US Customs seized the ships for violating an archaic sugar law and for landing passengers without clearance. The passengers were the Works, their daughter Margaret, and their son John, visiting their kin, Jane Work Tolmie.[86] During the extended family reunion over Christmas, they were doubtless struck by American hostility to the HBC, in defiance of the Oregon Treaty (1846). There was "intense excitement" in the new Colony of Vancouver Island to rescue the vessels.[87] As well as encroaching on company land, some newcomer Americans were derisive of fur traders' Métis wives. Two years later an American suitor of Letitia, who was often at Nisqually helping her sister Jane with the children, wrote to Dr. Tolmie of "the mean prejudice which bad characters" entertained toward her.[88]

FIG. 3.02. Hillside, Residence of John Work and family, c. 1880s.

The Works were detained at Nisqually until February, when they returned to Victoria. Whether the American detention reconciled Josette to settling in British territory is unknown, but Work, having given up thoughts of moving east, purchased nearly six hundred acres outside Fort Victoria in 1852. Although the land was partially cleared from Indigenous harvesting of camas, he began a new farm reluctantly. While their Hillside Farm manor house was being built, the Works moved in with the Finlaysons at Rock Bay.[89]

Settling in Victoria, Josette was reunited with her mother. In 1854, Pierre (known among the family as Pierrish or Pierish) brought their "mother and other Indian relatives from the interior" to Victoria.[90] Her mother died six months after their reunion. Catholic burial records identify Emme Lagassé, *femme des Têtes-Plattes, veuve de P. Lagassé*. Her name was finally recorded by her death.[91]

Since Josette had adopted her husband's Anglican denomination, it was probably Pierre who supplied the priest with the initial "P." for Emme's late husband, his father. Intriguingly, the spelling Lagassé is David Thompson's variant. Têtes-Plattes (Flatheads) was a French-Canadian name used in the fur trade for Interior Salish people generally, as well as a specific nation. The priest noted that Emme was about sixty years old. She would thus have been in her teen years when she bore Josette and Pierre.

The brief reunion was bittersweet, with Josette's last child, Suzette, born after Emme's arrival. Curiously, the Works did not name any of their eight daughters after Emme. Perhaps coincidentally, David Thompson had named a daughter Emma the year before he crossed the mountains west.

John Work had anglicized his name from the Irish "Wark" when he joined the HBC in 1814. While his letters refer to Josette, her name was later anglicized to Suzette, including on her tombstone. Granddaughter Jean Tolmie, however, took umbrage at this when critiquing Dye's manuscript, sent to her by Edward Huggins: "No one ever called Grannie 'Suzette,'—grandfather called her Josette, the French pronunciation, and not even her most intimate friend, Lady Douglas, ever addresses her as Suzette, but always Mrs. Work, and I do not think it nice to speak of her as Suzette, as if she had no other name and was a servant."[92] Although accepting her grandmother's French heritage, Jean also revealed class bias.

Jean also took exception to Dye's portrayal of her mother, aunts, and uncles: "Do you think it likely that if grannie was dressed in black silk, that her children would be dressed in skin? That should be changed, also calling the children 'papooses.' They were not Indian."[93] Jean's sensitivity echoed her aunt Letitia's. In 1903, Huggins informed a friend, "Madame Dye talks of visiting me, and I dread her coming...My wife doesn't fancy this lady coming here and asking questions about her mother's family."[94] In her study of five founding families in Victoria, Sylvia Van Kirk demonstrated the increasing pressure on fur traders' wives and children to assimilate to its burgeoning colonial society,[95] accelerated by the gold rush.

Although exceptionally fortunate that their eleven children survived childhood, the Works bore another loss in Victoria in 1856 when their son Henry died of rapid consumption (tuberculosis). In comparison, of the Douglas family's thirteen children, only six survived childhood. Both families were considerably larger than average; Jennifer Brown's 1980 study of officers' families found they had an average 7.3 children in a similar period.[96] Pierre, who lived in Victoria during his mother's residence, lost his youngest son the same year. But the Works' Hillside Farm prospered, growing similar crops to Colvile decades earlier, and Work doubled his land holdings.

Victoria's bucolic settlement of mostly fur trade families was overwhelmed by the Fraser River gold rush in 1858. Reacting to the influx of California miners, London sent a British Boundary Commission of Royal Engineers. Its secretary, Lieutenant Charles Wilson, initially demonstrated the typical newcomer's attitudes to the fur trade families. First meeting the "half breeds" aboard a Royal Navy ship, he felt they had "as many of the propensities of the savage as of the civilized being."

His attitude shifted after spending New Year's Day at Hillside, where "we had a large dinner party, no stiffness or formality & we would up with a 'hain' dance (as an Indian would say) which means no end of a jollification." Returning from a summer in the interior, he got "amongst civilized people" in Victoria again and immediately went to Hillside: "The Works are about the kindest people I ever came across; 'my western home' I call it." He was deeply indebted to the young ladies, who had been taught sewing by Josette, for the mosquito-net head bags they made for the boundary party. Often riding with them on Saturdays, he admired their "ease and gracefulness" even at full gallop, another skill probably learned from their mother. By 1860, he decried the newly arrived English who "pretend to look down upon the old settlers, which has split the people up into sets...however I stick to my old friends who...have in every respect the advantage of most of the newcomers with their pride."[97]

Well might Wilson have appreciated the mosquito protection. In the fall of 1861, Work had a relapse of malaria that he had contracted in California twenty-eight years earlier and died in December at age sixty-nine. Widowed the same year as Queen Victoria, Josette had a portrait done in mourning striking a similar regal vein. The death of the fur trade patriarch could mean loss of social standing, but Josette inherited much of the Hillside Farm, revealing Work's distrust of his alcoholic sons, and speaking to Josette's important role as matriarch of her family, considering the unusualness at the time of naming an Indigenous spouse as primary beneficiary.

Pierre Lagacé moved back to Victoria to help at Hillside but lived in one of the outbuildings with his son, Peter. Despite the Works' earlier attempts to assist them, Pierre's sons got in trouble with the law. In 1865, Peter stabbed an Indigenous farmhand in the back, critically injuring him.[98] A Pend d'Oreille girl living at Hillside was a court witness, likely one of the relatives who arrived with Josette's mother. Leaving clues to complex family dynamics, the press reported the "Indian" victim's name, Stanislaus. His name reappeared as Dr. W.F. Tolmie's 1870s source for the "Selish, Kullēspelm" vocabulary, obtained at Victoria, in his book of Indigenous languages.[99] Evidently, Josette continued to provide a Hillside home for her Kalispel kin decades after her mother died. John Work Jr. was the victim's court interpreter, indicating familiarity with the language. Despite the serious crime, Peter had a short sentence for assault, suggesting intervention by the Work family, headed by Josette.

Josette's large family provided mutual support. Two of her sons-in-law were already chief factors in Victoria where, like Work, they owned extensive property. In 1859 Dr. Tolmie built a mansion on his neighbouring 1,100-acre farm, Cloverdale, where Jane, similar to her mother, raised a family of twelve, though two girls died young in 1865. Jane also echoed Josette's experience in hosting visiting scientists, among other guests.[100] Mary's husband, James Allan Grahame, would become the HBC Chief Commissioner in North America. Reflecting the changing economy, four of the younger daughters married outside the fur trade, to men employed as a farmer, bank managers, and merchants. Despite their general success, Kate's husband, Charles Wentworth Wallace, had disastrous misfortune with the declining gold rush, losing Point Ellice House (a gift from John Work, and now a museum) to bankruptcy. Kate moved in with her sister Jane Tolmie, and then with her mother at Hillside, where she died of consumption. Josette raised Kate's only surviving daughter, continuing her active role as a matriarch.

Although John Work wasn't particularly close to James Douglas, the Work women's relationships with the Douglas family helped to protect their social standing through changing times. As Governor of Vancouver Island, the gold rush propelled Douglas to become governor of the new colony, British Columbia, and he was knighted for his service. Despite his relinquished ties to the HBC, the ties of his wife Amelia (now "Lady") Douglas with Josette only strengthened.

Youngest daughter Martha Douglas, the same age as Suzette Work, her "great friend," reminisced about the "rejoicing when Mrs. Work came to pay us a visit. She was such a lady. Such a loving friend, so true and sympathetic, and stood by my dear Mother on so many sad occasions. One of these occasions was the death of my dear sister, Mrs. Helmcken. Mrs. Work came and comforted my Mother and remained with her until the end.... I have never met such a grand woman. She was so clever she helped Dr. Helmcken in his work and saved the life of one of my nieces when the Doctors had given her up." She also recalled in loving terms the kindness of Work's daughters Jane Tolmie and Sarah Finlayson.[101]

Like Martha and Suzette, Douglas daughters of similar ages became close friends to the Work daughters. Oldest daughter Cecilia Douglas Helmcken in 1857 wrote a rare surviving letter to Jane Tolmie at Nisqually, revealing their sympathies. Describing the local wedding of an English bride, she shared her wish "to see next spring a little McD, I sincerely hope two at once, for she is always turning us all into ridicule for having little ones so soon."[102] This ridicule insinuates the aspersions of white colonists toward fur trade women's Indigenous heritage, which they associated with lascivious tendencies.[103] Cecilia's retaliatory remark assumes graver significance knowing that Cecilia had a twin sister who died in infancy. Both mothers, Cecilia and Jane were familiar with childbirth risks, particularly as Captain McNeill, of the steamer *Beaver*, lost his first wife, Mathilda, giving birth to twins in 1850. As Martha noted, sadly Cecilia herself would die soon after giving birth to her last child in 1865.

Further showing the families' close ties, Sarah Finlayson was entrusted with the care of the motherless newborn. Sarah's sensitivity to newcomers' censure might explain her reluctance to meet English fur trade surgeon Dr. Helmcken when he arrived in early colonial times. As he recalled, she was "bashful and at the same time but recently married."[104] While living at the fort, a daughter recalled her mother Sarah giving milk to gold miners, declining any payment. In addition to charity, she emphasized the genteel aspect of the Finlaysons' later estate at Rock Bay, bordering Hillside, with its imported California redwood construction and terraced gardens of well-kept lawns and flowers. Among their Royal Navy officer visitors, she recalled Lord Charles Beresford.[105]

Douglas had appointed Work, the colony's largest landowner, to Vancouver Island's Legislative Council in 1853. Four of Work's sons-in-law were elected to government, both colonial and post-confederation, and a grandson became a BC premier. As Van Kirk noted in her study of Victoria's founding families, Premier Simon Fraser Tolmie, reminiscing of his father and childhood, barely mentioned his mother and omitted his remarkable grandmother Josette.[106] Despite listing several measures about livestock and weeds that Dr. W.F. Tolmie introduced as a member of BC's Legislative Assembly, Simon also neglected to include that his father was the first to propose female suffrage in 1875, decades before it would pass.

Yet political participation extended to the women of the fur trade families. The suffrage support of Tolmie's wife, Jane, was shared by some of her sisters. Like Josette, her fourth daughter, Margaret Work Jackson, took in a married daughter and granddaughter, Chase. Chase Going Woodhouse recalled her grandmother taking her to polling stations in Victoria and angrily declaring her regret as an unrepresented taxpayer. Turning to Chase, she would say, "But you will have the vote." Indeed, she would, becoming a US Congresswoman. Contending that her grandmother inspired her career, Woodhouse remembered looking out her window "seeing Indians sitting at the back door waiting for Granny... [to] help in getting a son out of jail or because something had happened to their homes.... I grew up with the same sense of community obligation and duty."[107] Stating "Granny was my law and gospel," Woodhouse did not, however, mention her grandmother's name, or her Indigenous heritage.

Woodhouse's mother also inspired her career in teaching; Harriet Jackson was one of the earliest women teaching professionally in BC. Likewise, her cousin Ettie (Josette) Tolmie became a nurse, taking the aptitude inherited from her grandmother Josette into the professional realm. Josette lived to see children and grandchildren become active in charities and community groups, continuing her own role.

Outliving her husband by thirty-five years, the matriarch lived on until nearly the turn of the century, dying at Hillside in 1896. Addressing the legislature, the premier recognized her as "one of the honoured pioneers" of the province, helping new arrivals and "ready to lend a hand of sympathy to all in sickness and trouble." The legislature passed a resolution of sympathy to her family for the loss of Mrs. Work, "who before her death was the oldest resident of British Columbia, and who will be remembered for her usefulness in pioneer work and many good deeds."[108] Despite her questionable paternity and uprooted past, Josette maintained her familial and societal place through transitions from the fur trade to agriculture and gold-rush commerce, and through BC's colonial transition to confederation. The premier's parting words echo those of historian Hubert Bancroft, who two decades earlier had been so struck by Josette's intelligence and resilience to declare she was "strong and elastic as steel."

NOTES

1   Bancroft, *Literary Industries*, 534.
2   Brown, *Strangers in Blood*, 73–74; Van Kirk, *Many Tender Ties*.
3   Watson, *Lives Lived West of the Divide*, 542.
4   Perry, "Historiography that Breaks Your Heart," 81–92.
5   Van Kirk, *Many Tender Ties*, 6.
6   Thompson, *Columbia Journals*, 7–11.
7   Schaeffer, "Le Blanc and La Gasse," 6–8.
8   Thompson, *Columbia Journals*, 193–94.
9   White, ed., *David Thompson's Journals*, 117.
10 Brown, *Strangers in Blood*, 85–87.
11 Van Kirk, *Many Tender Ties*, 46–47.
12 LaGasse, Charles (fl. ca. 1800–), Biographical Sheets, Hudson's Bay Company Archives, Provincial Archives of Manitoba, last modified 2018. https://www.gov.mb.ca/chc/archives/_docs/hbca/biographical/l/lagasse_charles.pdf.
13 North West Company ledgers, 1811–13, Hudson's Bay Company Archives, Provincial Archives of Manitoba.
14 Edward Huggins to Eva Emery Dye, June 27, 1904, accompanying "Suggestions (for corrections) relating to Mrs. E.E. Dye's new book," Fort Nisqually Living History Museum, Tacoma, WA.
15 Van Kirk, *Many Tender Ties*, 50–51.
16 Dye, *McDonald of Oregon*, 24–25.
17 White, *David Thompson's Journals*, 235.
18 Wade, *The Thompson Country*, 13–14.
19 Van Kirk, *Many Tender Ties*, 28–30.
20 Wallace, ed., *Documents Relating to the North West Company*, 211.
21 Thompson, *David Thompson's Narrative*, 1784–1812, 305.
22 Cox, *The Columbia River*, 185–89.

23 White, *David Thompson's Journals*, 117.
24 Edward Huggins to Clarence B. Bagley, April 19, 1906, call no. 979.778 H873hu, *Letters Outward: The Letters of Edward Huggins 1862-1907*, Fort Nisqually Living History Museum.
25 Edward Huggins to Dye, February 8, 1904, Fort Nisqually.
26 Maloney, "John Work of the Hudson's Bay Company," 100.
27 Edward Huggins to Bagley, May 18, 1904, Fort Nisqually.
28 Williams, "The Daughter of Angus MacDonald," 111.
29 White, David Thompson's Journals, 244.
30 Halliday, ed., *Fur Trade Letters of Francis Ermatinger*, 64.
31 Brown, *Strangers in Blood*, 202-3.
32 Elliott, "Journal of John Work," 265-66.
33 Van Kirk, *Many Tender Ties*, 46-50.
34 Van Kirk, *Many Tender Ties*, 108-9.
35 Elliott, "Journal of John Work," 270-71.
36 John Tod to Edward Ermatinger, February 27, 1826, PR-0947, Edward Ermatinger Correspondence, BC Archives.
37 Thompson, *David Thompson's Narrative*, 305.
38 "Mrs. Work Dead," British Colonist (Victoria, BC), January 31, 1896, BC Archives.
39 John Work to Edward Ermatinger, March 28, 1829, PR-1506, Correspondence outward, File A/B/40/W89, John Work fonds, BC Archives.
40 Maloney, "John Work of the Hudson's Bay Company," 100.
41 Tod to Edward Ermatinger, February 14, 1829, PR-0947, BC Archives.
42 Anne Huggins to Eva Emery Dye, January 20, 1904, MSS1089, box 1, folder 15, Eva Emery Dye Papers, Series A1: Incoming Correspondence, 1845-1942, Oregon Historical Society Research Library, Portland.
43 Edward Huggins to Bagley, November 4, 1903, Fort Nisqually.
44 Work to Edward Ermatinger, August 5, 1832, PR-1506, BC Archives.
45 Work to Edward Ermatinger, February 24, 1834; "Appalled by Fever," 164.
46 Perry, *Colonial Relations*, 75.
47 Maloney, "John Work of the Hudson's Bay Company," 103.
48 Perry, *Colonial Relations*, 42-43.
49 Edward Huggins to Dye, January 24, 1904, citing Fort Nisqually Journal, December 2, 1836, Fort Nisqually.
50 Halliday, ed., *Fur Trade Letters of Francis Ermatinger*, 216.
51 Perry, *Colonial Relations*, 40.
52 Tolmie, *The Journals of William Fraser Tolmie*, 332-33.
53 Anne Huggins to Dye, May 9, 1904, Oregon Historical Society.

54 Meilleur, *A Pour of Rain*, 165.
55 Work to Edward Ermatinger, February 15, 1841, PR-1506, BC Archives.
56 Meilleur, *A Pour of Rain*, 168.
57 Work to Edward Ermatinger, February 15, 1841.
58 Halliday, ed., *Fur Trade Letters of Francis Ermatinger*, 128–29.
59 Work to Edward Ermatinger, February 15, 1841.
60 Work to Edward Ermatinger, October 11, 1841, PR-1506, BC Archives.
61 Rich, ed., *The Letters of John McLoughlin*, xi–xii, 25n3.
62 Anne Huggins to Dye, February 3, 1904, Oregon Historical Society.
63 Rich, *The Letters of John McLoughlin*, 88–89, 154–55, 371.
64 Rich, *The Letters of John McLoughlin*, 372.
65 Rich, *The Letters of John McLoughlin*, 359.
66 Rich, *The Letters of John McLoughlin*, 46.
67 Finlayson to Mackenzie, August 16, 1842, in Rich, *The Letters of John McLoughlin*, 389.
68 "Mrs. Work Dead," *British Colonist*, January 31, 1896, BC Archives.
69 Anne Huggins to Dye, May 9, 1904.
70 Donald, *Aboriginal Slavery on the Northwest Coast of North America*, 33–35.
71 Ruby and Brown, *Indian Slavery in the Pacific Northwest*, 223–31, 246–50.
72 Meilleur, *A Pour of Rain*, 181.
73 Perry, *Colonial Relations*, 131.
74 Lugrin, *The Pioneer Women of Vancouver Island*, 62–63.
75 Ann Huggins to Dye, December 29, 1905, Oregon Historical Society.
76 Halliday, ed., *Fur Trade Letters of Francis Ermatinger*, 203.
77 Smith, *Captain McNeill and His Wife the Nishga Chief*, 180.
78 Meilleur, *A Pour of Rain*, 192.
79 Anne Huggins to Dye, May 9, 1904.
80 Douglas, *Journal Kept by David Douglas*, 180.
81 Anne Huggins to Dye, May 9, 1904.
82 Work to Edward Ermatinger, January 10, 1846, PR-1506, BC Archives.
83 Van Kirk, *Many Tender Ties*, 108–9.
84 Van Kirk, "Tracing the Fortunes," 160.
85 Douglas, *Fort Victoria Letters*, 156.
86 Isaac Burpee, "The Story of John Work," (1943), BC Archives.
87 Douglas to Earl Grey, HM Secretary of State, in Douglas, *Fort Victoria Letters*, 249.
88 Lang, *Confederacy of Ambition*, 60–62.
89 Dee, "An Irishman in the Fur Trade," 263.

90 *Fort Nisqually Journal*, September 2, 1854, in Crooks, "Pierre Lagace: The Life of an Extraordinary Hudson's Bay Company Man."
91 St. Andrew's Cathedral, Burial Register, March 5, 1855, Victoria, BC.
92 Edward Huggins to Dye, June 27, 1904.
93 Edward Huggins to Dye, June 27, 1904.
94 Edward Huggins to Bagley, April 16, 1903, Fort Nisqually.
95 Van Kirk, "Tracing the Fortunes," 150, 161.
96 Brown, *Strangers in Blood*, 154.
97 Wilson, *Mapping the Frontier between British Columbia & Washington*, 28, 44, 71, 87–88.
98 "The Hill Side Stabbing Case," *Daily British Colonist* (Victoria, BC), March 31, 1865, BC Archives.
99 Tolmie and Dawson, *Comparative Vocabularies of the Indian Tribes of British Columbia*, 123 B.
100 Lugrin, *The Pioneer Women of Vancouver Island*, 65.
101 Martha Douglas Harris, "Reminiscences of Early Life in Victoria," Harris family letters, journals and publications, MS-2789, file 12, BC Archives.
102 Cecilia Helmcken to Jane Tolmie, Add. Ms. 505, March 17, 1857, MS-0505, box 14, folder 3, Helmcken family papers, BC Archives.
103 Perry, *On the Edge of Empire*, 51.
104 Smith, ed., *The Reminiscences of Doctor John Sebastian Helmcken*, 82.
105 Lugrin, *The Pioneer Women of Vancouver Island*, 42–43, 70.
106 Tolmie, "My Father: William Fraser Tolmie."
107 "A Pioneer Feminist Savors Grandmother Role," *New York Times*, May 10, 1981, accessed February 16, 2023. https://www.nytimes.com/1981/05/10/nyregion/a-pioneer-feminist-savors-grandmother-role.html.
108 Lugrin, *The Pioneer Women of Vancouver Island*, 63–64.

Four

Caroline McNabb and Culturally Adaptive Practices of Métis Kinship[1]

by Jade McDougall

BORN AT THE RED RIVER SETTLEMENT IN 1862, CAROLINE (McNabb) Kirkness experienced a number of transitions over the course of her life, including political upheaval and the westward migration of Métis families from Red River. Her family identity is inflected by early experiences with customary adoption and convent education and in many ways expressed through her lifelong handcrafting. Caroline's story, along with those of her husband, son, and other relations, are found in two Saskatchewan (SK) community history volumes: *Communities of Courage and Cordwood* from the district of Red Deer Hill, SK—where the family lived and farmed from the late 1870s until the late 1920s—and *A Homesteader's Dream* from the area of Cookson, SK, where they relocated in 1929.[2] The narrative connections of Caroline's life within her wider social network show a thread of inter-familial and inter-communal solidarities wherein women take up roles of authority and cohesion. Caroline's story also asks us to consider what it means to be a matriarch: though she did not raise a large family, she did take up a similar role to those modelled by the women in her own kin circle through practices of community stewardship, knowledge-sharing, and adoption. By examining the stories and photos Caroline's descendants chose to share about her—along with other documents which illuminate her family's place within the network of Métis fur trade families at Red River and later Red Deer Hill—we can gain insight into the complex dynamics of Métis kinship in contexts of mobility and change.

Self-Location

My given name is Jade, and I also go by J.D. My father's family are historically Michif-speaking Red River Métis who relocated to the Southbranch[3] area in present-day Saskatchewan in the nineteenth century. My mother's family are historically Scots Halfbreed[4] Red River Métis who migrated first from Poplar Point to Red Deer Hill in the late nineteenth century, and then to the Shellbrook area in the 1920s. Though I was born and have extensive roots in Prince Albert, I was raised in Saskatoon, away from most of my extended family. Like others with similar experiences, my journey as a human being involves coming to understand my place within my community and the role it encompasses. As a literary scholar, my process of coming-to-know has been the slow interpretive unspooling of my family's narrative across the centuries and across the land, from James Bay, York Factory, and Red River to Southbranch and northern Saskatchewan. This is how I came to study Caroline McNabb's life story; she was my great-great-grandmother. However, her narrative thread is not a solitary line unfolding in a linear spatial and temporal arc. Rather, it forms a connective piece within a much larger whole of kin and relationship.

Methods and Guiding Knowledges

As Elder Maria Campbell explains in a conversation with Métis scholar Anna Louisa Flaminio, the trauma of colonization and the violent upheavals that disrupted Métis communities left our "kinship circles shattered" and, to this day, the legacies of "formal and informal policies and practices continue to affect the strength of our kinship relationships, responsibilities, and obligations."[5] As Campbell recognizes, a key element of rebuilding our nation is restoring those kinship circles and the knowledges embedded within them. Mvskoke Creek scholar Tol Foster echoes this epistemology when he contends, "History and events are part of the story, but they are not the determinate parts. Relations are the primary axis through which we can understand ourselves and each other."[6] Knowing our collective history and culture must then be centred in understanding how to be in right relation with one another. Knowing our relations must involve reaching further than the mere act of tracing genealogical descendancy.[7] We must relearn how we relate within our communities writ large, finding a way forward in honouring our shared obligations as Métis. Ancestors are the key to that journey; intergenerational continuity, flowing through the past and present into the future, shapes the knowledge we create and the outcomes we make of it.

In accordance with relational models of knowledge, my primary framework for reading Caroline McNabb's life narrative is a combined archival/genealogical/kin-based approach, which Métis scholar Brenda Macdougall argues can present scholars "an analytical framework for Métis history that explores their family life as the root of their humanity."[8] As Heather Devine notes, numerous thinkers and writers have established that kinship is "the 'glue' that bound [Indigenous] societies together."[9] Those social bonds reach far beyond the hearth; within Métis communities kinship "provides structure to society; infuses institutions with meaning; establishes protocols and frameworks for interaction and behaviour; [and] is the foundation for pursuing any economic, political, social, or cultural activity."[10] By digging into the family relationships uncovered within written narratives and archival documents, unpacking not only their structures but also the philosophies of kinship by which those bonds were made and maintained, we are able to expand beyond the limitations of a genealogical framework, seeking out our relations in history with the ultimate aim of finding "evidence of their voices, thoughts, and ideas"[11] within a community complex.

Central to this approach is wāhkōhtowin,[12] a Cree term describing an "overarching law of respect and belonging" mapping reciprocal relations between all spheres of creation.[13] Krystl Raven glosses the term as "'to belong to one another,' or 'relationship'" and notes that it expresses "the virtues that an individual should personify as a family member,"[14] which in Macdougall's research include values of "reciprocity, mutual support, decency, and order."[15] Caroline and her husband, George, much like other Métis who settled in the Prince Albert area, "were part of an extended, regional family system that shaped their cultural identity," wherein the community was "connected in a chain of history and memory defined by their acceptance of, and adherence to, their regional narrative."[16] Kinship alliances formed and maintained in accordance with wāhkōhtowin principles of "inter-familial...connectedness"[17] manifest at various points in the life story of Caroline McNabb as told in community histories and archival materials, which branch outward to reveal the intertwined lives and stories of many Métis families belonging to a complex and expansive kin group. These Métis communities "lived according to a worldview defined by...the responsibility individuals had to their immediate and extended family, and their relation to the geography and landscape."[18] Reading for relationship thus serves to recontextualize individual narratives within their wider social circles, reaffirm the breadth and depth of kinship ties and continuity of culture in Halfbreed family stories, and reinscribe Indigenous community back into the documents in which they are found. My analysis therefore focuses on unpacking what Caroline McNabb's life story reveals about her kin circle, and by extension the social and cultural landscapes of the Métis in Red River, Red Deer Hill, and Cookson during the years of transition in which she lived.

Caroline's Self-Fashioning: The Anniversary Portraits

One common challenge of studying Indigenous women's narratives in history is the long-standing practice of omitting them from the "official" documentary record[19] or only seeing their presence "coloured by the [colonial] male perspective."[20] The elision of women within written archival records highlights how conventional practices of historical memorialization and record-keeping have "failed to understand female presence and authority" especially within Indigenous communities.[21] However, Celeste Pedri-Spade has made the case for photographs as "technologies of memory" which, despite their fraught history, constitute "significant historical documents rich with information" about Indigenous knowledges, kinship, history, and cultural geography, and as such may provide us a lens through which to "reclaim a hidden or lost past."[22] Because, as Pedri-Spade argues, photography is a "social and relational" act which "happen[s] at a particular time and place" and demands active engagement, photographs operate as "unrealized documents that are active, powerful, open, and impossible to restrict in terms of meaning."[23] Caroline can speak to us in this way; her portraits and the self-fashioning she

FIG. 4.01. George Kirkness and wife Caroline (née McNabb), portrait taken in a Winnipeg studio on their wedding anniversary, c. 1895.

enacts within them tell us something of how she viewed herself and her place in the world. We do not have Caroline's words, but we do have her image.

Caroline McNabb and George Kirkness are depicted in a set of two 1895 photos taken in Winnipeg to mark their fifteenth anniversary. She wears a long fur-trimmed woolen peacoat and hat. He wears a heavy plainsman-style coat, likely intended to keep him warm on winter freighting trips. In the second photo reproduced here (see Figure 4.01), they are positioned in a "conventional pose of married couples in the second half of the nineteenth century," as described by Sarah Carter: "The bride stands, her hand on her husband's shoulder, demonstrating her submissiveness, obedience and devotion."[24] Their faces are difficult to read. George looks directly into the camera, his chin tilted upward. Caroline angles toward him, looking off to the side, the faintest trace of a smile quirking the corner of her mouth and rounding the apple of her right cheek.

Commemorative photos such as George and Caroline's might be intended to communicate the couple's health, prosperity, and hope for future anniversaries. It stands to reason that George and Caroline opted to wear some of their best clothing for this special occasion. Aileen McKinnon, in her study of dress and textiles within the Red River Settlement, notes that clothing is widely understood as "a source of unspoken communication" which the viewer may "readily identify with its visual cues."[25] The signifiers at play may include cultural influences, gender relations, class dynamics, and a range of other elements. Métis dress is no exception. Though by the middle of the nineteenth century, "the mixed-blood wives and daughters of the officer class attempted to keep up with English fashion," Sylvia Van Kirk does note that "in general, mixed-blood women evolved a more practical costume" which was distinct to them.[26] Caroline was herself a farmer's wife with a fur trade heritage, but I would argue that her clothing reflects the same distinctive sensibility described by Van Kirk. Her coat is styled with a Victorian influence, given its structure, double row of buttons, puffed shoulders, and the high furred collar framing her face. She wears a pleated wool hat with fur trim. The pieces are all beautifully constructed, but their design is equally concerned with warmth and sturdiness.

Despite her otherwise buttoned-up appearance, and in a departure from outdoor fashion norms of the day, Caroline does not wear gloves. She reveals her bare hands, the left one curled gently with a wedding band visible on her ring finger. I notice that her fingers are as stout and weathered as her husband's; they too are working hands. Caroline, like many of her ancestors, was well-versed in the numerous arts required to maintain the family's material well-being, and she was further trained as a young girl. Her handcrafting skill remained a topic of family pride long after her death. According to various family conversations, Caroline almost certainly sewed the clothing that she and George are pictured wearing in the portrait. The photoset of them dressed in their winter finery might then be read as an affirmation of her skilled knowledge, and of the relationships which formed that knowledge. These relationships will be explored in the sections below.

The McNab/McNabb Family in Red River Society

In order to situate Caroline and her family within the social fabric of her time and place, we might reach backward in her family's history to pick up the narrative thread. The written record of the family on this continent begins at James Bay with Caroline's great-grandparents. The surname McNabb was often spelled with variations including McNab or Macnab. In Caroline's family, earlier generations appear more often as "McNab," while later ones are more likely to be styled "McNabb." The author follows the spellings most commonly documented for each person mentioned. Hudson's Bay Company (HBC) servant John McNab (c. 1755–1820) was born in Scotland, arrived at Fort Albany in 1779,[27] and married a local Indigenous woman. After an HBC career of some thirty years, McNab was released in 1810,[28] and as a private employee of the Earl of Selkirk, he became embroiled in Selkirk's settlement plans and subsequent conflicts with North West Company (NWC) rivals. By 1818, Selkirk had undergone "serious financial loss" from his Red River venture.[29] McNab purchased Selkirk's Baldoon estate for £2,000, half of which was "generously" advanced to Selkirk on a loan against John's own land holdings in Scotland.[30] However, Selkirk left Canada still owing McNab over two years' worth of back pay, and with no signed record of their arrangement, John's written pleas were "ignored" by both Selkirk and the HBC.[31] McNab fell into his own financial hardships, "moved to Baldoon with [his] family,...borrowed any money he could, [and] died in debt, of malaria,[32] sometime after May 1819."[33] Selkirk died in 1820 without paying McNab's estate, and the Baldoon property was "subsequently subdivided and resold at public auction."[34] Evidently, John McNab's life of corporate service and personal loyalty to Selkirk did not result in the long-term gains he may have hoped.

From these records assembled by Norma Jean Hall, we know something of how John McNab's involvement in fur trade power struggles impacted his wife and children. In May 1817, at Selkirk's behest, McNab arrested several Nor'Westers at Fort William and took charge there for three weeks, before being arrested himself on an NWC warrant. His wife, who had accompanied him, was "ejected with [the] children from the fort [and] threatened with a search of her possessions."[35] During John's imprisonment and overseas furlough in 1817–18, Mrs. McNab and the children "stayed at Point Meuron...'among her relations,'" and later "with the T[homas] family" in Vaudreuil, Quebec.[36] These details illustrate Mrs. McNab holding her family together, maintaining community ties, and asserting her social position in times of duress while her husband was either absent or putting the family through upheaval for a stake in the profits of settlement. For all McNab's efforts, he would ultimately find himself without lasting allies among his patrons. However, his descendants who relocated to Red River did continue their mother's work of creating and maintaining kinship ties.

The McNabs' son Thomas (c. 1781–1866) entered HBC service in 1797 and served as a labourer, steersman, and assistant trader, retiring shortly after the merger between HBC and NWC in 1821.[37] His first HBC assignment was at Point au Foutre/Fort Alexander[38] (present-day Sagkeeng First Nation), situated at the south end of Lake Winnipeg. Thomas married a Saulteaux woman named Mary/Mary Jane around 1801 and remained stationed around Lake Winnipeg for the majority of his career.[39] Records from 1827 show he had taken up farming at the parish of St. Clement's, by the northeast edge of the Red River settlement nearest to Lake Winnipeg.[40] The parish was populated largely by former HBC employees who had accepted river lot land grants upon retiring, but the McNabs may well have chosen to stay and settle there at least partly to remain near Mary's family. On December 18, 1827, Thomas and Mary were married at St. John's Anglican Church in Red River alongside their son John (who married Jane Sandison the same day).[41] Mary was baptized with her daughter Eleanor in 1830.[42] She died in December 1856 at the approximate age of seventy,[43] and Thomas lived on at the settlement until he died on October 23, 1866, at the age of 86.[44]

Thomas and Mary's son, Charles McNabb (1820–1895), also had experience with HBC service and farming in Red River. On

April 3, 1850, at the Upper Church (St. John's), Charles was married to Marie Anne McLeod[45] (1835–1870)[46] "with consent of parents."[47] Their wedding was witnessed by Anne McDermot[48] and John Pruden.[49] It is somewhat uncertain who Marie Anne's parents were. She died at the age of thirty-five on November 12, 1870, and Charles is simply listed as a widower living at Poplar Point west of the Red River settlement in the 1870 census.[50] However, St. François Xavier parish records show official witnesses to the burial of "Marianne McLaud" were Antoine McLaud (b. 1824) and Joseph McLaud (b. 1829).[51] Antoine and Joseph were brothers born to Joseph McLeod (1805–1849) and Angelique Azure dit Lessard/Lacerte (1810–1850).[52] While no definitive relation is established, given the family's presence in the St. François Xavier records, Marie Anne likely belonged to this branch of the McLeods.

The McLeods may have been among a number of Pembina Métis hunting families who relocated to St. François Xavier (formerly Grantown) under the leadership of Cuthbert Grant in 1824.[53] Brenda Macdougall and Nicole St-Onge, in their analysis of Métis buffalo hunting brigades, acknowledge that while St. François Xavier is "largely described as a French Métis parish because of its Roman Catholic heritage,"[54] its sacramental records illustrate that "intermarriage between the so-called English-and French-speaking Métis families at Red River was...fairly widespread," and the permeability of these categories is especially evident in the concentration of patronymic crossover between Scottish and French names at this parish.[55] If these relational readings hold true, the records above fit into Macdougall and St-Onge's analysis, placing Caroline's family in a circle of Scots Halfbreed HBC trading families as well as the Métis hunting families of St. François Xavier.

A few years after Marie Anne's death, in 1873, Charles McNabb remarried to widow Elizabeth (Badger) Cameron (b. 1835).[56] The

Badger and McNab/McNabb families shared numerous marital connections around nearby St. Peter's reserve, and within both families there are those who accepted scrip, those who took treaty, and those who presented administrative headaches for colonial officials. Elizabeth was herself denied Halfbreed scrip on the basis that she had already accepted treaty annuities; in her 1877 application, she insisted that she "never understood the treaty properly" and "accepted it, not knowing the consequence," maintaining that she "never lived in the Reserve with Indians, [and] always led the life of a white settler."[57] Since she had remarried to Charles, a non-treaty halfbreed, officials were instructed to have her "struck off the [treaty] pay list" and rendered eligible for scrip instead.[58] Perhaps due to clerical oversight, Elizabeth was never removed. She "died while she was in receipt of Indian annuities," and thus her daughter Isabella (Cameron) Thorp's "alleged claim...could not be entertained" in her 1886 scrip application.[59]

This incident emphasizes once again the "mutable and multifaceted" nature of cultural identity in Red River,[60] challenges the idea of "hermetically sealed populations" among the various groups and parishes at the settlement,[61] and highlights the absurdity of bureaucratic attempts to impose race logic and classificatory systems onto them. Just as the boundaries between French-Catholic and Anglo-Protestant Métis families were nominal and largely imposed by colonial officials, the same is true of Métis and First Nations families of the area. While the groups did see themselves as somewhat differentiated, these distinctions meant little to the community as a whole until colonial mechanisms imposed divisions and hierarchies on the basis of language, religion, and traditional lifeways. Red River was a site of long-standing interfamilial and intercultural exchange, strengthened and enacted via "intergroup transfers," which created "extended kinship support networks through child and adult adoption, spousal exchange, and marriage."[62] The importance of those adoptive (and adaptive) kinship practices is illustrated within Caroline's early life.

Caroline's Early Life and Adoptive Family

Caroline, the seventh child of Charles and Mary, was born on March 5, 1862, and was eight years old when her mother died in 1870. Although Elizabeth Badger was her stepmother by marriage, Caroline apparently also had a "foster mother," known to my family as "Mrs. Ballantyne." Customary adoption was a relatively common occurrence in places like Red River, as "nineteenth-century Métis communities tended to de-emphasize direct genetic lineage, and embrace those connected by blood or need within their family."[63] Moreover, these adoptions were undertaken "following the concepts of *wahkootowin* [wāhkōhtowin]" in that they "drew the adoptee into a web of relations that went beyond the family and into the greater Métis nation."[64] We see this pattern recur in Caroline's family narrative, beginning with her own adoptive mother, Mrs. Ballantyne. Below is a copy of an image posted by my cousin to an online family group, a photo of Mrs. Ballantyne, which has remained in his family for years. In the photo I recognize Anne "Annie" (McDermot) Bannatyne,[65] a community leader among women at Red River and a witness to Charles McNabb and Mary Anne McLeod's wedding. A copy of the same photo is in the McCord Museum holdings in Montreal (see Figure 4.02).

The McDermot family, to whom Annie was born in 1832, was closely linked with other trading families in the region. Caroline's aunt Sarah Mary McNab married Irish merchant Andrew McDermot and was Annie's mother. Though Annie and Caroline were first cousins, the McDermot family river lot, known as Emerald Grove, was located several parishes away

FIG. 4.02. Anne (née McDermot) Bannatyne, Caroline's adoptive mother figure. Portrait taken at the Notman & Sandham Studio in Montreal, c. August 31, 1882.

from the McNabs. It adjoined the five-hundred-acre common area surrounding Fort Garry, which had been set aside by HBC "as a camping space for the plains traders when they came in from the West."[66] When in 1851 Annie McDermot married merchant Andrew Graham Ballenden (A.G.B.) Bannatyne, the couple lived in the adjacent river lot on the north side of her father's property.[67] The layout of these lots bespeaks their residents' familial ties, as well as their proximity, both spatial and symbolic, to sites of social and economic importance in Red River. In 1871, the Bannatyne home served as the literal seat of political power in the province as it was determined to be the "best and most commodious building" to temporarily house Manitoba's new provincial legislature.[68] Given their home's status as a hub of the community, it is unsurprising that both Andrew and Annie took up key roles in politics, philanthropy, and leadership in Red River.

It is beyond the scope of this chapter to enumerate the Bannatyne family's activities in the public sphere, but Annie's community role is of particular interest to understanding Caroline's story. In addition to extensive community organizing and fundraising, Annie famously horse-whipped Canada First agitator Charles Mair in February 1869 for his defamatory comments about the Métis women of Red River. As Todd Lamirande argues, Annie's actions were likely less about Métis political activism than they were about "defending her status as an elite mixed-blood woman"; however, later that year, when "events moved to open resistance," Annie's husband, Andrew, "became quite actively involved on the Metis side" and "it is an open question as to how much his wife influenced his sympathies to the Metis cause."[69] There is much speculation around these events, but their significance can perhaps be read forward in the lives of those who may have been likewise influenced by Annie. If we consider Caroline McNabb's early experiences—losing her mother at the age of eight, being taken on as an adoptive daughter to the Bannatynes, and having a family association with key players in the events of 1869, including one of the most powerful women in the community—we can make some inferences about the profound impact this customary adoption had on the trajectory of her life.

Convent Education, Cultural Capital, and Community

While the community history narrative of Caroline and her husband, George, does not describe Caroline's childhood with any specificity, her grandchildren do mention her educational background, stating in *Communities of Courage and Cordwood*: "Grandma received her early education at a convent in Manitoba."[70] My grandmother often mentioned that Caroline learned both the French language and the art of sewing from the nuns who educated her. Given the location, timeframe, and specific use of "convent" to describe the institution, I speculate that Caroline's schooling may have been carried out by the Sisters of Charity of Montreal (Grey Nuns), who established themselves in St. Boniface in 1844 and by the 1860s had developed an expansive educational franchise throughout the Red River settlement with the intent to "'civilise' the Métis population."[71] For the girls' schools, this meant creating "wives and mothers who would ensure that their families adhered to Catholic and European norms of behaviour."[72] Though Caroline's family was Protestant and the order was Catholic, we may gain some insight by noting that Annie Bannatyne may have had a similar Catholic education. Norma Jean Hall notes that while "specific details about her childhood are sparse...it is generally conceded that Anne was educated. Her long association with the Catholic Church at St. Boniface suggests she was schooled in the tenets of that faith," perhaps on the basis of her father's Irish

Catholic background.⁷³ If she had taken on responsibility for Caroline's education, then it is possible Annie opted for an institution toward which she had already shown interest.

Caroline's convent education was seen as a marker of status and social prestige. The majority of the nuns' boarders belonged to well-off families with a mercantile or farming background. Lesley Erickson notes that for "financial and sectarian reasons, the clergy largely catered to the daughters of this class because they perceived them as more 'civilised' than the hunting class."⁷⁴ A key part of the schools' mission was to encourage the Métis as a whole to adopt a "Catholic, sedentary, and agricultural" lifestyle.⁷⁵ To that end, the schools attempted to "attract more bourgeois children" from socially prominent families, and hoped "their reputation would bring in the rest."⁷⁶ This approach seems to have been successful to some degree, as Rita McGuire writes: "There was a certain status in the 1850's to having one's daughters entrusted to the careful, competent instruction of the Grey Nuns. One notes in class lists such pioneer names as Connolly, Sinclair, D'Eschambault, Kittson, and Bannatyne. [T]he daughters of Hudson's Bay Company families were considerably attracted to the Sisters' school in spite of the river crossing."⁷⁷ Leaving aside McGuire's adulatory tone and assumption of "pioneer" primacy, here we may see colonial strategies of cultural and class division manifesting in the scholarly research around the Grey Nuns' boarding schools.

Erickson argues that the Church's recruitment strategy reflects a clear social hierarchy at Red River, with the clergy "recognizing that wealthy, influential, and Catholic HBC officials did not want to send their daughters to the Grey Nuns' day school, where they would rub shoulders with Métis, Mixed-blood, and Saulteaux girls of the hunting class."⁷⁸ To complicate Erickson's analysis somewhat, previous sections of this chapter would suggest that these social boundaries were more the product of outside imposition or encouragement than a widespread community inclination. It is indeed true that the practice of removing Indigenous children from their homes and cultural surroundings was already well entrenched among HBC officers who were "particularly anxious" to "inculcate in their daughters proper feminine virtues," and, recognizing Indigenous women's key educational role in their families, saw a pressing need to keep their children "isolated from Indian women."[79] In the York Factory correspondence books for 1806–07, Caroline's own great-grandfather John McNab advocated for a "Matron" to be sent to York Factory, arguing that "native women as attendants on these young persons seems improper" as "their society would keep alive the Indian language & with it, its native superstition which ought to be obliterated from the mind with all possible care."[80] As invested as men like McNab may have been in this assimilatory agenda, the integrative familial patterns followed by his own descendants suggest that they were not concerned with isolating their families from any of the other Indigenous populations in the area. Whether or not the missionary tactic of isolating children from their homes was truly reflective of merchant families' desires to segregate their daughters from the hunting classes, we may equally recognize convent schools' popularity as a product of increasing pressure and economic uncertainty created by the changing settler population of Red River.

To further contextualize the Grey Nuns' appeal to their target demographic of wealthy Métis families, it is important to note, as many scholars have, "the evolution of Indian and metis [*sic*] women's position from an economic advantage during the early years of the fur trade to a social disadvantage by 1870."[81] Whereas Indigenous women had taken on key labour roles in the early fur trade era, the entrenchment of Euro-settler gender dynamics had profound effects on their place in the economy, as they became "increasingly relegated to a purely social position among the higher socio-economic classes."[82] HBC officers in particular placed considerable pressure on their daughters to marry fellow traders and thus strengthen the family's economic alliances.[83] However, even at Red River, Métis women's social status was on a steady decline, influenced by ideologies of "race, respectability, and progress,"[84] and with the midcentury influx of white settler women, success in conforming to an increasingly popular "'acculturated' ideal" was correlated to perceived desirability as wives.[85] Perhaps recognizing this social shift and the economic anxiety it produced, the nuns "created a curriculum for their boarders that was on par with European finishing schools."[86] Whereas the day schools taught "the rudiments of reading, writing, religion, and sewing," the boarding schools took on a more "advanced" approach to preparing students for prospective roles "as wives to future HBC officers."[87] In 1862, Father Richot boasted that the boarding schools' "program of studies is exactly the same" as "our fine convents in Lower Canada."[88] Positioning their program as able to compete with eastern schools undoubtedly helped to attract trade families looking to secure their daughters' future prospects.

Caroline's husband, George Kirkness, was not a wealthy HBC officer; he was a farmer's son who grew up on a nearby river lot. However, he appears to have been determined to give her a life of relative comfort. Around 1875 or 1876, George headed west by Red River cart through the Red Deer Hill district as a freighter, hauling telegraph wire from Winnipeg to Edmonton. As freighting was a lucrative business, George was able to secure a quarter-section of land and have a large house "of Red River frame construction" built by Jerry Cook[89] at Red Deer Hill in 1877.[90] Once he had made a home for his wife, in 1880, "George returned to Fort Garry to marry his sweetheart, Caroline McNabb,...now

18 years old."⁹¹ George's stopping at Fort Garry, rather than Poplar Point where both his and Caroline's families resided, may indicate that Caroline was living at the St. Mary's convent, which opened near to Fort Garry in 1869,⁹² the St. Boniface convent across the river junction where the girls' boarding school had operated since 1854,⁹³ or indeed the Bannatyne house a few lots away from the fort itself.

While Caroline's convent education may be viewed as an expression of social privilege, it did also hold an important practical and relational value as she committed to a life of farm labour alongside her childhood "sweetheart" George in Red Deer Hill and later Cookson. Not only would her knowledge of reading and writing have been useful in navigating the "burgeoning government bureaucracy in the Northwest,"⁹⁴ these skills were highly valued in Métis and homesteading communities, particularly when families had to be resourceful with limited materials or they supplemented family income through the wives' handiwork. Caroline was, by all accounts, "a tremendous seamstress," who devoted much of her time "sewing surplices [and] garments and spent hours sewing for the grandchildren."⁹⁵ Caroline also "took an active part organizing the Willing Workers (W. A.) [women's auxiliary] at MacDowall, was a member of the Homemaker Club and organized the first Sunday School and W. A. at Cookson."⁹⁶ This litany of Caroline's talents reflects the social value of her education and the relational ways Caroline was able leverage it with the explicitly "active" role she maintained in expressing religiosity through her labour (for instance, by sewing surplices and organizing committees).

The confluence between Caroline's extensive knowledge of various skilled crafts and her involvement in community service through women's industry is undoubtedly inflected by the religious educational structures of her youth. Erickson argues that a number of the Métis and Halfbreed women who went on to become novices and missionaries "adapted women's traditional role as cultural mediators in the fur trade to the Catholic traditions of female congregations and community service."[97] I read a similar possibility here. Caroline enacted her service in an outwardly Christian faith-centred forum, mirroring those Métis women at Red River and elsewhere who were educated by the Grey Nuns and who in turn took up their project of acculturation to Anglo-Canadian norms of behaviour. In addition to lending her labour to the service of the local church and community organizations, she also "taught many young girls knitting and tatting and knew the art of spinning, leatherwork, furrier and needlecraft."[98] Given the nuns' emphasis on "teaching the Métis girls to become exemplary wives and mothers,"[99] it is possible that Caroline saw her community role as an extension of her maternal identity, particularly since she had no daughters. It is also possible that she sought to pass on some aspect of the feminized community in which her own schooling took place, or that she was following her own adoptive mother's example as a community organizer, modelling the guidance and mentorship she received as a girl.

Alongside the dynamics discussed above, Caroline's activities also fit well within Métis women's practices of knowledge-sharing and kinship. Her focus on using her gifts and skills for the benefit of the community also demonstrates a broader kinship praxis inflected by wāhkōhtowin. As Lawrence Barkwell, Anne Carrière, and Amanda Rozyk note, within Métis customary law "the first requirement to be counted as a family member is the ability to contribute from one's talents to the good of the whole family unit, clan, or the community at large."[100] Women in particular "have a positive obligation to work for initiatives that will strengthen the community" and are "expected to look after the girl children of the community."[101] The repeated use of the term *active* in this context drives home the conscious initiative central to wāhkōhtowin. Caroline took up the responsibility of sharing her knowledge by teaching local girls the art of sewing and beading. In this way, I read potential for Caroline to have enacted kinship practices by taking on this role of stewardship and education, creating and maintaining good relations through passing on important skills to younger generations.

Maintaining Kin-Based Caretaking Networks in the Midst of Mobility

Though they married in 1880, George and Caroline did not have their first (and only) biological child until 1889—a son, Sam. This was, as members of my family have remarked upon, unusual for families at this time. One cousin speculated that it must have been lonely in their large house with so few children. As I will discuss, this was not necessarily the case. Caroline continued to take on family through adoption and integration, as had been done for her when she was a young girl. The most significant illustrative example of this is John Edward Cook (1885–1946), or "Jack, as he was known by his friends."[102] Jack was the son of George's sister Catherine Kirkness and her husband, John Cook; when Jack's parents "passed away at an early age,"[103] he "resided with his Aunt and Uncle."[104]

Census records illuminate this relationship in interesting ways. Jack does not appear in their household in 1891, but in 1901 and 1906 the Kirkness household enumeration includes George, Caroline, and two sons: Samuel James, born 1889, and John (Jack).[105] It isn't until 1911 that Sam (age twenty) and Jack (age twenty-six) are distinguished as "son" and "nephew," respectively. Perhaps because Sam had now reached the age of majority and would be married that same year, matters of legal descendancy may have made this distinction more relevant. It appears that George and Caroline considered Jack their son in a very real sense, duly stating this relationship until it became necessary to distinguish him from their biological son. By the time of the 1916 census, the Kirkness family structure had changed significantly. "Nephew" Jack at thirty-one years old had served in WWI and, after a stint in a sanitorium, returned home to live with George and "Carry," along with Sam, Sam's wife, Mary (née Attig), and their two eldest children, Clayton and Daisy.[106] In the 1926 census, Jack is listed as a "ward" at the age of forty-two.[107] Though his familial role in the census records would shift over time (at least in Canadian property law and ever-changing census language), Jack was as much a core member of the family as Sam.

It is made clear in the community history texts that Jack was coping with chronic poor health—a result of his military service and subsequent battle with tuberculosis. However, he is not treated herein as the passive "ward" which the census terminology applied to him. Rather, his agency is expressed through a model which resonates with discussions of wāhkōhtowin and mutual caretaking. His nephew mentions Jack had "many hobbies; crafts, basket weaving, carving, carpentry, reading, and a love of horses," noting that "he spent many happy moments playing the fiddle because it gave him great pleasure to see people dance."[108] The varied interests Jack cultivated, shaped at least in part by his health struggles and perhaps also encouraged by his adoptive mother Caroline, do explicitly contribute to the well-being of the family and community. I find his place in the Kirkness family to be most fully understood through his niece Daisy's remark that Jack "made his home with his cousin Sam Kirkness."[109] The active phrasing is again significant here; the language implies an ongoing role in not only occupying a home, but also constituting and maintaining—*making*—the home unit itself.

The entire Kirkness family, including eight grandchildren with more on the way, lived in George and Caroline's house until the late 1920s, when they moved to Sam's new homestead just north of Shellbrook. Sam and Mary chose a section of land on which Mary's parents, John Attig[110] and Harriet Stevens, had also settled. Sam, who narrates his own entry in Helen Larsen's 1981 volume *A Homesteader's Dream*, states that with the help of his father-in-law, he "built our first homestead shack which was our residence while working on our new house of logs."[111] George and Caroline's lot was located kitty-corner to Sam's, with the other two properties making up the section of land belonging to the Attigs.[112] Though George filed for his second homestead at the same time as his son, he and Caroline didn't arrive until 1929 when Sam and Mary's house was completed. As the grandchildren recall, Caroline and George "lived in a small house in their son's yard,"[113] most likely the smaller, provisional house built by Sam and Mr. Attig. Evidently, George's quarter-section was only used for the purpose of farming rather than habitation.[114]

The family was now recentred around Sam and Mary as the primary heads, and the narrative emphasizes that their cousin and elderly parents are valued contributors to the household. The language of nuclear family is rather limited in describing the full complexity of kinship and family labour structures, but here again wāhkōhtowin principles emphasize the ongoing mutual obligations and contributions each family member makes to the collective well-being of the group. Jack "helped with farm chores and would always find something to do,"[115] and though he had no biological children, he "was keenly interested in religious education for the young people," serving on the "board of trustees for the organization of the Cookson school."[116] George likewise "enjoyed helping with the chores,"[117] and his "evenings were spent entertaining the young people with his novelty whistling and stories,"[118] while Caroline "kept busy sewing and knitting for the children"[119] and passing Sunday evenings "around the table singing hymns; she was a good singer."[120] Here we see the Kirkness/ McNabb/Attig unit—including Jack—electing to live together on the same parcel of land, choosing not to spread out their living arrangements even within the same small township, but rather to *make their home* together, consolidating their family and keeping interfamilial, intergenerational bonds intact.

George died on November 22, 1932, the year his twelfth grandchild was born. Caroline went with Sam and Mary when they moved to Prince Albert in 1940, along with Jack, who spent time in the Prince Albert sanitorium before his death in 1946. Caroline, in her final years, lived in an outbuilding in the backyard of her eldest grandson, Clayton. As with the previous arrangement in Cookson, this living situation granted her independence and privacy while maintaining close proximity to family. When she died on November 23, 1954, she was buried in the Sturgeon River cemetery alongside George.

Over the course of her life, Caroline passed on her skills to many of her grandchildren and other young people. How far her teachings may have carried from her community circles is unknown. Some of her great-grandchildren still have memories of seeing her sitting quietly—even enigmatically—in her small living space, working the foot-powered treadle of her sewing machine. Through to the time of her passing, Caroline continued practising her art, "always making something,"[121] creating connections upon the fabric of her family circle, just as she had done all her life.

We might initially read Caroline McNabb's passing on of her convent education as a translation of cultural hegemony and class hierarchies, but there is much to be said about the ways in which her actions uphold principles of Métis customary law and kinship. Caroline, who herself never had a daughter or a large number of children, remained committed to a matriarchal role much like that modelled by her own surrogate mother, Annie Bannatyne. As a woman with skilled knowledge to pass on to other young women in the community, Caroline sought a role of active engagement and caretaking outside a nuclear family model. In a similar vein, she continued taking on kin through customary adoption of her nephew—a tradition that continues in our family to this day. Her ongoing maintenance of family and community ties demonstrate practices of caretaking and responsibility, reflecting traditional Métis understandings around wāhkōhtowin. The multidimensional relationships embedded within Caroline's life story and historical record illustrate tight-knit structures of Métis kinship obligations across vast geographic distances, as well as the significance of deep-rooted mobility to constructions of Métis family. By following the arc of Caroline's family narrative, we can unpack the key relational roles of women who are so often overlooked within the documentary record. An expanded kin-based view shows a consistent connective thread of matriarchs taking up roles of authority within their communities and kin circles, which may shift and adapt through the generations but ultimately remains unbroken.

NOTES

1 Author's note: this chapter is adapted from parts of my doctoral dissertation. I would like to thank my mother, Jackie Mitchell, as well as my cousins Pat Lavoy and Ryan Kirkness, for sharing their knowledge and photos.
2 Tait and Olson, eds., *Communities of Courage and Cordwood*; Larsen, ed., *A Homesteader's Dream*.
3 The Southbranch region includes Batoche, St. Louis-de-Langevin, St. Laurent-de-Grandin, and numerous smaller Métis settlements in the surrounding area south of Prince Albert, SK.
4 Though many Métis remain uncomfortable with the pejorative term "Halfbreed," it was also a common form of self-identification

for Scottish Métis, particularly in the latter part of the nineteenth century; see Flaminio, "Gladue through wahkotowin," particularly p. 3. Members of my own family's kin circle historically used this term to identify themselves, and it is used alongside the term "Anglo-Métis" to distinguish the community from their Michif or French Métis cousins when applicable. The term Métis is used to encompass all subsets of the community, and to acknowledge that these distinctions are highly fluid and contextual.

5   Flaminio, "Gladue through wahkotowin," 29.
6   Foster, "Of One Blood," 151.
7   See Darryl Leroux's *Distorted Descent* for further discussion of the issues surrounding genealogical Indigenous identity claims.
8   Macdougall, "Speaking of Métis," 29.
9   Devine, *The People Who Own Themselves*, 209.
10 Macdougall, *One of the Family*, 7.
11 Macdougall, "Speaking of Métis," 29.
12 Macdougall uses the spelling "wahkootowin" in her work, and Flaminio uses "wahkotowin." I use the spelling "wāhkōhtowin," from Arok Wolvengrey's Saskatoon-published Cree dictionary based upon y-dialect Plains Cree. Wolvengrey, *Cree–English*, 232. This is a geographic choice and, in some ways, a cultural one: as my Métis ancestors have done, I am trying to practise good relations by honouring the language of the place where I have been raised, which I call home, and from which my work originates. I will maintain the authors' original spellings wherever they are directly quoted.
13 Roan and Waugh, "Relationships."
14 Raven, "Beyond the Battlefield," 18.
15 Macdougall, *One of the Family*, 8.
16 Macdougall, *One of the Family*, 6.
17 Macdougall, *One of the Family*, 8.
18 Troupe, "Mapping Métis Stories," 62.
19 Millions, "Ties Undone," 11–14. See also Millions, "'By Education and Conduct,'" 11–12.
20 Van Kirk, *Many Tender Ties*, 16.
21 O'Brien, *Firsting and Lasting*, xvi.
22 Pedri-Spade, "Waasaabikizo," 48.
23 Pedri-Spade, "Waasaabikizo," 48.
24 Carter, *The Importance of Being Monogamous*, 22.
25 McKinnon, "Dress in Red River Settlement," 1.
26 Van Kirk, *Many Tender Ties*, 95.

27 "McNab, John [Dr.] (ca. 1755–ca. 1820) (fl. 1779–1812)," Biographical Sheets, Hudson's Bay Company Archives, Provincial Archives of Manitoba, last modified 2018, gov.mb.ca/chc/archives/_docs/hbca/biographical/mc/mcnab_john1755-1820.pdf/.
28 "McNab, John [Dr.]."
29 Mitchell, "Lord Selkirk's Baldoon Settlement."
30 Mitchell, "Lord Selkirk's Baldoon Settlement."
31 Hall, "McNab."
32 Mrs. McNab also succumbed to malaria in the same year. Hall, "McNab."
33 Hall, "McNab."
34 Hall, "McNab."
35 Hall, "McNab."
36 Hall, "McNab."
37 HBCA, "McNab, Thomas (b. ca. 1781) (fl. 1797–1821)," Biographical Sheets, Hudson's Bay Company Archives, Provincial Archives of Manitoba, last modified 1999, gov.mb.ca/chc/archives/_docs/hbca/biographical/mc/mcnab_thomas1797-1821.pdf/.
38 HBCA, "McNab, Thomas."
39 HBCA, "McNab, Thomas."
40 Hall, "McNab."
41 "Parish Registers: Manitoba: H-1344," Kipling Card index 1-1344, images 2609 and 3426, Canadiana Heritage, Library and Archives Canada, accessed November 14, 2022, http://www.heritage.canadiana.ca.
42 "Register of Baptisms, 1820–1841," Red River Settlement records, "Extracts from registers of baptisms, marriages and burials in Rupert's Land sent to the Governor and Committee (1820–1851)" series, E.4/1a fo. 74d, location code H2-136-1-1 (E.4/1-2), microfilm number 4M104, image number HB16-004402, Provincial Archives of Manitoba.
43 "Item: Mary McNab," reference number MG 25 G62, item number 5311, Kipling Collection fonds, finding aid FA-1368, "Births, Marriages and Deaths Recorded in Canada" index, Vital Statistics: Births, Marriages, and Deaths, Library and Archives Canada, accessed July 14, 2020, https://www.bac-lac.gc.ca/eng/discover/vital-statistics-births-marriages-deaths/births-marriages-deaths-recorded/Pages/item.aspx?IdNumber=5311&.
44 Hall, "McNab."
45 "Scrip affidavit for McNabb, Marie Anne; died: Nov. 11, 1870; husband: Charles McNabb; heirs: her children Ellen, wife of George Atkinson; Jane Mary; wife of Samuel Cook; James; David; Thomas; Caroline; Alexander; and Charles; claim no: 2910; scrip no: 12413; date of issue:

Jan. 30, 1879; amount: $160," RG15-D-11-8-a, "Métis and Original White Settlers Affidavits" series, volume 1322, microfilm reel C-14931, Department of the Interior fonds, Library and Archives Canada.
46 Sometimes styled as Marianne, Mary Ann, or simply Mary.
47 "Parish Registers: Manitoba: H-1344," image 2576.
48 Charles's niece, as will be discussed further in the next section.
49 In all likelihood, the same "John Peter Pruden, Esquire, Retired, Chief Factor at H. B. Co." who had retired to Red River and married his second wife in the same parish; see "Parish Registers: Manitoba: H-1344," image 117.
50 "Chs McNab," item number 11454, microfilm reel C-2170, line 1259, Census of 1870, Manitoba, "MG 9 E3 Manitoba Census Returns," Library and Archives Canada, 366.
51 Collection générale de la Société historique de Saint-Boniface, Fonds Paroisse de Saint-François-Xavier, 1834–1883, vol. 4, Index and Registers, 1864–74 (pt. 2), "Marianne McLaud," Digital Archives Database Project.
52 Barkwell, "Descendants of Daniel Lillie," 3.
53 After Angelique's death, Joseph McLeod's subsequent marriage took place at Pembina.
54 Macdougall and St-Onge, "Rooted in Mobility," 27.
55 Macdougall and St-Onge, "Rooted in Mobility," 27.
56 "Parish Registers: Manitoba: H-1344," image 2584.
57 "That Isabelle Thorp (nee Cameron) applied before the Commission for share of Scrip she alleged to be due to her deceased mother Elizabeth Badger widow of Thomas Cameron whose name appears on the list of HB Heads her claim was refused The said Elizabeth Badger having died while she was on Indian Treaty," microfilm reel T-12043, file number HB 8375, RG15-D-11-3, Department of the Interior fonds, "Dominion Lands Branch" series, Métis files sub-series, volume 219, Library and Archives Canada.
58 "That Isabelle Thorp…"
59 "That Isabelle Thorp…"
60 Hall, "A 'Perfect Freedom,'" 56.
61 Hall, "A 'Perfect Freedom,'" 54.
62 Hall, "A Perfect Freedom,'" 54.
63 Raven, "Beyond the Battlefield," 19.
64 Raven, "Beyond the Battlefield," 28–29.
65 Ballenden was the maiden name of AGB Bannatyne's mother, Eliza Ballenden, who married James Bannatyne, AGB's father. The family name Ballenden was given to AGB as a middle name. It seems that in

both spoken and written usage over the years, the names Ballendine, Ballenden, and Bannatyne were often conflated, used interchangeably, and/or merged into versions like the one my family remembers ("Ballantyne").

66 Healy, *Women of Red River*, 139.
67 Healy, *Women of Red River*, 139.
68 Mitchell, "Andrew Graham Ballenden Bannatyne."
69 Todd Lamirande, "Annie McDermot (Bannatyne)," Winnipeg: Louis Riel Institute, 2008, GDI Media filename 07426.Annie McDermot.pdf, Virtual Museum of Métis History and Culture, Gabriel Dumont Institute, accessed January 10, 2024, metismuseum.ca/resource.php/07426, 8.
70 Berggren and Kirkness, "Kirkness, George Thomas and Caroline," 204.
71 Erickson, "At the Cultural and Religious Crossroads," 1.
72 Erickson, "At the Cultural and Religious Crossroads," 6.
73 Hall, "Anne 'Annie' McDermot Bannatyne."
74 Erickson, "At the Cultural and Religious Crossroads," 6.
75 Erickson, "At the Cultural and Religious Crossroads," 1.
76 Erickson, "'Bury Our Sorrows,'" 27.
77 McGuire, "The Grey Sisters," 25–26.
78 Erickson, "'Bury Our Sorrows,'" 23.
79 Van Kirk, *Many Tender Ties*, 97.
80 Van Kirk, *Many Tender Ties*, 97.
81 McKinnon, "Dress in Red River Settlement," 9.
82 McKinnon, "Dress in Red River Settlement," 10.
83 Van Kirk, *Many Tender Ties*, 91.
84 McKinnon, "Dress in Red River Settlement," 9.
85 McKinnon, "Dress in Red River Settlement," 9.
86 Erickson, "'Bury Our Sorrows,'" 23.
87 Erickson, "'Bury Our Sorrows,'" 23.
88 McGuire, "The Grey Sisters," 27.
89 George's cousin and Caroline's brother-in-law.
90 Berggren and Kirkness, "Kirkness, George Thomas and Caroline," 204.
91 Berggren and Kirkness, "Kirkness, George Thomas and Caroline," 204.
92 McGuire, "The Grey Sisters," 27.
93 Erickson, "'Bury Our Sorrows,'" 21–23.
94 Millions, "Ties Undone," 21.
95 Berggren and Kirkness, "Kirkness, George Thomas and Caroline," 204.
96 Berggren and Kirkness, "Kirkness, George Thomas and Caroline," 204.
97 Erickson, "'Bury Our Sorrows,'" 20.

98 Berggren and Kirkness, "Kirkness, George Thomas and Caroline," 204.
99 Erickson, "At the Cultural and Religious Crossroads," 1.
100 Lawrence Barkwell, Anne Carrière, and Amanda Rozyk, "The Origins of Métis Customary Law within a Discussion of Métis Legal Traditions," Winnipeg: Louis Riel Institute, 2007, GDI media filename 07232.Metis law feb 07.pdf, Virtual Museum of Métis History and Culture, Gabriel Dumont Institute, accessed December 15, 2023, https://www.metismuseum.ca/media/document.php/07232.Metis%20law%20feb%202007.pdf, 12.
101 Barkwell, Carrière, and Rozyk, "The Origins of Métis Customary Law," 12.
102 Berggren, "John Edward Cook," 353.
103 John Cook died in 1884, and Catherine Kirkness died in 1886. They left behind three children. Norma Jean Hall notes that their daughter Adelaide Cook was adopted by Elizabeth Greenleaf-Settee, the daughter of Reverend James Settee and George's aunt Sarah Sally Cook. See Hall, "Sinclair." Eldest son Gilbert was adopted by George and Catherine's brother Henry Kirkness and his wife, Catherine Adams. See "Gilbert Cook," item number 4774010, microfilm reel T-6426, Census of Canada, 1891, "RG31 – Statistics Canada," Library and Archives Canada. There is no record of Jack being adopted or taken in by anyone other than George and Caroline.
104 Kirkness, "Cook, John Edward," 130.
105 "Geo Kirkness," item number 1037723, microfilm reel T-6554, Census of 1901, "RG31 – Statistics Canada," Library and Archives Canada, 5; "George Kirkness," item number 385500, microfilm reel T-18361, Census of the Northwest Provinces, 1906, "RG31 – Statistics Canada," Library and Archives Canada, 15.
106 "George Kirkness," item number 1415599, microfilm reel T-21942, Census of the Prairie Provinces, 1916, "RG31 – Statistics Canada," Library and Archives Canada, 19.
107 "George Kirkness," item number 855131, Census of the Prairie Provinces, 1926, "RG31 – Statistics Canada," Library and Archives Canada, 6.
108 Kirkness, "Cook, John Edward," 130.
109 Berggren, "John Edward Cook," 353.
110 Alternate spelling: Attick.
111 Kirkness, "Sam Kirkness, as told by Sam Kirkness," 397.
112 Larsen, ed. *A Homesteader's Dream*, 579.
113 Berggren, "George Kirkness," 397.
114 The same is likely true of Jack Cook's land, which, as mentioned in his passages, was awarded to him under a Soldier Homestead Grant. Though the homestead map found within the Homesteader's volume

shows that Jack held title to those sections, he lived with the rest of the family on Sam's quarter. Kirkness, "Sam Kirkness, as told by Sam Kirkness," 398.

115 Kirkness, "Cook, John Edward," 130.
116 Berggren, "John Edward Cook," 353.
117 Kirkness, "Sam Kirkness, as told by Sam Kirkness," 398.
118 Berggren, "George Kirkness," 397.
119 Kirkness, "Sam Kirkness, as told by Sam Kirkness," 398.
120 Berggren, "George Kirkness," 397.
121 Pat Lavoy, personal communication, November 14, 2022.

Five

"She Did Lead a Rough Life, but She Lived a Good Life"
The Life of Julia Lamotte

by Gabrielle Legault

THE QUOTE IN THE TITLE OF THIS CHAPTER—"SHE did lead a rough life, but she lived a good life"—captures the sentiment that emerged from many exchanges with family members and family friends about my great-grandmother Julia Lamotte (née Fayant). It also comes from a conversation I had with my great-aunt Marge Liboiron in August of 2014.[1] We sat in the basement of her daughter Paulette's house in Ponteix, the small town in southwest Saskatchewan (SK) where I was born and was staying with my Grandma Tova Lamotte. I was pregnant, partway through my PhD, and had returned to Ponteix that summer for the hundredth anniversary of the town, a celebration held at the hockey rink, where I could be sure to run into cousins and old family friends. I knew my great-aunts Terry (or Theresa) and Marge (Marguerite) were my late grandpa Connie's sisters, but I knew little about their lives. One thing was certain: it was a special occasion, as my great-aunt Marge was visiting from her home in India. At the age of eighty-five, Aunty Marge's trips back to Canada were becoming fewer and further between.

My PhD research focused on Métis identity, particularly for folks living outside of the Métis homeland in British Columbia's Southern Interior region, but had led me to ask many questions about my own family histories and identity.[2] Unlike many Métis people, I had the privilege of growing up knowing I was Métis and, even rarer, being told that it was not to be a source of shame. The tagline "Proud to be Métis" has become widespread, found on T-shirts, hats, and bumper stickers across the Métis Nation, likely because so many people have had to push back against the lack of pride so long associated with being Métis or, in the case of my mother's and grandfather's generations, what was known as being a "half breed." I, with the exception of a few ignorant comments from classmates in high school, had been spared the shame, never having my Métis ancestry hidden from me. This I attribute to my great-grandmother Julia Lamotte, whom I call Grandma Julia.

Grandma Julia has always been a source of fascination to me, for a number of reasons. The areas of her life I describe in this chapter are the parts of her that are of most personal interest to me, that I can strongly relate to, or characteristics she possessed that I aspire to demonstrate in my own life. Despite never meeting her, through the stories others have told me about her, I have always understood Julia to be our family matriarch, and she has long been a source of strength and guidance. Though it is easy to think of historical research as a strictly intellectual pursuit, my research has been an extension of my spiritual practice of connecting with my ancestors and an emotional journey of understanding my own Indigenous identity and sense of belonging. Throughout this work and during difficult moments in my life, I have felt my grandmother's hands on my shoulders, supporting me.

This research didn't happen suddenly but has built slowly over the course of nearly a decade, prompted by interviews in 2014 with my great-aunts in the heat of the prairie summer. It didn't begin as a systematic review of historical documents or with a trip to the archives, but with long phone calls, visits over coffee at Grandma Tova's kitchen table, and included a slow trickle of family photos, old postcards, and thick town history books, all making their way into my hands. This chapter is but a small snapshot of Grandma Julia's life as I understand it at this point, and I am sure this understanding will only deepen as I learn more about her life and relations. Yet, it is important that I share this work not only with my own relatives (some of whom are her descendants), but for other Métis, who might see their own family histories reflected in Julia's life, and might seek inspiration from her, as I have, along my own path.

The life story that follows is drawn from several interviews between 2014 and 2021 with my great-aunts Terry and Marge, my grandmother Tova (Connie's wife), my mom, Barb, my mom's cousin and Julia's eldest granddaughter, Paulette, and Lamotte family friend and relative, Métis Elder Cecile Blanke (née LaRoque).[3] As mentioned, I've also drawn on local history books, photos, postcards, the written works of Julia's father, Hugo Maguire, and archival documents such as birth, baptismal, marriage, and death records, census documents, homestead records, scrip records, as well as notes shared with me by Cecile Blanke. There are other material objects passed down to me that I cannot do justice to through writing but that speak to Julia's life, including her created work, which includes beautiful pheasant feather hats, a tanned cattle-hide, a birchbark basket she made, and her fiddle. These records, family heirlooms, and family stories converge to piece together the puzzle of Julia's life; but I share this story knowing full well that many pieces remain missing, some purposely hidden, others forgotten over time.

FIG. 5.01. Julia's postcards and photos.

Southwest Saskatchewan

The land where Julia spent her life can be described as southwest Saskatchewan. This area is not only where Julia lived amongst her relations but where her extended kin network lived and moved through and within. Included in this region, along the present-day Alberta/Saskatchewan border, is Cypress Hills, a significant wintering site for Métis and the location of the Cypress Hills Métis Hunting Brigade, a place where Métis people unsuccessfully petitioned for a reserve in 1878, and one of the last places where buffalo could be found in the Prairies.[4] It was not uncommon for Métis to cross the US-Canadian border, known by Plains Indigenous people as the Medicine Line, "in recognition of its power to mark different national jurisdictions," southwards to and beyond the Milk River.[5] Julia's relations moved from Willow Bunch to Saskatchewan Landing, where she was born, but wintered in Cypress Hills and hunted along the Milk River, eventually returning to settle at Lac Pelletier (see Figure 5.02).

Julia's Relations

Piecing together the familial web into which Julia was born was not as easy as I had anticipated, a common stumbling block faced by myself and other relatives who require clear genealogical links to their Métis ancestors when applying for provincial Métis citizenship. The story of Julia's biological mother names her as Marie or Mary,[6] but contradictory descriptions of Julia's parentage, found across multiple sources, describe her mother as potentially being Marie Genevieve Cabe, Madeleine Lavallée, Caroline Fayant, or Marie Angelique Fayant.

Caroline Fayant is listed as the mother of Julia Lamotte on her birth registration.[7] According to Julia's eldest granddaughter, Paulette Strand, this discrepancy resulted from Julia's attempt to claim her Old Age Pension in the 1960s, when she falsely listed her aunt Caroline (her mother Mary Angelique's sister) as her mother, as Caroline was alive and able to confirm Julia's date of birth.[8] Cecile Blanke's notes describe Julia as the daughter of Madeleine Lavallée and a niece of the Fayants and say that she grew up on the Fayant homestead.[9] Nowhere else has a connection to Madeleine Lavallée been indicated, and the provenance of Blanke's notes is unclear, however this may still be a possibility as the Métis Lavallée families are described as having lived in proximity to the Fayants at Lac Pelletier.[10] The well-known genealogical volumes

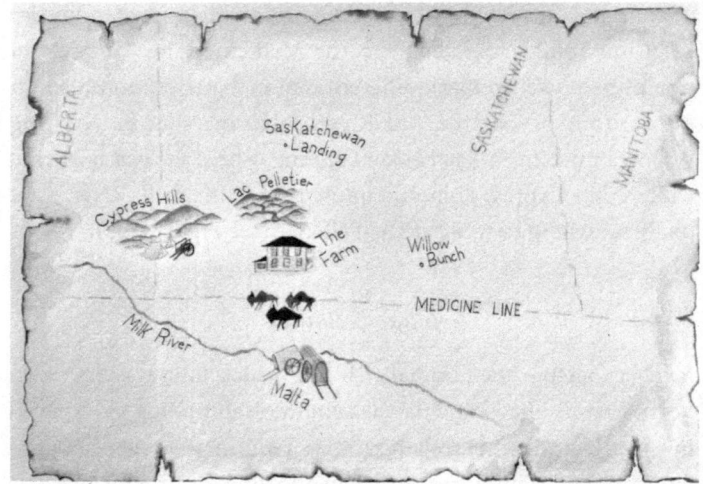

FIG. 5.02. *(top)* Map of southwest Saskatchewan, hand drawn and painted by Denica Bleau.

FIG. 5.03. *(bottom)* Grandma Adams (née Elise LaPlante) sitting with her great-grandchildren and great-great-grandchildren. From left to right: Louise Lamotte, Robert Moyer, Bertha Moyer, Ronald Moyer, Elise Adams, Raymond Moyer, and Edna Moyer.

of Métis families compiled by Gail Morin describe Julia's mother as Marie Genevieve Cabe, citing microfilm reel number C-15003 (a collection of scrip records) as the source of this information.[11] However, Marie Genevieve Cabe was, according to scrip records, married to Thomas Sinclair, George Sinclair's brother.[12]

In all likelihood, Julia's mother appears to have been Mary Angelique Sinclair (née Fayant), who was married to George Sinclair, born at Fort Walsh, Saskatchewan (SK), the son of Métis William Sinclair and Marie Chartrand.[13] This is supported by family history books describing Julia as Julie St. Claire[14] as well as 1906 Census records that list Julia (age four) as Julia Sinclair, living with George Sinclair and Mary Sinclair and their other child Nellie Sinclair (age two).[15] Birth records for Albert, Nellie, and Jennie Hazel Sinclair list Mary Fayant or Mary Angelique Fayant as their mother and George Sinclair as their father.[16] Marie Angelique's husband was George Sinclair; however, he was not Julia's biological father. Interviews and postcards indicate that Julia had long-standing relationships with George and Mary Angelique's children (Julia's half-siblings), namely Nellie and Agnes Sinclair.[17] Julia did not appear to live with her mother and her mother's new family for long, and family stories indicate she was raised primarily by her grandparents Jean Louis Fayant and Elise Fayant (née LaPlante), due to the stigma associated with being born out of wedlock.[18] Julia's biological father is described as having little relationship with his daughter until he was older.[19] Julia's daughter Marge, describes him as "a cowboy" who would "just come and go."[20] His name was Hugo Maguire, who my own mother affectionately referred to as Grandpa Pipe.[21]

The adventures of Hugo Maguire could themselves fill a book, and fortunately for his descendants, he was an avid writer and poet, leaving behind his writing documenting life along the Medicine Line during the turn of the century. Hugo, a cowboy and scout for the North West Mounted Police, was born in 1874 in Carleton Place, Ontario, and left his family in 1891 to move to the Northwest, where he worked on ranches throughout the Cypress Hills area before acquiring his own ranch Northwest of Shaunavon, SK.[22] He is described in Beth Ladow's *The Medicine Line* as a "largely forgotten Eastend area cowboy" who "with a touch of lyricism recalled with relish the isolated outdoor living his job required." As Maguire wrote, "I would rather hear a meadow lark sing, crickets chirp or frogs croak around a slough, than to hear Gilbert and Sullivan orchestras or Shuberts lofty music." He declared it a "happy and carefree life," in which he would "rather be bitten by a sage tick than any housefly."[23]

His writings offer rich descriptions of those he calls "half breeds" camping throughout "the south country," receiving scrip, putting on dances and parties in the winter, hauling buffalo bones, trading hides for horses, and running from police for hunting illegal game and rustling cattle. In particular, he tells numerous stories about Métis Norbert Adams, whom he travelled with, describing him as a "bronc buster," wolf and coyote hunter, and an "Indian belonging to the Métis Wolves Tribe."[24] Norbert Adams eventually married Julia's grandmother Elise Fayant (née LaPlante) after Jean Louis Fayant's passing, rendering her as (Great) Grandma Adams to Julia's children.[25] Yet, despite clearly living in the same area and among Julia's relatives, nowhere in Hugo's writing does he refer directly to his daughter. Family stories suggest he had no relationship with her until after Julia had children and grandchildren, when he arrived at her doorstep, unable to care for himself, and asked Julia if she would care for him.[26] She offered him a room in her house, and cared for him until his passing in 1969.[27] Julia was ultimately considered an illegitimate child, being born out of wedlock, a mark of impropriety amongst the local settler and Métis Catholic community.

FIG. 5.04. Julia on the farm with son Louis.

Like other Métis families who participated in the mass exodus from Manitoba in the midst of the 1869 Red River Resistance, Julia's grandparents Jean Louis and Elise left the Red River region and were married at the Qu'Appelle Mission.[28] They moved to Willow Bunch with other Métis families (both English and French), eventually reaching Saskatchewan Landing, just north of Swift Current.[29] In the 1901 census, Jean Louis is enumerated as a "Saulteaux FB" (French Breed) and Elise (or Elsie) as a "Cree FB." Their mother tongues are listed similarly (as Saulteaux and Cree), and their children are listed as speaking French and Cree. Jean Louis and his eldest son Antoine are both listed as being hunters and trappers. Living in the same household as Jean Louis and Elise are their eight children and two grandchildren. They appear to have lived among others who were presumably Métis, Cree, and Saulteaux, including Pelletiers, Dumonts, and Lemires.[30] In Cecile Blanke's notes, she shares the following recollection about Jean Louis and Elise Fayant, as told by Susie Penner Adams:

> Jean Louis Fayant came from Ontario or Eastern Manitoba. He was a mailman and hauled mail with horses and a wagon on horseback from Swift Current [North-Western Territory] to Battleford. Jean Louis and his family along with the Lemeres [sic] from Lac Pelletier and several other Metis families travelled each winter in a caravan to an area around Malta, Montana where they lived, in the bush, along the Milk River. Each spring they returned to their homes in the Swift Current area hunting and fishing along the way. One summer Jean Louis and Xavier Lemere went to Montreal with a cartload of buffalo bones. They were gone for three months. In 1898 Jean Louis was hired as a guide on the Smart Jones cattle drive to Klondike. After 29 days he left the drive at Edmonton to return home to Saskatchewan Landing. Mrs. Fayant's maiden

name was Elsie LaPlante. Before her marriage she had worked for her brother-in-law Joe LaRoque, caring for his three boys after her sister's death. Mr. Fayant was then 65 years of age. They had eight children. Their log house was built on the banks of the Swift Current Creek. After they left the homestead they lived with their son Alex at Lac Pelletier. Jean Louis died there on Jan 21, 1929. He is buried at Ste. Anne's Parish Cemetery at Lac Pelletier.[31]

It appeared that Jean Louis and Elise Fayant wintered among relatives in the Cypress Hills, and south of the US border, where many of their relations remained.[32] The lives of Jean Louis and Elise Fayant illustrate what may be considered a "typical" Métis experience for the time period, and reflect the often-repeated historical narrative of the Métis Nation in terms of their exile from the Red River in 1869, mobility westwards and seasonal crossing of the Medicine Line, intermarriage practices, and ways of life as hunters and trappers, and hauling buffalo bones.[33] Only with more permanent settlement at Lac Pelletier was it possible for their descendants, including Julia, to adapt and transition to a more "Canadian" agrarian lifestyle.

From Lac Pelletier to Farm Life

The history of Lac Pelletier and the Métis families who lived there have been well documented by Cecile Blanke (née Larocque) and Louise Moine (née Trottier).[34] Lac Pelletier, formerly named Spirit of the Eagle Lake and renamed by Métis who settled in the area,[35] was originally considered to be along the road allowance.[36] As Teillet explains, "having lost their lands to the speculators through the survey, homestead and scrip processes, the Métis lived wherever they could as long as they could, and then, when pushed off their lands, they moved to the public lands available along railroads, roads and Crown lands."[37] There were a number of such "road allowance communities" that existed in typically unserved areas throughout Saskatchewan and Manitoba, where Métis peoples built cabins or small shacks and attempted to survive.[38] Many Métis, like Julia's grandparents, were eligible for scrip and filed applications for their children,[39] but few actually settled permanently or attempted to homestead. The Fayants were among a number of Métis families that intermarried and moved through these same areas, namely the Adams, Alary, Gunn, LaFrambois, LaPlante, Laroque, Lasante, Lavallee, Lemere, Parenteau, Pritchard, Sinclair, Stout, Trottier, and Whiteford families.[40] Cecile Blanke's recollections of life at Lac Pelletier are rich in details, describing the log homes Métis families lived in, foods they ate, local festivities and rites of passage, the work they engaged in, traditional stories of the area, the local flora and fauna, and the common practice of visiting.[41]

Cecile Blanke's notes tell a story of Julia's early life at the Fayant home at Lac Pelletier as follows: "While on a visit with children to the homestead Julia (Fayant) told a Gowan family of a childhood experience. Left alone at home (Fayant homestead) one day in winter, she pulled a small beautiful-crafted horse sleigh (built by the Fayant boys and made from willows) to the top of a steep hill near the house. At the end of her one thrilling downhill ride near the bottom of the hill she crashed into a huge boulder and demolished the sleigh. Needless to say, she was not very popular when the family returned home."[42] Family stories suggest Julia grew up speaking Michif with her family[43] but taught herself to read and write English and French despite no clear evidence of any formal schooling.[44] Michif was the common language among Métis at Lac Pelletier.[45] Many of Blanke's contemporaries at Lac Pelletier, including her relatives, attended the Qu'Appelle Industrial School, also known as Lebret Indian Residential School.[46] She describes her recollections as follows: "The local priest would come and gather the kids, seven years old and up. They would take them in a wagon to Swift Current and put them on the train to Regina. From there, they went to Lebret, which was the nearest residential school for Métis kids."[47] How Julia escaped this fate remains unknown. While living at Lac Pelletier as a young woman Julia worked cleaning fish, helping her grandmother who took in laundry, and taking other odd jobs including cleaning houses, which is how she eventually met my great-grandfather Leon Lamotte.[48]

Julia lived at Lac Pelletier until going to work as a house cleaner for Leon as a teenager.[49] At the age of twenty-one, Julia married Leon. He was twenty-one years her senior, and had moved to Canada from Daverdisse, Belgium, with his family in 1889 and homesteaded in Redvers, SK, before moving to Willow Bunch, and finally purchasing land at the place our family calls "The Farm" as well as ranch lands south of Val Marie.[50] Family stories describe a tense relationship between Julia and Leon's sister Jeanne, who disapproved of her brother's marriage to an (illegitimate) Indigenous woman.[51] Family stories describe Julia experiencing discrimination from Euro-Canadian settlers both while living at Lac Pelletier and following her marriage to Leon, as it was common knowledge among locals that she was "part Indian."[52] Yet her Indigenous background and pride in being Métis didn't appear to be a problem for her husband. The farmhouse (where my aunt and uncle still reside) was built by Leon in the 1920s. In my conversation with Cecile Blanke, she remembers how the kitchen was built to suit Julia's six-foot-tall frame as all the counters and cupboards were raised.[53] Their marital relationship was described as a loving one, where they listened to one another and Leon was described as an accommodating man. It was clear from our conversations that upon moving to the farm,

Julia became the manager of the family's ranching and farming business, as Leon preferred to stay on the ranch land near Val Marie, away from the family.[54] My grandma Tova explained the situation as follows: "I don't like to say that Grandpa [Leon] kind of run away and left her with all the work, but that was kind of the impression I got. But then by the time I knew him, he was already old. I don't know how to say it, she did most of the work around the farm. There was nothing to have two or three hired men, and she looked after them and fed them and made sure they were working, and looked after her family."[55] Though it may have been unusual for Leon to spend extended time away from the farm, Julia's work ethic and contribution to the household aligned with the ways in which Métis women's skills, abilities, and labour have been described elsewhere.[56] A local history book about the nearby town of Cadillac confirms Julia's hands-on approach to farm operations, stating that "every fall you could find Julia stooking sheaves and surprising the best of stookers with her abilities."[57]

The relationship dynamic between her and Leon and how she came to run the family farm has long been a source of interest for me. Her strength, determination, and work ethic were also described by Cecile Blanke, who described her as

> a very clever woman and strong, [who] knew how to do things. I was told that in the early years when the kids were young, she would get up at five o'clock in the morning or maybe earlier and feed the horses and have them all fed and then come in and make breakfast. And when the men got up, they were ready to go in the field or whatever they were doing. And then I heard that she could butcher a cow or a beef all by herself. That's how strong she was. And then probably did the canning and butchering in those days. They have to can the beef because you couldn't keep it. You didn't have electricity.[58]

Julia's fortitude and household contribution was clearly known to those even outside of the family, but was not unexpected among Métis families. As Maria Campbell illustrates, "it was always the women—our grandmothers, mothers, and aunties—who were the cultural, spiritual, and in more recent times, economic strength of our families and community life. Without them, times would have been much harder."[59] Similarly, Diane Payment describes Métis women as "the backbone of society, the ones who kept the family together and passed on values of caring, giving, and sharing. 'Work, work, and more work' was their motto."[60]

Julia had seven children of her own. After Louis and Louise, her first two children, she struggled to conceive and, a devout Catholic, she prayed to St. Joseph for a child. Becoming pregnant, she named her third child Josephine.[61] She then had four more children: Marguerite (Marge), Joseph, Theresa (Terry), and my grandfather Constantine (Connie). Her children attended church-run schools and convents where they stayed as far from home as Gravelbourg (110 kilometres east of the farm), where they had mixed experiences, some negative and traumatizing, but for others, going to school at the convent was remembered fondly.[62] Her eldest son Louis enlisted in the military, while several of her children married other Métis from Lac Pelletier, including the Whitefords (or Whitfords), with whom our family was closely tied.[63]

Julia and Leon supported their children as much as they could financially. My grandpa Connie eventually worked and lived on the farm, where my mom was raised and where I spent my childhood holidays and summers. As part of a province-wide effort by Métis Peoples to politically organize in Saskatchewan, which depended significantly on the labour of Métis women,[64] my grandpa Connie and his sister Marge, started the first Métis association in nearby Ponteix, around the same time that Cecile Blanke started the Swift Current Local in the late 1970s. Cecile

FIG. 5.05. Julia as a child with her grandmother Elise Adams (née LaPlante).

and Marge were among the first women to be involved in starting local Métis associations, as documented by Dr. Jennifer Adese.[65] Connie and Marge were both very proud to be Métis, something Julia instilled in her children through speaking openly about her identity as "part-Indian" or Métis.[66]

Julia engaged in many traditional activities that can be associated with Métis culture, including playing guitar and fiddle; tanning hides; making winter coats lined with fur, feather hats, and birchbark baskets; sewing clothes from the fabric that packaged sugar and flour and other materials; spinning and looming wool; embroidery; and using medicines from the land for different ailments.[67] As Stringer explains, "it didn't matter what Julia did, she seemed to get much enjoyment from just doing it."[68] She grew a sizable garden, planted an orchard, and preserved food for the harsh prairie winters, sustaining her family from the land.[69] Her granddaughter Paulette recalled a time when Julia took the women in the family to find what she called ki-ni-kin-nik, which she loved the smell of as it reminded Julia of her grandparents.[70] Cecile Blanke describes the practice of smoking the inner cambium layer of the red willow (ki-ni-kin-nik) as a common practice among Métis relatives at Lac Pelletier.[71] The Métis practice of nicknaming was also common within the family, as Julia referred to all of her grandchildren with nicknames.[72]

Julia was remembered very fondly by her grandchildren, each of whom she told were her favourite, and each of whom believed it to be true.[73] She was actively involved in her grandchildren's lives, including that of my own mother, who describes her as "a good example of a mother, a grandmother-type person, a matriarchal, strong individual with plenty of courage," going on to say, "I thought of her as a brave person. I don't know why, but I always thought: she would have been brave."[74] She was an affectionate and loving grandmother, and her grandchildren defended her to those who commented upon her appearance, being that she was six feet tall, Indigenous, and born with strabismus, also known as "crossed eyes."[75]

A Complicated Life

In interviews, Julia is described as having faced considerable discrimination not only for being known at the time as a "halfbreed," but also for being "a big woman" with crossed-eyes.[76] Julia's life was complicated by her disability, as strabismus would have likely caused her to see double until she had her vision corrected in the 1960s.[77] Given that she was described by everyone interviewed as being an expert seamstress who could sew without a pattern, excelling at embroidery, and a painter, it appears her disability did not limit her from doing the things she enjoyed.[78] My mom explained it saying: "I've seen pictures of her when I'm sitting beside her and I'm little, but I didn't think anything of it. For someone who had vision issues, she was an excellent sewer. She did lots of fine work like embroidery and crocheting and sewing. So you know, it wasn't a disability in any means."[79]

When I was younger, I heard stories about certain families refusing to sit near to Julia on the train because she was stigmatized as Métis; yet Julia was proud to be Métis and never attempted to hide her ancestry or family ties from anyone. However, nearly every interview with family noted that she had a distanced relationship with her own family, due to their struggles with alcoholism. Interviews explain she refused to touch alcohol "like she was allergic to it,"[80] despite making different wines from locally grown fruits.[81] This was one reason she tried to keep her children away from the Métis at Lac Pelletier, as she didn't want her children to "know the life" of her relatives that included drinking and violence.[82] Yet Julia's daughter Marge recollects with fondness several summers spent with her great-uncle and great-aunt, Donald and Julia Gunn, while photos and postcards suggest Julia continued to communicate and visit with her half-sisters, mother, grandmother, cousins, and other Métis relations stretching as far as Pryor, Montana.[83]

FIG. 5.06. Julia surrounded by her family. From left to right: Julia's children Joe, Terry, Josephine, Louise, Marge, Louis [Connie missing] (back row); her father Hugo Maguire holding her grandson Dennis, Julia with her granddaughter Paulette, and Leon holding grandson Paul (front row).

Julia's life demonstrates the complicated and at times paradoxical position of a Métis woman living between and among societies on the verge of transition from old ways to sedentary farm life. She grew up travelling the cart paths with her relatives at Lac Pelletier. In some ways, she was thrust into the new world of her husband, where she moved from being the hired help to running the family ranch and becoming the matriarch of our family. Yet she held on to many of the old ways, speaking Michif to her children and following a spiritual path that included both Catholic beliefs and Indigenous spiritual practices, including what Cecile Blanke calls "premonition."[84] Julia is remembered for having read tea leaves and having predicted her daughter Marge's life of travel (she has lived in India for thirty years), the death of relatives, her husband's death, and even her own death, which happened at a funeral service in Eastend in 1973.[85] Cecile explains this aspect of her life as follows: "A lot of people did that at that time. And it was true for her. You would have premonition. You could see the sky or the way the horses acted or something. She probably had that in her. Because most of the Métis people did. It's how the horses acted or how the sky or the wind or the moon. And that's what they studied. And that's how they would predict weather and what was to come. Yeah, she probably had that in her."[86] Yet such "premonition" was not considered to clash with her Catholic beliefs as she remained devout for her entire life, travelling to Montreal to Saint Joseph's Oratory, then returning home to paint a mural of it at the farm, which remains today.[87] Clearly Julia's upbringing at Lac Pelletier shaped her and impacted the ways in which she raised her own children and grandchildren, as she was able to pass on Métis traditions and values.

The story of Grandma Julia is one of strength, resilience, adaptation, and familial devotion, all in the face of discrimination, family dysfunction, abandonment, and other consequences of settler colonialism. She had a lasting economic impact on my family through managing the farm and passing on the values of hard work and determination. Her lived experience as a Métis woman was likely not unusual for her time. Despite appearing unremarkable at first glance, Julia's instrumentality, determination, and strength against the odds paints a picture of an incredible woman who earned the title of matriarch. In closing, I want to offer my gratitude to the women I interviewed and who shared materials with me to assemble this puzzle: Paulette Strand, Marge

Liboiron, Terry Whiteford, Tova Lamotte, Barb Tofte, and Cecile Blanke. I would also like to thank Genna Moyer (a student in one of my classes) and her grandfather Andrew Moyer (son of Julia's good friend and cousin Edna Moyer) for sharing family documents with me.

Julia left behind a beautiful legacy, having had seven children, who had their own children, many of whom are working to reconnect to their Métis identity through her and the legacy she left behind. For the entirety of my life, I knew I was Métis, and I have my great-grandmother Julia to thank. I was told I was Métis from a young age and have spent the bulk of my career trying to better understand what it means to be Métis. For me, this means I carry with me particular traditions, philosophies, and responsibilities passed through my lineage, inherited from my mother's family. I don't only look to the past but continue to be an active participant in the local Métis community, working for future generations of Métis peoples, while continuing to share these traditions and ways of being with my own children. Connecting to my Grandma Julia by learning about her life has been very meaningful for me in connecting to my own Métis identity. My grandmother Tova summed it up, saying, "She was truly a magnificent woman," and I can only hope to be half the woman she was.[88]

NOTES

1 Marge Liboiron, interview by Gabrielle Legault on family history, August 2, 2014.
2 Legault, "Stories of Contemporary Métis Identity in British Columbia."
3 Barbara Tofte, interview by Gabrielle Legault on Grandma Julia Fayant Métis family history, November 25, 2021; Paulette Strand, interview by Gabrielle Legault on Grandma Julia Fayant Métis family history, November 2, 2021; Tova Lamotte, interview by Gabrielle Legault on Grandma Julia Fayant Métis family history, October 28, 2021; Cecile Blanke, interview by Gabrielle Legault on Grandma Julia Fayant

Métis family history, October 27, 2021; Barbara Tofte, interview by Gabrielle Legault on family history, August 8, 2014; Terry Whiteford, interview by Gabrielle Legault on family history, August 3, 2014; and Liboiron, interview. Participants consented to be identified and provided permissions to share historical family materials in both UBC Behavioural Ethics H21-01963 and H13-00050.

4   Ens and Sawchuck, *From New People to New Nations*, 217–38.
5   Hogue, *Métis and the Medicine Line*, 4.
6   Strand, interview.
7   Julia Fayant, birth registration, Saskatchewan Vital Statistics.
8   Strand, interview.
9   Cecile Blanke Historical Notes on Mrs. Fayant (Elsie LaPlante), shared with author in November 2021. Note: Blanke could not recall when she wrote these notes and where this information was gathered from.
10 Blanke, *Lac Pelletier: My Métis Home*, 26.
11 Morin, *Company Men: James Peter Whitford*, 49, 140, 227, 226.
12 Scrip application of Geneviéve Sinclair, July 9, 1900, RG15-D-II-8-C, Volume 1367, microfilm C-15003, Library and Archives Canada.
13 Morin, "Company Men: James Peter Whitford," 226; George Sinclair, birth registration.
14 Lamotte and Lamotte, *The Lamotte Family: Reunion 1894–1994*, 2–3.
15 1906 Census of Northwest Provinces, microfilm: T-18358.
16 Birth registrations for Albert, Nellie, and Jennie Hazel Sinclair, Saskatchewan Vital Statistics.
17 Strand, interview.
18 Liboiron, interview.
19 Tova Lamotte, interview.
20 Liboiron, interview.
21 Tofte, interview, 2014; Tofte, interview, 2021.
22 Hugo Maguire obituary, "Cowboy Dies at 94," *Val Marie Bulletin*, 1969, courtesy of Tova Lamotte.
23 Ladow, *The Medicine Line*, 105.
24 Maguire, *Stories of the West*, 7, 14, 16.
25 Liboiron, interview.
26 Tofte, interview, 2014.
27 Hugo Maguire obituary.
28 Jean Louis's scrip application states he moved from St. François Xavier to the Qu'Appelle Mission with his father in the fall of 1869, where he married Elise LaPlante in 1878. Scrip application of Jean Louis Fagnant,

April 11, 1885, RG15-D-II-8-b, Volume 1327, microfilm C-14938, Library and Archives Canada.
29　Whiteford, interview.
30　1901 Census of Canada, Item Number: 1024321.
31　Blanke Historical Notes.
32　Scrip application of Jean Louis Fagnant, heir to his deceased daughter, Marie Fagnant, July 5, 1900, RG15-D-II-8-c, Volume 1346, microfilm C-14967, Library and Archives Canada.; Scrip application of Jean Louis Fagnant, heir to his deceased daughter, Elizabeth Fagnant, July 5, 1900, RG15-D-II-8-c, Volume 1346, microfilm C-14967, Library and Archives Canada; Jean Louis Fagnant Land Transfer, July 17, 1906, 1229013.
33　Teillet, *The North West Is Our Mother*.
34　See Blanke, *Lac Pelletier*; and Moine, *Remembering Will Have to Do*.
35　Blanke, *Lac Pelletier*, Appendix A.
36　Liboiron, interview; Strand, interview.
37　See Teillet, *The North West Is Our Mother*, 420.
38　See Teillet, *The North West Is Our Mother*, 422.
39　Scrip application of Angelique Fagnant, July 5, 1900, RG15-D-II-8-c, Volume 1346, microfilm C-14967, Library and Archives Canada.; Scrip application of Antoine Fagnant, July 5, 1900, RG15-D-II-8-c, Volume 1346, microfilm C-14967, Library and Archives Canada; Elizabeth Fagnant Scrip Application; Scrip application of Julie Fagnant, July 5, 1900, RG15-D-II-8-c, Volume 1346, microfilm C-14967, Library and Archives Canada; and Marie Fagnant Scrip Application.
40　Blanke, *Lac Pelletier*, 26.
41　Blanke, *Lac Pelletier*.
42　Blanke Historical Notes.
43　Blanke, interview.
44　1926 Census of the Prairie Provinces, Item: 1008311.
45　Blanke, *Lac Pelletier*, 10.
46　Blanke, interview; Moine, *Remembering Will Have to Do*, 42–67.
47　Blanke, *Lac Pelletier*, 32.
48　Liboiron, interview; Whiteford, interview.
49　Whiteford, interview.
50　Lamotte and Lamotte, *The Lamotte Family: Reunion 1894–1994*, 8.
51　Liboiron, interview; Tova Lamotte, interview.
52　Tova Lamotte, interview.
53　Blanke, interview.
54　Strand, interview.
55　Tova Lamotte, interview.

56   Campbell, "Foreward: Charting the Way," 1.
57   Legros and Jordan, *Cadillac: Prairie Heritage*, 638.
58   Blanke, interview.
59   Campbell, "Foreward: Charting the Way," 1.
60   Payment, "'Une femme en vaut deux—Strong Like Two People,'" 265.
61   Strand, interview.
62   Whiteford, interview.
63   Blanke, interview.
64   Stevenson and Troupe, "From Kitchen Tables to Formal Organization," 229.
65   Adese, "Restoring the Balance," 129.
66   Liboiron, interview; Tova Lamotte, interview.
67   Whiteford, interview; Tova Lamotte, interview; Legros and Jordan, eds., *Cadillac: Prairie Heritage*, 638.
68   Legros and Jordan, eds., *Cadillac: Prairie Heritage*, 638.
69   Whiteford, interview; Tofte, interview, 2014; Tova Lamotte, interview.
70   Strand, interview.
71   Blanke, *Lac Pelletier*, 67.
72   Tofte, interview, 2014; Strand, interview.
73   Strand, interview.
74   Tofte, interview, 2021.
75   Strand, interview.
76   Tofte, interview, 2014.
77   Tova Lamotte, interview.
78   Whiteford, interview; Tova Lamotte, interview.
79   Tofte, interview, 2021.
80   Liboiron, interview; Tova Lamotte, interview.
81   Whiteford, interview.
82   Strand, interview.
83   Postcards passed down to me include Julia's correspondence with her relations living at Pryor Montana, her cousin and close friend Edna Moyer, Angelic Fayant (presumably her mother), and Nellie Sinclair.
84   Blanke, interview.
85   Tofte, interview, 2014; Tova Lamotte, interview; Strand, interview.
86   Blanke, interview.
87   Tova Lamotte, interview.
88   Tova Lamotte, interview.

Six

On Becoming Sovereign
Generations of Métis Matriarchal Resistance

by Janice Cindy Gaudet

> *"I am not courageous, my girl. We were raised that way."*
> —NORMA GAUDET (NÉE MORRISON)
> Mother of Janice Cindy Gaudet, daughter of Auxile Lepine Morrison, granddaughter of Margaret Boucher and Josephte Lepine

JULY 15 IS THE BIRTHDAY OF AUXILE CAROLINE LEPINE Morrison. It was the perfect day to begin writing on the ancestral land along the South Saskatchewan River that she and her women kin would have intimately known for more than a century. Within our family conversation, we still remember Auxile's birth date yearly, thirty-seven years after her death in 1985, when I was fifteen. On this day, we acknowledge her with memories, circulating around the kitchen table, in social media or in passing. I had rarely considered her life within the context of how our family is shaped and influenced by generations of Métis matriarchal resistance until now. Yet I am comforted by the knowledge that "memories can act as a catalyst for self-recovery and *renewed* community."[1] The sharing of memories as stories are themselves a way of resisting against the erasure of Métis life and kinship wellness grounded in matriarchal resistance. The way of storying offers a space of being visited by our matriarchs and embodying more deeply the heart of their values. Memories of Auxile bring me closer in relation to the power that Métis women held and still hold. Closer because in visiting with my relatives and extended kin, I hear their voices, see their faces, and feel their sentiments in relation to Auxile and her family. It is embodied. We exchange stories (the ones that inspire, strengthen, and sadden us). In doing so, Auxile becomes epic, a recognized matriarch in all of our lives. In connection to her, we recognize ourselves as an integral part of her community. We recover and reclaim a part of ourselves in relation to our matriarchs, and the endured pride and love of being Métis flourishes and becomes visible in all generations.

In 2006, Auxile inspired my graduate studies research that focused on the collective memory of 1885, intergenerational trauma, and Métis women. She visited me and, without mincing her words, stated that I needed to change my story about her and therefore how I perceived myself.[2] We did not belong to the stories of victimhood. Instead, she was pointing me to generations of Métis women's matriarchal resistance. It has taken fifteen years to give voice to her teachings through this chapter and through visiting with relatives of all ages over the past decade. It is through their generosity of stories and perspectives that I am able to change my story. Their experiences of Auxile, alongside my own reflection, are included with their permission. Some family members have generously reviewed, clarified, and commented on my drafts, including the knowledge keepers I quote in this chapter. When weaving together the resilient threads of memories with literature, it is evident that Métis women loved and valued family and their freedom. They resisted collectively against the harmful colonial ideologies and actions that threatened all that they loved.³ I learn that their existence and freedom was under threat with the

FIG. 6.01. Margaret Boucher, holding her daughter, Auxile Lepine.

growing racialization and land dominance shaping the 1869–70 and 1885 Métis Resistances.

I started to think of how resistance and violence are responses to one another. In this context, love as a practice and a power is rarely discussed nor considered as critical to exist and to live freely.[4] Yet it is what sustains, "unites...and binds all life."[5] I also draw inspiration from Black feminist theorist bell hooks, who researched love in relation to Western patriarchy dominance so as to reimagine the place of love within the context of my research. She redefines love as "a combination of care, commitment, knowledge, responsibility, respect and trust."[6] I consider hooks's critical analysis of love as a form of decolonial love, as it invites a conscious return to the Métis matriarch's role in healthy kinship and a departure from self-recognition in the systems that dominate, devalue, and punish women for being women. I chose the term *sovereign* as it signals what I come to understand as the continuity of freedom, kinship love, meticulous care, and owning one's self. My chapter honours the generations of Métis matriarchs that I belong to, and my learnings with family and community. It is a collective approach of drawing strength in Auxile Lepine, my Maymair (grandmother in Michif).

Drawing Strength in Auxile Lepine

Drawing strength in relation to Auxile as my Métis matriarchal lynchpin brings me in proximity to generations of Métis women. As I mention earlier, I cannot think of Auxile in isolation from the generations of Métis women who shaped her life and their place in Métis people's social and political resistances. Knowing who we belong to, how we are related, and what and who keeps us related is part of a Métis health and well-being perspective.[7] In shifting my lens, I can reimagine matriarchal resistance as a foundational principle of rematriating kinship health and well-being, thereby refusing distorted representations of womanhood.[8] Zoe Todd's Métis feminist research reminds me that "kinship has a powerful way of continuing to assert itself across time and space."[9] Although Auxile is her own person, I became aware of the importance of celebrating Auxile within the Métis social and political consciousness of resistance shaped by matriarchal kinship. In other words, her umbilical connection to generations of female kin was nourished by the way of visiting, a deliberate and reciprocal approach for the taking care of one another and their land.

Our Métis kinship practices, resistance, and love are bound to this collective identity. My mother adamantly reminded me of this during the difficult COVID-19 pandemic. In my discomfort in assisting her with body care, I acknowledged her individual courage. She replied, "I'm not courageous, my girl. We were raised that way." In her refusal of my imposition even in the midst of seemingly distressing life changes, she, without any commotion, corrected me by naming a life principle that was true to her living, true to her sovereign way of being.

As I turn my attention to Auxile, the bond to my own mother deepens. I recognize Auxile now in my mother's life philosophies, choices, and leadership. I understand more deeply the way in which her vision, actions, and being-ness were influenced by generations of Métis matriarchs. She too was shaped by women's social and political resistances, kinship, spirituality, sovereign food systems, and what is so little talked about, love. In this way, I recognize spiritual stability as rooted in matriarchal commitment, strength, and service. Métis matriarchs shape and lift up community, making them foundational pillars of resistance; resisting a culture of domination that rejects the value of sustaining female well-being.[10]

During some of my visits with Mom, she tells me how much she still misses her mother even decades after her passing. Their love for one another is unwavering, reciprocal, profound, and life-affirming. My moonoocs ("uncle" in Michif) and mataants ("auntie" in Michif) echo the same fondness toward Auxile, as do her grandchildren. Such ways of being loved and loving give "courage to risk being and sharing of ourselves, being honest and revealing."[11] Auxile embodied this form of love as part of her family value system and as an enactment of Métis women's resistance. Diane Payment begins to provide evidence that "Métis women resisted Western patriarchal value, especially in the case of mothers with many young children to care for."[12] Auxile is one of these many Métis women. To make this connection, I am compelled to physically shift my view on my matriarchs from the photos, archives, and family stories to the place where she was born and her maternal and paternal kinship. I also visit the location of her family home and walk the landscapes they would have known and in return would have known them.

This land is tended by my matriarchs. Knowing this, I can confidently depart colonial myths and move toward our matriarchal ways of upholding "a culture of love."[13] In every step, I re-educate and re-centre my belonging to generations of insistent, sovereign, affectionate, and intellectual Métis women. I write

FIG. 6.02. Cindy Gaudet, granddaughter of Auxile Lepine, walking on the foundations of Auxile Lepine's homestead in Hoey, Saskatchewan.

for the generations of kin so they too may know their matriarchal belonging and add to their stories. Placing my attention on Métis matriarchs resists the patriarchal ideology that power and privilege belong solely to men. It is an ideology that justifies and prioritizes the voices, labour, intellect, and needs of men as superior to women.[14] It further invites a deeper inquiry into the ways men and children too are deeply affected and harmed by Western patriarchal dominance, though they are less vocal about it.[15] When we centre matriarchs within the lens of social and political resistance, Métis women's resistance becomes more visible. We can enact it consciously and adapt and model it for future generations. My focus on resistance does not imply nor negate Métis women's experiences of violence, struggle, injustices, loss, trauma, and ill health. To the contrary, Auxile's identity was not bound to these; her identity was bound to something much greater. This is my first matriarchal teaching of resistance.

Learning from the past, we can theorize Métis matriarchs' praxis of kinship love as an ongoing form of resistance. In doing so, research contributes to a regenerative understanding of sovereignty that centres Métis women's wisdom, knowledge, stories and perspectives. It connects us to Métis governance that was organized around buffalo hunting laws, which included the care, freedom, and protection of the social and economic organization of the broader Métis community.[16] The economic, political, and social positioning of Métis women is too often lost, or deliberately excluded, in male-centred narratives. Yet, increasingly, Métis women's scholarship is making visible historical and contemporary literature, material culture, traditional practices, language, and oral stories. For example, research by Brenda Macdougall and Nicole St-Onge demonstrates that "women played a pivotal role in the creation, formation, leadership and maintenance of brigades."[17] Their research demonstrates a pattern of interrelated sisters strengthening "social and economic cohesiveness" by connecting kin as part of the "buffalo-hunting economy" patterns. Auxile's great-grandmothers, Julie Henry and Marguerite Grenon, would have been accustomed to this lifestyle and deeply steeped in a kinship way of life. Macdougall and St-Onge explain that the most cohesive sister communities existed in the 1700s and 1800s with the integral influence of First Nations women's traditional knowledge. Similarly, Cheryl Troupe's research demonstrates how Métis women's kinship influenced the historical Trottier brigade's success.[18] The long-standing history of Métis kinship points to the ways in which matriarchs kept order, adapted, and kept us related and living as les gens libres ("the free people") and otipemisiwak ("people who owned themselves"). Payment describes patterns of "female-led resettlement."[19] Those patterns shaped Auxile's way of being and thinking. The matriarchs, before, during, and after the resistances of 1869 and 1885, and the generations they raised, connect our families to a long history of resistance, sovereignty, and kinship love.[20]

Born to a Courageous People

Auxile was born in 1908 in her family home, in a place that the Plains Cree people refer to as See Seep SaKayegan, known today as Duck Lake. The lake, referred to as a "small body of water," was home to a diversity of ducks that migrated to this area, hence the name.[21] I have frequently returned to Duck Lake, north of present-day Saskatoon, searching for anything I could learn about her parents. In doing so, I learned that there were several clusters of families that lived on the road allowance in the Duck Lake area. They would have seen themselves as one community stretching across the geography in family groupings. I called Maria Campbell, Métis matriarch and mentor, to share my surprise that some family members recalled Auxile speaking of life on the road allowance. Maria went on to share her memories as a young girl stopping to visit her relatives in the communities when her family travelled to Gabriel's Crossing in the South Saskatchewan River region to fish, harvest, and/or attend the community rodeo in St. Louis.[22] The undeveloped road allowance on which these Métis families lived was land set aside in the Canadian government's Dominion Lands Survey for the building of roads, the land between the township sections that was not owned by settlers. Some Métis families had no other choice but to build homes on these unused portions of land when displaced from their own home lands. They became known as "Road Allowance People."[23]

Cheryl Troupe situates Métis road allowances as "sites of resistance."[24] Métis families created homes in these places, continuing their cultural practice of "owning themselves" despite land dispossession, political violence, and growing representations of them as second-class citizens, lazy, rebels, squatters, and savages. The negative representations justified life-threatening actions directed toward families involved in the resistances. This, alongside what Maria Campbell recalls as a "miserable life of poverty, which held no hope for the future,"[25] resulted in shame of being and living as Métis. Shame seeped into our bones and our homes.[26] The intersecting forms of violence are, too, part of my family story of resistance and love. As I deepen my inquiry into Métis matriarchal resistance, it is evident that Métis women had to deal with unimaginable circumstances in their decision making. Knowing the roots of colonial violence helps me to make sense of what matriarchs endured, and gather perspective on the ways that Western patriarchal dominance still persists today.[27]

The roots of gendered violence and its many evolving forms in Canada's nation-building efforts and ideologies have been well documented. For example, Sylvia Van Kirk's research on women in fur trade society provides insight into the influence of Victorian ideals, patriarchal thinking, religious morals, and Western notions of femininity and power structures on Indigenous women.[28] Harmful representations of Indigenous women as sinful led to punishment, which involved denial of food rations and medical attention. Demeaning and ridiculing women along with their governing roles and labour brought about the rise of harmful patriarchal systems that sought to replace an egalitarian structure. The arrival of non-Indigenous women into fur trade society and the development of Western Canada were devastating for First Nations and Métis women. Even when they had adopted British manners and styles, racism grew toward them. They were perceived as "not being of moral character," and were therefore not seen as equals by settler societies. They became a threat to church-centric marriages and Eurocentric social norms. Métis-Cree scholar Kim Anderson's research addresses the negative representations of Métis and First Nations women through the power of reconstructing native womanhood.[29] She demonstrates the disconnection from kinship roles and responsibilities as a form of gendered violence that reshaped our matriarch-led communities. Negative representations perpetuated harmful attitudes toward Indigenous women as "squaws," a narrative constructed to obstruct their authority and power, rendering them less than, useless, and easily disposed of.[30] Stereotypical imagery fostered "cultural attitudes that encourage sexual, physical, verbal or psychological violence against Indigenous women."[31] Yet Janice Acoose noted that "Indigenous women exercised autonomous control over their bodies and relations with others."[32] This shift from female-centred ways of living to Euro-Canadian patriarchal ways of living meant that First Nations and Métis women's meaningful social, political, and spiritual ways are largely undocumented. Changing my story of negative perceptions, as Auxile demanded, I have come to recognize an enactment of resistance grounded in a long history of Métis women's sovereignty.[33]

Métis Resistance and Land

Many changes occurred following the 1869–70 Red River Resistance, a resistance fuelled by the Canadian government's intentional neglect of Métis peoples' inherent right to lands that they used and occupied. Assimilation efforts were harshly enforced to settle the West and remove Indigenous peoples from sight. Métis people sent letters of petition, but they went unanswered. As noted by historians, the resistance during 1869–70 forced the government to negotiate with the Métis and bring Manitoba into Confederation. The Manitoba Act (1870) made allowances to provide 1.4 million acres of land in exchange for the extinguishing of Métis title to land, but it never mentioned scrip as the way that this would happen. It was only through an Order in Council that scrip was decided upon.[34] The government created scrip policy as a way to extinguish Métis title to the lands they had known, loved, stewarded, and proudly created as their homes for decades.

The Scrip Commission of Canada was later extended from Manitoba to Saskatchewan. Troupe explains: "This was part of the reason for the 1885 resistance—government was not acting on what it promised to Métis. The Métis that were outside Manitoba in 1870 did not receive scrip but they continually pressured government to provide it. In 1885, at the same time as the resistance, they started providing land scrip to Métis that were in the northwest at the time of the creation of Manitoba."[35] Auxile's maternal grandmother Caroline Lesperance's scrip was issued on August 20, 1876, as were those of her great-grandmother Julie Henry and her grandfather Maxime Lepine Sr. My relatives would have received the 1870 land scrip, along with many other Métis families. I was unable to find out when or whether my families' scrip was redeemed for land or cash. The government's incompetence in regulating scrip justly for Métis people is another form of dominance that resulted in mishandling, breakdown of kinship, land loss, and stereotypes.

Caroline's scrip record identifies her as "Halfbreed." Halfbreed was the term commonly used to identify the Métis at that time, but there are important distinctions to be made, as Maria Campbell has explained.[36] The identities of Michif and Halfbreed were different, based on the people themselves, where they lived, their relatives, their language, and the religion they practised. In Caroline's case, her family and other Métis families with whom they would have been related by marriage left the Red River region in the 1880s due to land disputes, racial hostility following the 1869–70 Resistance and the creation of the Manitoba province, and state policies that increasingly privileged white settlers.[37] These families were collectively enacting their resistance, rights, and responsibility to exist and to live freely.[38] Métis lawyer Jean Teillet provides a vivid picture of the oppressive colonial legacy of fear and silence that attempts to deny Métis people's right to exist freely. She explains the circumstances that increasingly pushed them out of their homeland and their resistance of being controlled.[39] Her research offers important social and political context for the way in which Auxile's relatives would have lived. It further contextualizes the thread of resistance carried in my mother's living, that "we were raised that way," to be a courageous people.

Margaret Boucher: Born during the 1869 Resistance

Auxile's mother, Margaret Boucher, was born between 1866 and 1869. The baptismal records indicate ties to the Métis families of the parish of St. François Xavier in the Red River Settlement. These

FIG. 6.03. Auxile as a young woman.

families were mainly Catholic and Michif-speaking.[40] Margaret's parents, Caroline Lesperance and Jean-Baptiste Boucher, had fifteen children. Caroline was the daughter of La Loche Boat Brigade leaders Alexis (dit Bonami) Lesperance and Marguerite Grenon. They supported the 1869–70 Red River Resistance. Little is written about Auxile's grandmother, aunties, and great-grandmothers. We do know that, in 1882, Caroline, along with her husband and their family, travelled from Red River with other Métis families.[41] At the time, Métis people were fleeing and seeking refuge and safety from the distress of increasing racial prejudice and the loss of their land that were brought about by changes to the Manitoba Act. Their trajectory has been described as taking fifty days in ox-drawn carts to land along the South Saskatchewan River, which became known as Boucherville, and later St. Louis de Langevin.[42] Margaret would have been sixteen when her family made this long journey. Her thirteen siblings at that time would have ranged in age up to twenty-three, the youngest having been born in 1882 on the Carleton trail. Métis Matriarch Sophie McDougall (née Boyer) refers to this movement as the *trail of babies*, signalling the unspoken labour of the women and demonstrating how life carried on for families as they were on the move.[43] This was something that they were used to; it was not unusual for women to give birth while on the move. Métis Matriarch Yvette Cyr (née Boucher) shared that Caroline's youngest child, Ernest, was born in the midst of the 1885 Métis Resistance in Batoche. Auxile's mother, grandmother, and aunties would have all directly experienced the strength of family structures and the "continuation and persistence of traditional customs"[44] during this period.

On February 18, 1889, Caroline and Jean-Baptiste applied for homestead entry to River Lot no. 12, comprised of 121 acres of land along the South Saskatchewan River. It was not until February 29, 1904, that they received patent, or title, to the land. This is where they continued to enact their sovereignty and rebuild their lives. Auxile's mother and maternal aunts, uncles, and cousins would have continued to contribute to the social, economic, and political system, as they did at the Red River. I name them to honour their lives and to strengthen our kinship ties: Caroline (b. 1859), Marie (b. 1859), Jean-Baptiste (b. 1861), Solomon (b. 1862), Charles (b. 1864), Rose (b. 1865), Emma (b. 1871), Frederic (b. 1872), Alvina (b. 1874), Elise (b. 1876), Sarah (b. 1877 or 1879), Joseph (b. 1878), Delima (b. 1882), and Pierre-Louis/Ernest (b. 1885). The stories of our ancestral land and the love of this land continue today to be stewarded by members of the Boucher family. They also proudly honour the life of our Matriarch Caroline Lesperance and their families who first settled along the South Saskatchewan River.

With the 1882 relocation from the Red River to the South Saskatchewan region, "the Boucher and Lepine family constituted by themselves almost the entire population of St. Louis."[45] These northwestern Métis-centric settlements were traditionally identified by family names. The adjoining regions of St. Laurent, Batoche, Gabriel's Crossing, Fish Creek, and Duck Lake were settled or had been settled by Métis kinship systems, creating a broad relational network of "family" systems.[46] Teillet's research speaks to the Métis understanding of family as being distinct from the Eurocentric concept of family: "For the Métis, family was the basic unit of life, the relationship, or wahkootowin, around which all life revolved, including social customs, marriage, trade and the economy. The family was a worldview that guided all Métis values and behaviour. Family was deeply treasured and no man or woman advanced alone. Reciprocity, mutual support and the sharing ethic were central values of the Metis family."[47] Auxile's relatives experienced firsthand what Payment calls the "migration" of Métis families to the South Saskatchewan region. Some of our old people recall the devastation that followed, and the continuity of community strength in its rebuilding. Auxile's parents were nineteen years old at the time of the 1885 Resistance. They were married a year later, in 1886.

Grandmother Josephte Lavallee

Auxile's father, Maxime Lepine, was the son of Josephte (née Lavallee; also written as Josette in some texts) and Maxime Sr. Much has been written about Maxime Sr. and Auxile's uncle Ambroise Lepine, given their leadership in Riel's provisional government during the 1869–70 Resistance. In August 1885, at the age of forty-eight, Maxime Sr. and nine other Métis men were sentenced to seven years in prison for high treason. While sources differ on the length of time Maxime Sr. spent in Stony Mountain Penitentiary, it is evident that his time there impacted him and the family greatly. Maxime Sr. died in September 1897. Marie Anne McDougall (granddaughter of Josephte) recounts her grandmother's memories of having spent twenty-eight years raising a family without Maxime: "Sadly, prison had left him discouraged and humiliated, and Josephte believed that the war shorted her husband's life."[48] Marie Anne writes that Josephte believed that "those years in prison undermined his health, and often said, Maxime was built to live one hundred years."[49] Josephte would have been fifty-three years old during the 1885 Resistance. Although Maxime Sr. received scrip the same day as his mother, dated 1876, oral accounts indicate that he later was denied his scrip because of his involvement in the Resistance.[50] Punishment was another form of dominance and violence that Métis families faced.

Payment's research gives insight into Métis women's presence at Batoche from 1870 to 1920 and describes the active role Métis women played before, during, and after the resistance.[51] Our

FIG. 6.04. Auxile feeding chickens on her farm in Hoey, Saskatchewan.

ancestral stories deepen my conviction that the wisdom and guidance of Métis matriarchs through the recounting, still today, will carry forward the persistent labour of resistance as, undoubtedly, a practice of love. I continue to search for knowledge about Métis women such as Josephte and Caroline, who would have lived during this period of war, public hangings, public humiliation, political coercion, and loss of family and land rights. Payment's research helps us to see Josephte in her agency, love, and stature as she warns Maxime and other Métis leaders of the consequences of war. Josephte, and most likely Caroline and Margaret, were part of the community of Métis matriarchs who cared for the children and the wounded, made bullets "by melting lead kettles,"[52] rallied to salvage material goods, dug and hid in caves, guided the men, and fled to Minitinas Hill for refuge. These Métis women shared in the spiritual, emotional, and physical labour that resisted the cruelty of war by upholding an atmosphere of what Payment describes as a "camp of solidarity and exchange."[53] Such cruelty included the sexist acts by soldiers who ridiculed in their reports the "appearance and condition of squaws."[54]

During one of our visits, Métis Matriarch Sophie McDougall shared that her mother, Leona, was dear friends with Auxile. They were also related through Bremner, Boucher, and Boyer family ties. Sophie's grandmother Nancy Boyer also survived 1885: "She was camped with their two small children on what was known as 'no man's land.' Bullets blazed all around but Mrs. Boyer and her children miraculously escaped."[55] Sophie recalls that neighbouring Métis families knew and respected Josephte as "Koohkoom Lepine." This speaks to Josephte's ongoing community role of assuming cultural practices that persisted long after 1885. She and Maxime Sr. lived with their kin a few miles along the South Saskatchewan River, close to what is known as the Hudson's Bay Company South Branch trading post. The Lepine families lived in the place that became known as Lepine Flats. Josephte and Maxime were stewards of this place. They operated a ferry from this river lot.[56] Josephte and Maxime hosted Sunday mass, community gatherings, and community meetings at her kitchen table. Given that their home was located on the road following the river, visitors were frequent, and in that Métis way of being, the family welcomed and fed guests even during scarce times. Auxile and her children's and grandchildren's households have carried on this cultural way of being. This was of utmost importance, an unquestioned practice, and many who knew Auxile remember how food was plentiful and shared as an ongoing act of resistance, agency, and love.

Family Kinship Ties

In 1886, Margaret Boucher, at the age of twenty, married Maxime Lepine Jr. in St. Louis de Langevin, North-West Territories. Payment explains that "Métis people of St. Laurent, St. Louis and Batoche rarely married outsiders. Endogamy was practised, almost without exception, until 1940. This was common practice for societies having a distinct cultural identity and national consciousness. Social class and economic status or parents' occupation were of prime importance in the choice of a spouse."[57] To date, I have found no official records that would confirm whether their marriage was conducted in what is often described as "customs of the land" or in the custom of the Catholic Church. It is unclear where they lived after they married. Margaret and Maxime's respective families would have directly experienced both Métis Resistances (1869–70 and 1885), the tail end of the fur trade era in Red River, the changes in food sources, the beginnings of agricultural industry, the changing worldview of land ownership, the hardship of flu and tuberculosis epidemics, and the encroachment of settler society.[58] Oral accounts suggest that Margaret, Maxime, and their children (including Auxile), along with other Métis families, may have lived on the road allowance in the Duck Lake region, as discussed earlier. As with many Métis families displaced from their lands, road allowances would have become their homes for a period of time.

After 1885, Métis economic systems became unstable. Some men went to Montana, some stayed in Batoche, some left to find jobs in other provinces, and some went to the bush for seasonal logging and fishing.[59] Movement was common. Maxime Jr. and his relative Frederick Boucher left for the Yukon during the gold rush of 1896–99 with hopes of making money. Auxile's father was newly married. He moved away with the intention of coming back. Having to leave his wife, six young children, and extended family behind must have been devastating, especially with the recent experience of war on their bodies and lands. Terry McDougall shared an oral account of their trip to the Yukon on social media, explaining that they would have taken the train from Duck Lake to Vancouver, a boat north to Skagway, and then made their way over to Chilkoot. One account speaks of Maxime coming back poorer than when he left,[60] while Terry says that his great-uncle Frederick returned with six hundred dollars a year later. Margaret would have continued to take care of their children, Arthur (b. 1886), Agnes (b. 1889-1890), Berthe (b. 1894), Corinne (b. 1895), Blanche (b. 1899), and Auxile (b. 1908). Ancestry records indicate that five of her children died in childbirth or at an early age. At an annual Batoche veterans' memorial gathering in November 2022, Maria Campbell spoke of and honoured the children and women who died post-1885. They died of hunger, illness, cold, and lack of medical care. "More died than the soldiers in the battle field,"[61] she said. We rarely discuss their compounded grief at the loss of loved ones, cultural birth and death practices, and ways of tending their families' health during these times.

FIG. 6.05. Auxille and her siblings. From left to right: Mataant Blanche (née Lepine) Rousset, Norman Morrison, Moonooc Oscar Leblanc, Mataant Bertha (née Lepine) Leblanc, Moonooc Charles Pilon, Moonooc Louis Rousset, Auxile (née Lepine) Morrison, and Mataant Agnes (née Lepine) Pilon, holding Auxile's twins, Marilyn and Evelyn. Photo taken at Moonooc Louis Rousset's house at Duck Lake, Saskatchewan.

Margaret, like many Métis women left alone after 1885, would have provided for her family during her husband's absence. Like Auxile later on, Margaret would have grown large vegetable gardens, harvested from the land, and relied on community. Catherine, Auxile's auntie, would have done the same, tending to her seven children. We know little of these women's experiences and the labour required to survive this period. They would have dealt with the demands of childcare and the household necessities of food, wood, warmth, shelter, and water. Like their matriarchs, they would have taken care of one another and made collective household decisions.

Upon Maxime's return from the gold rush, he and Margaret obtained land in Duck Lake through the Dominion Lands Act (1872). Maxime was later employed as a farm instructor at the neighbouring Kapeyakwaskonam (One Arrow) and Kamiyistowesit (Beardy) First Nation communities.[62] Auxile would have been influenced by these relationships and grown up hearing Cree spoken. As I drove through the town of Duck Lake, on the now-paved street where their homestead would have been, I found that their family home no longer stands; only its memory lives on, in a few people. Moonooc Duncan, Auxile's son, remembers visits to his Grandmother Margaret's little log house in Duck Lake. He said it was still standing a decade ago, and he described where it was located. Moonooc also recalls Auxile bringing him to visit, and having to be extra thoughtful, given that Margaret was sick with cancer.

These golden nuggets of family stories leave me with mixed feelings, and many more wonders. My search remains an ongoing process of learning, and returning home to the memories and stories that exist within the diverse living experiences of my relatives. Storying in relation to place and to generations of Métis people acts like medicine; there is strength in the stories, as Kim

Anderson explains.[63] They serve to reimagine and to weave the resistant threads of the past, present, and future Métis matriarchs.

Born to Women of Resistance

There is much to be considered when thinking of the ways that Métis matriarchal resistance has shaped our kinship health and well-being. I need to make a generational distinction, so as not to lose sight of the context in which our matriarchs made decisions, and the tenacity of their resistance before, during, and after 1885. In this way, I can ground my words and actions in solidarity with generations of matriarchs and consider cultural identity in a long trajectory of relationality, resistance, agency, and love. Even though men were increasingly seen as superior within the family, Métis women carried household and political authority.[64] Payment speaks to the father being the "head," implying a patriarchal household. This idea of the head was tied to being the sole economic provider. The Catholic Church's reduction of the role of women to motherhood upheld this idea and "suggested a lower status."[65] Yet, the running of the household, including control over certain economic resources and the education of children, were Métis women's responsibility.[66]

Children's involvement in household labour was part of their education on kinship responsibilities and fostered a healthy self-esteem and belonging. Children contributed to the labour of the home and the farm. This practice was in line with what Payment calls Métis families' "principle of unity, the need to maintain traditional values, and the primacy of the collective over the individual."[67] Auxile's friend and neighbour Diane Roy (née Gaudet) spoke of the times she would look after Auxile's sons. They were neighbours and relied on each other. Auxile would instruct her to make sure the boys helped out and worked. Diane recognized this as Auxile's way of making sure her sons continued the kinship ethics of contributing to household responsibilities.

Formal education was also important to Auxile. All her children attended the Argon School, one mile from their Hoey homestead, a one-building school that taught grades one to eight. Auxile continued to invest in her children's education after grade eight. Her two daughters, Norma and Christina, attended the Sion convent in Prince Albert. Moonooc Duncan recalled going to a French Oblate missionary-run college near Winnipeg for his continued education. It was sport-centred, which he appreciated. The school property had a farm that required students' manual labour. He was accustomed to hard work, as he was to the way of visiting. Auxile's sister lived in Winnipeg, so she had arranged for moonooc to visit her for a few days at a time. Moonooc Ken shared that he and his brother Doug attended the St. Patrick's orphanage in Prince Albert when it functioned as a school. He explained that it was important for Auxile that they attend together, so Mooncoc could look after his little brother.[68] Moonooc Ken speculates that Maymair would have paid for their education with her own turkeys, chickens, and vegetables.

Family kinship care was also a priority for Auxile. I learned of the many intersecting forms of relationality within Auxile's household. For example, Diane spoke of the times when Auxile received a letter from her sisters: "Oh this was very precious, for Auxile. She would stop everything to read the letter."[69] Diane's account pointed to the important connection between sisters. Norma, Auxile's daughter, returned home from the Sion convent when her twin sisters were born. Auxile needed her older daughter's help. Mom was happy to return home, recalling how lonesome she felt being away from her family for a month at a time. Moonooc Ken credits his music career to Norma's piano lessons, which she learned at her convent stay; Auxile had saved enough money to invest in a family piano. Music in the home was a resource, a powerful influence on creating a bond with his sister, as Moonooc Ken shared.

Auxile moved to the city of Saskatoon in 1968 because her husband needed medical services. She learned to navigate the city and travelled on the bus to see Paypair ("grandfather" in Michif) in the hospital every day. She made sure her four children with disabilities attended a creative, respectful, and participatory school together. She found a way to navigate a new life and created a strong support network in the same manner that she did when living in a farming community. Her network was one of the strong resources she relied upon. She was described as resourceful, knowing who could help with what. Relational accountability to her broad kinship system fostered strength within her and therefore her kin. Mom reinforced this way of being by respectfully and repeatedly acknowledging that Auxile gave them a good life.

Auxile was described by Diane Gaudet as beautiful and feminine. She remembers Auxile wearing an elegant velvet burgundy dress. And "she had a strong heart," Diane said.[70] Sonny Vandale, from a nearby Métis family, drove the horse and cutter that picked up Auxile's children to go to Argon School. He vividly remembers being welcomed by Auxile in her house to come eat and to warm up on those cold winter days.

Spiritual Stability as Resistance

Auxile's own early school years were at Stobbart School in Duck Lake, Saskatchewan. At the school entrance, she was greeted by a constructed mobile devil. Images were a powerful tool of assimilation. This is all of her school experience she shared with mom. The devil was a mechanism to enforce a punitive system and a fear of God. Auxile resisted this fear-based schooling and religious influence. When I asked Mom about faith, she told me Auxile taught her that "God was loving and good to all."[71] Mom again reaffirmed that they were raised this way. Shirley, Auxile's granddaughter, described her quality as being inclusive, and feeling so welcomed and special in her embraces.[72] Through these women, I have come to understand faith as a current of consciousness as opposed to dogmatic and punitive rule.

Our family went annually to Our Lady of Lourdes Shrine, St. Laurent, a sacred site located along the South Saskatchewan River. This was a special time dedicated to visiting with family and with Mother Mary.[73]

Auxile identified deeply with Mary, as many Métis women and men did, and still do. They identify with her as a mother and a human being. Andy Boyer, a Métis priest and relative from Duck Lake, explained that for Métis people, Mary would have been perceived as a common person. They could relate to her struggle, her efforts of resisting dominance and oppression, and perhaps even her helplessness and fear in the face of it.[74] Maria Campbell shared

FIG. 6.06. Josephte LaVallee, Auxile's paternal grandmother.

with me another important perspective that was part of her healing journey. She said, "Mary, too, was colonized and silenced like my mother. Perhaps in their deepest selves they knew this and this is why [Mary] was and is so loved by them."[75] Perhaps being loved by Mary as Mother and continuing to love her became a way of upholding a kinship worldview that included a notion of God being good to all.

Auxile was a tenacious and spirited woman. She defined herself. She gave plenty, with sincerity and humility. She spoke her mind. She made decisions—tough decisions. She had her own bank account. She ran the farm. She was a skilled and gracious entrepreneur. She purchased and wore locally made fur coats. She valued education. She valued her helpers. She excelled in math and spelling. She loved her children, grandchildren, siblings, and friends. She spoke and lived in four languages: Michif, French, Cree, and English. She was a classy woman. She enjoyed travelling and was a joy to travel with. She had a daily practice of prayer. Auxile's granddaughter Mona remembers the importance of saying the rosary every night before bed.[76] It was a daily practice, which was part of living a good life, with an understanding that prayer was about protection and love and was not about appeasing a fearsome and judging God or acquiring salvation. It was about being in communion with the deepest part of oneself. Rosaries have become memorabilia, and for some, artifacts of relationality that hold the enactment of humility as a way to strengthen the inner life. Rosaries, for some, remain part of daily life. Auxile also believed in the power of novenas, a form of discipline where the intermittent practice of devotional prayer recitation is done for a specific period of time. Mom did the same, and both had tiny cards of devotion that could be found on their nightstands; my mom's is still on hers today. Discipline was a way of life that assured self-regulation and self-love, part of a spiritual stability that comes with owning oneself.

Auxile's son, Monooc Ken, shared his respect for her faith in a loving God. He believes that this helped her to remain positive, given her circumstances: "Mom had ten children, four with disabilities, and a hard-working husband who binge-drank."[77] During the difficult episodes of alcohol, my mom recalls that

Auxile would visit Madame Maria Vandale, a well-respected Métis seer, for support and wisdom. It was only during these binge episodes that her husband was mean toward her, replicating the deeply entrenched socialization of negative representations, as discussed earlier. These were described as fearful times, and Auxile or the children would call the neighbours over to help or to hide. Occasionally, the locally known doctor would be called in, and her husband would be tranquilized. These were hard times. Diane admired how Auxile would carry on taking care. She remained clear-headed, with perspective, knowing that he must have known that he did not own himself during his harmful episodes. In reflecting back, Mom described in a Michif expression a behaviour of being out of balance in the head. She would have learned this philosophy from Auxile and therefore learned to maintain her sovereignty in the challenges she, too, would have to face.

Auxile resisted the demeaning representation of her womanhood. She must have known that she was held, and helped, by generations of her Métis matriarchs. Laughter also filled her household. Norma's husband (my dad) recalls going to visit Auxile when he and my mom were dating. He complained that the women would stay up at night and their laughter kept him from sleeping. Auxile and her kin would carry on investing themselves in a culture of love while balancing their struggles in and with community. Diane admired her, saying that "she has certainly earned her heaven on earth." She was also alluding to the harms and to the efforts Auxile made to strategically sustain a caring and loving household.

Another important story that repeats itself is the time when Auxile got angry and dumped a crock of her husband's homemade whiskey into the pigpen. He had gone too far in serving alcohol to a family friend who suffered physically, which was a detriment to successful farm life. There is agency in these stories, as they indicate Métis women's authority to define treatment and behaviour in their respective households, and the ways in which the household extends itself. Auxile resisted the superiority of able bodies, and advocated for equitable treatment of her children in educational systems. Her four children's disabilities were no excuse for poor treatment. She was not shy about making this known.

Auxile lived her faith. It was not a performance, but rather a meaningful relationship to God. She did not need a mediator, nor did she need to flaunt her faith with hallmark notions of religiosity. Faith was living, not stagnant and not existing solely in the church pews once a week. As many shared and experienced, no one was refused at her door. Auxile was not embarrassed by her husband's binge behaviour and thereby resisted colonial views of Métis women as passive, submissive, and docile. Accepting these views, as my eldest sister Mona and I discussed, would have been giving away her power, depleting her life force. The cost would have been too high, and she had many children who relied on her wellbeing. Auxile knew this. Mona reflected on this insight, adding in a later visit that Auxile would have been confident in her relationships, knowing her love would not be distorted.

I experienced this courageous expression of love in my early twenties in a sudden and unexpected exchange with Mom. She sternly corrected my boyfriend due to his harmful behaviours toward me, her land. And when I defended him blurting out harsh words, she looked at me and said in a calm yet direct tone, "I would have never spoken to my mother this way." Inside of me, I understood, and I never spoke to her that way again. In reflecting on this, I realize Métis women held court. This was not a performance—it was about our survival and changing the future.

Food Sovereignty and Entrepreneurship

The garden was another area under Auxile's jurisdiction. She managed and maintained the sovereignty of food systems. She also relied on the gifts from the land, such as Saskatoon berries, pincherries, raspberries, and chokecherries. She fed and nourished her children, guests, and friends in need year-round. Annually, she canned her harvest of vegetables, chickens, geese, turkeys, ducks, and berries. She raised rabbits. She grew pumpkins. My sister shared how she cleaned even the tiniest of potatoes and canned them. Diane described the pond behind Auxile's home, remembering the times she came over to help pluck ducks. Planting, tending, harvesting, and preserving are laborious, as is plucking chickens, ducks, and geese. She had two large gardens and two house cellars. She paid local women helpers, who stayed with her when she needed them. Trust and friendship was held dearly in these relationships. Diane described the extensive process of making salted lard as part of butchering pigs. Another sister recalls a large steel bin containing cream of wheat that was part of morning meals, served with fresh cow cream. Auxile sold her chickens, ducks, and potatoes to Chinese restaurant owners in the nearby city of Prince Albert. She had well-established relationships with her buyers and was a well-respected entrepreneur. Moonooc recalls a Chinese gentleman giving them a free meal when they delivered the farm goods.

Food was a resource, and women were responsible for its production and distribution.[78] Métis women enacted their sovereignty through food systems. This ties to their matriarchal roles, carried forth from buffalo hunting laws and female-led settlements. Auxile was greatly involved in running the farm, as it was part of her household governance. This included the specialty preserves that she would keep in the cellar under the bed. Diane describes Auxile's house as having a small porch leading to a long kitchen table at the centre, a green-painted storage cabinet, and a large wood-burning stove where a kettle of water hung on a side handle to keep water warm. Auxile was known for her love of flowers, appreciating their beauty and their important role in maintaining healthy food systems.

Auntie Christina, Auxile's eldest daughter, recalled Auxile's leadership in organizing an annual turkey shoot competition at her farm. This is another example of how she provided for her family. She invested her resources in annual trips to the fair, buying a piano, hiring local seamstresses, her children's education, bingo outings, household help, and hosting community gatherings. Some recall that Auxile was one of the few who organized shoots. Shirley, her granddaughter, remembers the farmyard was full of people, and there were plenty of games for the children.[79] The turkey shoot parties also included local musicians, Paypair's jugs of wine, and plenty of food. Moonooc Duncan explained that whoever shot closest to the bullseye would go home with a turkey and a bottle of wine.[80] This was an important community event.

Auxile's kitchen table was an extension of her harvest, her land, and her generosity rooted in generations of matriarchal values and cultural resistance. This evidently included the "way of visiting," understood in the Michif Cree language as keeoukaywin, as a value and a vibrant system of exchange, reciprocity, and sharing of knowledge.[81] She was known for being hospitable, for her diplomacy, which is tied to giving and receiving as forms of recognizing self-sovereignty, community-building, and interrupting the ideology that only a certain type of people belonged at her table and that men were the only providers. To the contrary, Auxile would have understood "love as a practice," of resisting the pressures of feeling inadequate, powerless, and abandoned.[82] Jean Teillet clearly describes the Métis value of sharing, distinct from acts

FIG. 6.07. Caroline Lesperance, Auxile's maternal grandmother.

of charity.[83] The neighbouring community recognized Auxile for hosting her eldest daughter's wedding reception. Fifty people were in attendance, according to St. Louis historical news clippings.[84] Auxile, like her mother, Margaret, grandmothers, Josephte and Caroline, and numerous aunties, would have been accustomed to hosting many people at her home and treating them as family.

Auxile was born only twenty-three years after her Métis kin would have been recovering from the battle waged on their people by the federal government in 1885 in Batoche (with the first shots in Duck Lake, where her family lived). She was two when her grandmother Caroline Lesperance died in 1910 or 1911, and seventeen when her grandmother Josephte Lavallee died in 1925. Her mother, Margaret Boucher, died in 1946. Auxile would have been thirty-eight, married to Norman Morrison (son of Margaret Bremner and Jack Morrison) since the age of sixteen, and raising a family of ten children of her own on their homestead in Hoey, Saskatchewan. The Métis women in her life would have deeply influenced her values, her strength, her leadership, her survival, and her way of being. Auxile carried this forth into the lives of her children, family, and community. It is evident by the stories that her life was connected to generations of Métis matriarchal resistance. Anderson explains that "the guidance that women receive from their mothers, aunts, and grandmothers shapes the way they learn to understand themselves and their positions in the world. These teachings, these ways of working together as families build resistance."[85] My Métis matriarchs offer a courageous worldview to understand ongoing relationality and kinship wellness from a place of belonging to generations of resistance and sovereignty.

Recognizing myself in relation to my matriarchs' sovereignty is expressed in the way of visiting with our lands—my mother being my first knowing of land—and with generations of Métis women, community, and extended kin. In doing so, I carry my matrilineal connections, an intricate and strong web of relations tied to place, people, and spirit. Yet Auxile is not confined to location nor time, and neither is visiting. For this reason, the emotional and spiritual ties to Auxile are ever-present in her story's tellers, in their living memories. Even some younger relatives who have never met Auxile in person draw spiritual stability from her.

FIG. 6.08. Auxile Lepine proudly dressed up for the Saskatoon Fair.

Auxile commanded respect with respect. In sharing my learnings with my cousin Leo Morrison, he stated with such certainty, admiration, and love for our grandmother Auxile: "Maymair! She was the boss!"[86] A powerful story followed. In their own right, Métis women held authority within their respective family systems, as lived and shaped by their experiences and relationships. They carried forward a way of being as Métis women that came with great responsibility, holding multiple realities and generations of resistance. I feel deep appreciation for my maamaa, for showing a sovereign way of being that was unique to her and for also giving me a good life. Like Auxile, she is an exquisite part of the Métis matriarchs who practised and lives a life of resistance. Their enduring acts of kinship love carry me through everything that I do. After all, we were raised that way.

NOTES

1 Hua, "Diaspora and Cultural Memory," 205.
2 Gaudet, "Collective Memory, Historical Trauma, and Healing."
3 Todd, "Honouring Our Great-Grandmothers," 174.
4 hooks, *All about Love*, 76.
5 hooks, *All about Love*, 75.
6 hooks, *Communion*, 88.
7 Macdougall, *Land, Family and Identity*; Macdougall, "Knowing Who You Are," 127–46.
8 Anderson, *A Recognition of Being*.
9 Todd, "Honouring Our Great-Grandmothers," 172.
10 hooks, *Communion*.
11 hooks, *All about Love*, 185.
12 Payment, *The Free People*, 255.
13 hooks, *All about Love*; hooks, *Communion*; hooks, *Outlaw Culture*.
14 Anderson, *A Recognition of Being*; hooks, *All about Love*; hooks, *Communion*.
15 hooks, *The Will to Change*.
16 Macdougall, *One of the Family*; Payment, "'La Vie en Rose'?"; Payment, *The Free People*; Teillet, *The North-West Is Our Mother*.

17 Macdougall and St-Onge, "Rooted in Mobility."
18 Troupe, "Métis Women."
19 Payment, "'La Vie en Rose'?," 23.
20 Scofield, *Louis: The Heretic Poems*.
21 Town of Duck Lake, "How Did Duck Lake Get Its Name?" accessed December 15, 2023, http://www.ducklake.ca.
22 Maria Campbell, personal communication, summer 2022.
23 Campbell, *Halfbreed*.
24 Troupe, "Re/Storying Métis Road Allowance Communities," 58:52 tc 1:29:47.
25 Campbell, *Halfbreed*, 8.
26 Gaudet and Martin/Wapistan, "Learning through Conversation," 95–112.
27 Anderson, Campbell, and Belcourt, eds., *Keetsahnak*; National Inquiry into Missing and Murdered Indigenous Women and Girls, *Reclaiming Power and Place*.
28 Van Kirk, *Many Tender Ties*.
29 Anderson, *A Recognition of Being*.
30 Acoose, *Iskwewak*; Anderson, *A Recognition of Being*; Anderson, Campbell, and Belcourt, eds., *Keetsahnak*.
31 Acoose, *Iskwewak*, 55.
32 Acoose, *Iskwewak*, 45.
33 Campbell, *Halfbreed*; Anderson, *A Recognition of Being*.
34 Cheryl Troupe, personal communication, October 2021.
35 Cheryl Troupe, personal communication, October 2021.
36 Campbell, *Halfbreed*.
37 St. Louis Local History Committee, *I Remember*.
38 St. Louis Local History Committee, *I Remember*.
39 Teillet, *The North-West Is Our Mother*.
40 Payment, *The Free People*.
41 St. Louis Local History Committee, *I Remember*.
42 St. Louis Local History Committee, *I Remember*, 92–93.
43 Gaudet, "Metis Women's Stories."
44 Payment, *The Free People*, 52.
45 Payment, *The Free People*, 42.
46 Payment, *The Free People*, 42.
47 Teillet, *The North-West Is Our Mother*, 90.
48 St. Louis Local History Committee, *I Remember*, 65.
49 St. Louis Local History Committee, *I Remember*, 65.
50 Payment, *The Free People*.
51 Payment, "'La Vie en Rose'?"; Payment, *The Free People*.

52 Payment, "'La Vie en Rose'?," 26.
53 Payment, "'La Vie en Rose'?," 26
54 Payment, "'La Vie en Rose'?," 26.
55 St. Louis Local History Committee, *History in Print*, 44.
56 Virtual Museum of Metis History and Culture, Gabriel Dumont Institute of Native Studies and Applied Research. Collections, Biographies. https://www.metismuseum.ca/browse/index.php/971.
57 Payment, *The Free People*, 47.
58 Todd Paquin, Patrick Young, and Darren R. Préfontaine, *Métis Farmers*, Saskatoon: Gabriel Dumont Institute, 2003, GDI media filename Farmers.pdf, Biography and Essay Collection, Traditional Lifestyle, Occupations and Wage Labour, Virtual Museum of Métis History and Culture, metismuseum.ca, Gabriel Dumont Institute, accessed December 15, 2023, https://www.metismuseum.ca/media/document.php/00718.Farmers.pdf.
59 Payment, "'La Vie en Rose'?," 33.
60 St. Louis Local History Committee, *I Remember*.
61 Maria Campbell, speech at Louis Riel Day memorial gathering for Batoche veterans, Batoche National Historic Site, November 16, 2022.
62 Payment, *The Free People*, 75.
63 Anderson, *Life Stages and Native Women*, 240.
64 Carter, *Imperial Plots*; Kermoal, *Un Passé Métis au Féminin*; Payment, *The Free People*; Troupe, "Métis Women."
65 Payment, *The Free People*, 45.
66 Payment, *The Free People*.
67 Payment, *The Free People*, 44.
68 Duncan Morrison, personal communication, November 18, 2022.
69 Diane Gaudet, personal communication, September 18, 2022.
70 Diane Gaudet, personal communication, September 2022.
71 Norma Gaudet, personal communications, summers of 2018, 2019, 2020, 2021, and 2022.
72 Shirley Grenier, personal communication, November 2022.
73 Gaudet, "Keeoukaywin," 52.
74 Gaudet, "Keeoukaywin."
75 Maria Campbell, personal communication, 2009.
76 Mona Markwart (née Gaudet), personal communications, 2020, 2021, and 2022.
77 Ken Morrison, personal communication, October 2022.
78 Anderson, *A Recognition of Being*.
79 Shirley Grenier, personal communication, November 2022.

80 Duncan Morrison, personal communications, August 2019 and November 2022.
81 Gaudet, "Keeoukaywin."
82 hooks, *All about Love*, 165.
83 Teillet, *The North-West Is Our Mother*.
84 St. Louis Local History Committee, *History in Print*, 123.
85 Anderson, *A Recognition of Being*, 101.
86 Leo Morrison, personal communication, summer 2022.

Seven

Métis Matriarchs in kāministikominahikoskahk (Cumberland House)
mîkisistahikêwin—
Beading Together the Generations

by Allyson Stevenson

THE MATRIARCH ROOM IN THE KWECĪC MUSEUM, near the end of the road through the northern village of Cumberland House, holds exquisite treasures created by Cree-Métis women artists from the late nineteenth and early twentieth centuries. In 2019, several rare and finely crafted beadwork and embroidered items returned home to Cumberland House. Referred to as the Cotter Collection for the family who had kept them, they are now on display. Alongside photos of communities, families, and other significant cultural items, when placed together, each item contributes to re-storying the history of the people and place of kāministikominahikoskahk and the northern trapping and fishing economy that sustained them.[1]

Grounded in the Cree-Métis worldview, the recently reopened community museum was first established by kwecīc, Virginia McKay, a local historian, archeologist, curator, and author, as a space that tells the community's stories of deep and ongoing historical presence, changes to the northern economy, and the significance of the people and place of kāministikominahikoskahk.[2]

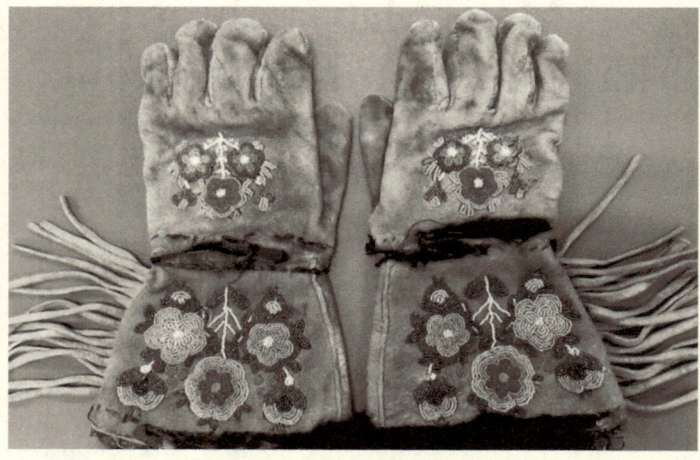

FIG. 7.01. Men's Beaded Gauntlets at the Cotter Collection, Cumberland House Museum.

Rather than focus on one Métis matriarch, this chapter focuses on the social relations between women in kāministikominahikoskahk, highlighting key Métis matriarchs and their beadwork, such as sisters Agnes Carriere and Margaret McAuley, as well as Isabelle Impey. The values in the community, and the process of intergenerational knowledge transfer between women, are an important nexus for examining the unique qualities of this community. These values and practices continue today and illustrate the strength of matriarchy as a core Indigenous system that contributes to community resilience. The Cree language and its embedded values, Métis historical memory of resistance, and the matriarchal familial context of kāministikominahikoskahk have created a distinctive social and historical milieux that is generative of profoundly important works of art and individuals whose influence has shaped the present and continues to transform the future.

In 2001, Sherry Farrell Racette wrote that a future direction in Métis material cultural research was to re-situate objects in their home communities, further arguing that "perhaps the most important need in future scholarship is to place the objects created by Métis women back within in their human context and resist their current decontextualized and dehumanized treatment in museums."[3] Unlike the museums that have long held captive works generated by Indigenous grandmothers, the kwecīc museum in kāministikominahikoskahk is a space that reunifies the community with its artistic heritage. Considering Farrell Racette's directive, illuminating the social and cultural context of kāministikominahikoskahk enables us to consider how Métis women's production of the distinctive apparel that adorned bodies and spaces gives voice to a love aesthetic that expressed Métis notions of beauty firstly encountered on our lands and territories.

This chapter considers the Métis matriarchy relationally through the lens of women's labouring, loving, teaching, dressing, and caring for beloved members of their community by examining the artistic production and influence of the Métis artisans of kāministikominahikoskahk, oral interviews of artists, and scholarship by kāministikominahikoskahk intellectuals and Indigenous historians. The cultural and material inheritance left by early kāministikominahikoskahk matriarchs reflects Cree-Métis matriarchal social relations expressed through women's artistic production. Connecting these pieces with their stories to the intergenerational transmission of the knowledge context in which they were created demonstrates how this influence can be seen in contemporary Indigenous artists, scholars, and community members who recentre these values in their work today.

The community of Cumberland House, situated in Treaty 5 territory, is home to Cree-speaking First Nations and Métis peoples who have inhabited the area since time immemorial. It is frequently credited as being the oldest settled community in the province of Saskatchewan.[4] kāministikominahikoskahk (a Cree term that means an island of many trees) is an island found in the largest inland delta in North America, the Saskatchewan River Delta.[5] Located on the shore of Lake Cumberland, the community is surrounded by the waters of the Bigstone River, the Saskatchewan River, and the Tearing River. East of kāministikominahikoskahk, the Saskatchewan River channels reconverge flowing easterly into Lake Winnipeg, to the Hudson Bay, and eventually into the Arctic Ocean. Many in the Métis and First Nations community are fluent Cree speakers (N-dialect) and retain a strong connection to the lands and waters of the delta through intergenerational water-based practices of trapping, fishing, and paddling.[6]

The northern village of Cumberland House and Cumberland House Cree Nation derive their names from the fur trade post built by the Hudson's Bay Company (HBC) on the south shore of Cumberland Lake in 1774.[7] HBC trader Samuel Hearne led a party inland and established the original post on the southern end of the lake, which was later moved a short distance north.[8] Hearne originally named it Pine Island Lake, but renamed it Cumberland Post in 1775.[9] The northern location was ideally situated for the water-based trade in furs enabling access to virtually all areas throughout the Northwest.

The Swampy Cree in the region traded with the Company, served as intermediaries, and provisioned the fur trade. Men's and women's labour supported the trade through hunting, fishing, and

FIG. 7.02. *(top)* The Matriarch Room at the Cotter Collection, Cumberland House Museum. FIG. 7.03. *(centre)* The Matriarch Room; Settlements and Families, Cotter Collection, Cumberland House Museum. FIG. 7.04. *(bottom)* The Matriarch Room, Cumberland House Museum.

providing moccasins, clothing, and other essential items.[10] The devastation of the 1781 smallpox epidemic resulted in mass deaths of Indigenous peoples along the Saskatchewan River, including many families at kāministikominahikoskahk.[11] The Rev. Henry Budd established a mission at kāministikominahikoskahk in 1840 as part of the push inland by the Anglican Church Missionary Society, but it was shortly after moved to The Pas.[12] Following the Métis Resistance of 1869–70, Métis from Red River, in present-day Manitoba, began to arrive in kāministikominahikoskahk. While the area had been a fur trade site with Métis families living in the vicinity, new families dispossessed or fleeing settler violence, including such families as the Chaboyers, Goulets, Richards, Carrieres, Cadottes, Nabisses, Cooks, McAuleys, McKays, and Fosseneuves, sought out kāministikominahikoskahk as a haven from racial intolerance. Of this influx, local kāministikominahikoskahk historians Virginia McKay, Jean Carriere, Pierre Dorion, and Marie Deschambeault wrote:

> [M]any Métis families began the trek north...Discouraged by humiliations, bewildered by government policies and uncertain about recognition of property rights they turned to the promised land of the north-west. There they would resume their favorite way of life, far enough away from regions where agricultural colonization and the more confining concepts of permanent settlements had surrounded them. They came to the Cumberland House District where traplines and generous fishing grounds would enable them to enjoy the free ways of living which had been their forefathers' birthright for so many years.[13]

In 1877, Father Paquette established a Roman Catholic mission southeast of the Post to minister to the newly arrived French

Catholic Métis families. In 1892, Rev. Ovide Charlebois built a school that is still standing today.[14]

These histories converge at the location of kāministikominahikoskahk and are simultaneously rooted in deep Indigenous presence connected to the lands, animals, waters, spiritual gathering sites, and ancestors, layered with the colonial impacts of disease, land dispossession, environmental degradation, the legal regulation of Indigenous identity, and kinship. In the re-matriation of kāministikominahikoskahk's history and material culture in the space of the museum, Indigenous women's centrality is reasserted powerfully as an act of remembrance and revitalization through mîkisistahikêwin—beading together the generations.[15]

Finding teachings and inspiration embedded in the past labours of Indigenous women is the basis for much of the decolonial work being done. In areas that include contemporary beadwork, restoring gender balance in families and communities, and the revitalization of Indigenous law and Indigenous literatures, often it is women's teachings, methods, and labour that inform decolonial efforts. As Jeannette Armstrong proclaimed in 1996: "We find our strength and our power in our ability to be what our grandmothers were to us; keepers of the next generation in every sense of that word—physically, intellectually, and spiritually."[16] She continues to describe the essence that empowered grandmothers as a weapon that one wields to both protect and nurture. This inheritance of fierce love from the grandmothers, she argues, is Indigenous women's original strength:

> It is the strength of this female force that holds all nations and families together in health. It is the bridge to the next generation. It is the female power that is the key to survival of us all, in an environment that is becoming increasingly damaged and unfit for all life forms. It is woman who holds this power

and becomes powerful only when catalyzing co-operation and harmony, and therefore health, at all levels—from the individual, outward to the family, the community, and to the environment.[17]

Colonialism attempts to destroy love and connection through the dismantling of the relational nature of Indigenous lifeways. The imposition of colonial laws, removals, racial theories of Indigenous inferiority, residential schooling, and the Sixties Scoop have attempted to remove Indigenous women from positions of authority in families and communities. The absence created through the loss of historical knowledge and the loss of women's artwork and its ability to speak to communities across generations is a felt injustice that fuels efforts to bring these items home.[18]

Empowered matriarchal love animates and activates efforts to return to loving communities through transmitting values and principles encoded in language and day-to-day sustaining activities. Lindsay Nixon argues that a return to Indigenous love brings about Indigenous feminist change in colonial institutions. She argues that "[e]thical love is a pedagogy of relationality taught to Indigenous peoples by their kin—siblings, aunties, grandparents, and other individuals of influence—and activated, its animated self, through attentiveness to kinship responsibilities."[19] In the work of contemporary curators and artists, Indigenous Relational Aesthetics (IRA) acts to disrupt the colonial project, which devalues Indigenous women's material cultural production such as beadwork and embroidery.[20] Further, she argues that "IRA makes space for materialist feminist considerations within curatorial and creative practices, resisting a sole focus of human to human relationalities within an extended kinship network and a limited understanding of material relations as enacted primarily between bodies and bodies. Materialities, objects like beading and quillwork, can love, be loved, and instill love, relating to the communities from which they derive."[21] The artifacts beaded for loved ones in the past sought to beautify, warm, comfort, and impress. As Sherry Farrell Racette has found, European men sought Métis women's artistic productions as desirable symbols of the western frontier, both practical and beautiful.[22] Sewing and beading into the twentieth century provided economic opportunities for skilled women to support families.[23] As these pieces are brought home by communities and individuals to be restored, the active force of love that generated its creation returns once more as a way to empower Indigenous relationalities.[24]

The significance of Métis women's artistic productions as both historical sources and as works of art has, until recently, gone unrecognized.[25] Past Victorian notions that devaluated "women's work," museum categorization that mis-attributed Métis works to other Nations in collections, and categorizations of such works as "craft" rather than art by museums and collectors, continue to have economic impacts in Indigenous communities as well as contributing to a legacy of misrepresentation of Métis art.[26] The fur trade, argues scholar Kathy M'Closky, undervalued women's work, in that

> many articles fashioned by indigenous peoples were treated as if they were renewable resources and marketed by the pound. Since these were not "raw resources" but finished products often involving hundreds of hours of work, the extraction of surplus was intense. The seeds of underdevelopment were sown in the non-Western world due to rampant depredation by colonial merchants.[27]

Farrell Racette's research has transformed our understandings of Métis beadwork, Métis women's artistic production, and has established a field for Indigenous material cultural research.[28] As an Indigenous interdisciplinarian and artist, Farrell Racette's reconnection with pieces found in museums and private collections, along with historical analyses and community-based understandings, have illuminated research methods for Indigenous cultural material items. These beloved articles from the past play a critical role for the future. As Farrell Racette states: "We search collections, not to replicate the past, but rather to learn from it and reclaim it in the present."[29]

Métis women's material cultural production offers a rare window to the past. As Farrell Racette has found:

> "Women's voices are often conspicuously absent from historic documents. Women have left few written records of their lives, and early observers and the anthropologists who followed them often ignored or diminished their activities, primarily being men interested in the doings of other men. However, if we remember that women created most of the material in museum collections, even if much of it was used by men, we can see it as a remarkable intellectual, technical, and artistic legacy."[30]

Beadwork, embroidery, rug hooking, and quillwork provides a rich historical source, especially so when community oral history and Indigenous languages are still spoken, or when the practice is still being undertaken.[31] With some exceptions, Métis women's voices were not often captured in the historical record, thus limiting knowledge of Métis women's lives. As individuals and collectively, Métis women's active engagements securing resources for families, enacting relational ethics, fierce love, collective labouring, and political activism speak to non-hierarchical Métis social relations and are embodied through actions that seek the well-being of the community.[32]

KÂMINISTIKOMINAHIKOSKAHK · 205

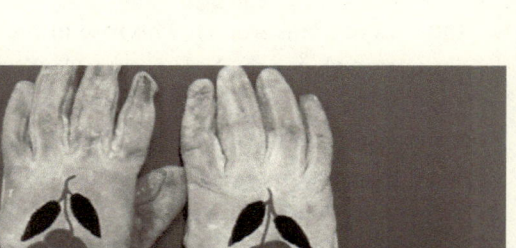

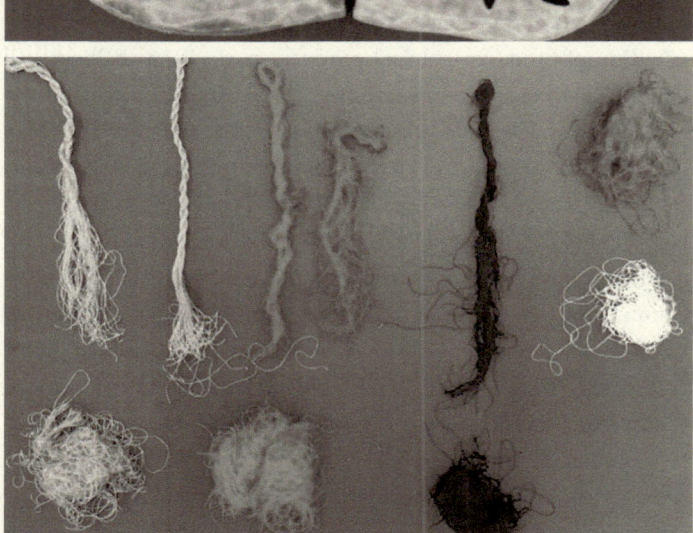

FIG. 7.05. *(top)* Women's embroidered gauntlets, Cumberland House Museum. FIG. 7.06. *(bottom)* Silk embroidery thread donated to Cumberland House Museum.

The lives of Métis women who rose to prominence can also be illustrative. Historian Doris Jeanne MacKinnon's biographies of Métis matriarchs capture the complex identities of Marie Rose Delorme Smith and Isabelle Clark Hardisty Lougheed. Their diverse experiences nonetheless highlight Métis women's work in supporting families in transitioning economies and societies.[33] Zoe Todd's scholarship on her great-grandmother Caroline LaFramboise honours her grandmother's efforts to preserve Métis autonomy in the twentieth century through her acts of resistance and refusal enacted in protection of Métis lands.[34] Family histories and community histories threaded together share a common core of gendered autonomy.[35]

Non-Indigenous historian Jan Noel's analysis of the Haudenosaunee "matriarchy" focused on the role women played in the distribution of food, agricultural production, decision making, and diplomacy in early colonial records.[36] Children belonged to the mothers, and Haudenosaunee women had the greater authority over children than fathers had. Collective labouring in the fields took place under the supervision of Elder women, and captive people and children assisted.[37] Hesitant to use the term "matriarchy," Noel concludes that the Haudenosaunee constituted a "Mothered Community." Haudenosaunee mothering, she argues, illustrated how the full potential of "mothering" as female authority in the village in turn shaped "public" political life.[38] Haudenosaunee women ensured that essentials such as food and resources were distributed in a manner that supported the health and well-being of the entire community. Women's authority over collective well-being and children's care extended outward to include protection of the health and well-being of the natural world, ensuring spiritual forces remained in balance and the kinship and clan obligations were met.

Métis matriarchs have been seen as exceptional individuals who amassed wealth, prestige, or embodied spiritual or political virtues. Oral histories, community histories, and material artifacts reveal a persistent pattern of Métis women acting as leaders, decision makers, knowledge holders, intellectuals, trappers, artists, and economic agents. Kim Anderson's ground-breaking work on Indigenous women, followed by her work on gendered relations and life-cycles, uncovers Indigenous women's empowerment and the balance maintained through centring children and communities.[39] She began with an interest in the "non-patriarchal and non-hierarchical social structures of many land-based Indigenous societies."[40] Sharing Noel's focus on community organization, Anderson's oral historians outlined the importance of genders working for the good of the whole community, which formed the basis of Indigenous identity and citizenship.[41] Elders, including Elders from the community of kāministikominahikoskahk, spoke of the importance of maintaining balance to ensure the well-being of community.[42] Adult women were responsible for providing for the community's essential needs, which included food and clothing, and acted as keepers of relationships who were responsible for maintaining the bonds of kinship, which often occurred through women's collective labour.[43]

kāministikominahikoskahk's distinctive historical and geographical context has enabled many to continue to practise Cree-Métis relational ethics well into the twentieth century.[44] Colonial influences of church and government indeed impacted balanced gender relations, but forces of Métis land dispossession operated differently than in the southern Plains regions. The Métis community remained a collective with a measure of control over its schools and the ability to engage in a (highly regulated) fishing and trapping economy into the twentieth century.[45] Evictions and removals experienced by Métis in agricultural areas and Indian Act provisions reducing mobility and removing children from family homes do not constitute the experiences of this community to the same extent.[46] Environmental degradation due to damming, its impact on the economic livelihood of fishers and trappers, and land losses and broken treaty promises do feature prominently in this community.[47] However, the lands and waters of the delta, the Cree language, Métis histories of resistance, and the matriarchal social system sustained artistic practices and enabled the intergenerational transference of Indigenous knowledges now being restored at the kāministikominahikoskahk Museum.

Turn-of-the-century Métis women's embodied experiences as artisans, seamstresses, and mothers were captured by Métis historians of kāministikominahikoskahk who valued Indigenous lifeways and saw the importance of preserving these stories for the future.[48] The values of hard work, bush skills, self-sufficiency, generosity, and strength are captured in these histories. The women hand-made dresses from material purchased from the HBC store.[49] Often married at an early age, many women bore fourteen or more children in the early twentieth century but died prematurely due to lack of medical care. Prior to the arrival of nurses and doctors, older women served as midwives, and plant-based medicines were used to treat illnesses. Women were responsible for looking after children, tanning moosehides, and making dry meat for pemmican. In addition, "women made teepees from tarp bought from the store. For heat they dug a hole in the centre of the tepee and made a fireplace from stones and they were kept warm during the winter."[50] Others lived in houses made of locally sourced logs with mud plastered on the outside. Because no furniture was available for the people, they would often spread tarps or a tablecloth on the floor, and this they used as their tables. In addition, women would make soap and quilts, and feather robes out of goose or duck down.[51] Flour sacks were turned into underwear and undershirts for babies, and the largest sacks would make pillowcases and dish towels.[52]

kāministikominahikoskahk historians described the incredible beadwork and embroidery the women did in an understated manner: "Moccasins were made by the women with bead and silk thread used to make designs and also porcupine quills added a lovely design. The hair of a horse tail was also used."[53] In addition to moccasins, the women made winter wear. "Parkas were also made lovely with moose hide, satin, beads silk threads and ribbons sewn on the hood. Gloves and mittens added to the lovely outfits which were made too with moosehide."[54] Not only did the women cut, sew, and bead or embroider the clothing and moccasins they made for their loved ones, they prepared and tanned the moosehide used for their clothing.

> Moosehide was made by women, and they used the moose brain to make it soft after the hair and inner layer of skin had been scraped off with a mataigen, the blade of an ax tied together by a good sized willow bent in half, dried in the sun and smoked in a pail or a washtub with Noskichatogoa. The hide was sewn up lengthwise like a bag and hung in a tree. The tissue (astisee) on the back of the moose was also dried and made a strong thread for sewing moccasins.[55]

The infusion of Cree terminology in the description of tools and processes, as well as remarks noting the extensive and, by our standards, gruelling labour that women dedicated to the production of garments, orients us in the present to dedicate this same level of attentiveness to our chosen tasks. These pieces honoured people who wore them and communicated to the human and non-human world through intricate designs that animated the hides.[56]

Children raised in the homes of parents, grandparents, or close relatives gained important cultural knowledge transmitted through the Cree language, teachings, and laws, including the teachings on love. In Leah Dorion's interviews with Cree and Métis Elders and knowledge keepers, they explain love as the nature of the universe: "Elsie Sanderson describes this as 'the traditional spiritual belief that all life is sacred and must be treated with loving kindness. *Kisewatotatowin* is one of the most important teachings placed into the traditional parenting teaching bundle. Within this teaching it is understood everyone is expected to play a role in raising children with love and kindness.'"[57]

Dorion's oral histories regarding child-rearing values and practices provide insight into the nature of a mothered community. She found that men's leadership in public forums and through administration of law gave the appearance of a patriarchal system. However, foundationally women as holders of law were decision makers: "James [Burns] expresses that the 'grandmothers are the keepers of all the medicines, laws, and stories.'"[58] This is reflected in the question "Who are your grandmothers?" commonly asked when establishing kinship connections and relations.[59]

Dorion's interviews further reveal how the home, and more specifically the kitchen table, was the space where teachings, including food knowledge, were shared:

> In both Cree and Métis homes the kitchen was always a place of intergenerational teaching for families. People in this study expressed gratitude for the storytelling, sharing, and knowledge exchanges that occurred over daily family meals and tea breaks. The grandmothers in particular played a significant role in teaching stories to both young girls and boys about food knowledge. A child's relationship to food is a learned behavior and reinforced by family members and they need to be given the Opikinawasowin food teachings at an early age and at an age-appropriate level. When children or young

people harvest and prepare foods from beginning to end this teaches them to become self-sufficient and increases their self-esteem.[60]

Women did their beading and trained the next generation of matriarchs at the kitchen tables.[61] Reflecting on her influences, artist and knowledge holder Isabelle Impey remarked:

> I think that the highlight of when I think back is when we had this big circle of people in the kitchen and they'd put all the lights on and they would throw a cloth on the table and we had benches and the women would gather and learn to bead.[62]

The older women would demonstrate the craft to the younger women around the table:

> women were showing us, this is how you bead and this is how you make this. It was a moose hide jacket. This is where I started and as soon as I could handle needles, I was allowed to participate and it was such a nice warm place to be and you'd have this, maybe burns lard pail or something with a lamp sitting on top so the light would spread throughout the table so everyone could see their needles and their beads. We would be making these jackets or different garments for the men in the family or else we made moccasins for ourselves.[63]

Isabelle's artistic creations are in the Gabriel Dumont Institute's Collection, as are many of her teachings on Métis beadwork.[64]

In the 1950s and 1960s, women in kāministikominahikoskahk continued crafting winter garments, moccasins, and gloves, and in doing so, passed down this knowledge to youth in the community. Isabelle remembered:

Some of the things we made in the community were garments for people to wear, particularly things that you want people to be warm in the winter. We did a lot of the leather work for jackets and shoes to keep your feet warm, so we ended up making a lot of moccasins and the wrap-a-rounds were very common because we had a lot of snow and so you would have these wrap-a-rounds so you could tie them around your leg and keep the snow out so your feet would stay dry. The other things that we made would be blankets. We made a lot of quilts and different kinds of blankets to keep the family members warm during the winter and the cold months.[65]

Scraps of leftover materials were stitched together to re-create beautiful and warm blankets. In the community, such creations were undertaken by many women in the community. Isabelle further recalled:

You had so many kinds of colours and they were common. Sometimes we used to think that the women had a competition in the community because they all had these long clotheslines and it'd seem like the same day, everybody would wash their "all kinds of blankets" and they'd have twenty of them hanging out there and they were so colourful. It's a shame we never got any pictures of these clotheslines because they were awesome to look at. And the moss bags, the people you knew how loved and how welcomed and how anxious people for this new child that was going to come and you would see this beadwork, would be just intricate and a lot of work for this little baby that was going to come along, so moss bags as well were made.[66]

The love, friendly competition, and joyful anticipation of new life animated women's creations, wrapping family and community in the priceless gift of belonging.

FIG 7.07. Moccasins made by Agnes Carriere at the Carriere Family Collection, Cumberland House Museum.

Picking up beadwork occurred as soon as girls could handle a needle and because the women were always beading, as it was part of the daily round of women's work. Isabelle recalled the matriarchal context in which women undertook their beading, noting the importance of visiting, having tea, and sharing stories. Each object they created was infused with the women's community-centred values for belonging and beauty:

> What was beautiful about it was it was always a social event. They all get together and there would be a big pot of tea and the women would sit around and they would bead and tease each other or tell stories, and it was wonderful and it was a nice way of coming together with other women in the

community. And there was some real awesome beaders in that community. Some of the work that they did, you know, you'd see the work even on the animals. Like you'd see a dog blanket, a beaded dog blanket...so they weren't just beading for family members but actually beading to decorate another part of their life, which would be their dog team, because that was the common transportation in the wintertime. We didn't have vehicles there. Later in life we had one truck, eh.[67]

Because of the prevalence of generations of women artisans in the community, kāministikominahikoskahk beadwork shares a traditional floral style, but there has also been innovation in styles and patterns. However, what remained constant is the intention behind creation. Isabelle recalled that if "you're not used to doing it and if you're not doing it for the joy, but you want to make something special for someone, it's your way of saying, 'You're special. I did all this for you,' and generally it would be the floral pattern."[68] The oldest kāministikominahikoskahk style was still undertaken by Agnes Carriere, which is unique to her. In recounting the artistry of beadwork, Isabelle reflected that "there's no particular I think rhyme to what you're putting together. What you're doing is putting a lot of beadwork with lots of nice colours and you're making sure what you are decorating is going to be fully decorated, it's going to be loved, will complement the person who is going to be wearing the garment or piece of clothing."[69]

For Cree-Métis children, the home was an Indigenous space that operated with Cree-Métis principles and values, clearly separate from the world of school. kāministikominahikoskahk Elder Irene Cook grew up speaking Cree, the language of her parents, and passed it to her own children and grandchildren, and only learned to speak English later.[70] Isabelle also recalled the importance of the Cree language. She too grew up speaking her mother's language. She referred to Cree, her first language as "the language of the home."[71] In the community of kāministikominahikoskahk, many families spoke Cree at home, and children learned English at the local public school, where corporal punishment was often used on students, confusing the children who lived in two separate worlds. Solomon Sanderson stresses these tensions and paradoxes in the community severely, "disrupted traditional parenting methods because of the colonial influence."[72]

kāministikominahikoskahk kehte aya Agnes Carriere (b. 1915)—whose father was Dougal McKenzie, grandfather Old Bill McKenzie, and grandmother mother Virginia Jourdain—had her mother pass away when she was eleven years old. Her mother was six months pregnant when she died. Her father took care of the children, and Agnes recalled that he was very kind and very knowledgeable in the traditional way of life.[73] She and her siblings grew up on food gathered from the land. She married Pierre Carriere and had eleven children, three of whom died. "Life was hard back then," she recalled, but her family was never hungry as they were able to obtain food mostly from the land. Pierre also trapped and fished, and she helped. She also tanned hides and sewed clothing for the children. Women prepared all the food, dried everything including meat and fish, and canned ducks in the fall. The women also picked berries, some of which were stored and others used to make jam. Berries included moss berries and cranberries, which were plentiful around kāministikominahikoskahk. It was her father, Dougal who taught his children to make bread and Bannock. "Us children would gather around the table, we were not very big," Agnes recalled. Her son John Carriere noted that his mother was also a fisherwoman who learned from helping her father as a child. During the war years, she also trapped and fished by herself with her sisters in order to feed her family. John shared that "until she was 85, she was making moccasins for us. I still have her jacket and I will always be proud of that."[74]

Beyond the individual tasks of physical labour for family, shared labour in beading, or child-rearing, women's responsibilities in the areas of governance and environmental and cultural knowledge were instrumental.[75] The late Anne Carrière-Acco, daughter of Agnes and Pierre Carriere, situates the health and vitality of the community in the ability of the land to provide for the physical, spiritual, social, cultural, and economic needs of the Métis people of kāministikominahikoskahk.[76] It is in the context of a healthy environment and balanced gender roles that the community remains Métis. Women kept the family history, which included birthdates and ancestral stories. Anne recalled: "My aunt Margaret McAuley told me that at the turn of the century, not only was the genealogy recited, but also the availability of female family members was currency in the marriage brokerage run by medicine people. Double cousins were tracked to keep any cousins as far apart as possible."[77] She likewise remarked on the importance of the matrilineal connection to grandmothers, pointing out that "details about family lineage are kept in the oral history among the women members. In assembly, women will come to ask who your grandmothers are. Most of the time they can share historical notes."[78]

Women also taught work ethic, since widows became heads of family, and the community valued women's education.[79] Women were responsible for making sure their family had an adequate supply of food, and for meeting their spiritual needs and praying for them. At the life stage of an Elder, women took on additional roles in governance. It was widely believed that a good community had women involved in the decision making, with Anne stating that "this was told to me directly."[80] Women held numerous other responsibilities tied to the health and well-being of the community, including that of passing on the hunting, fishing, and harvesting laws of the Métis: "Respect for the land and that which lives on the land is deeply ingrained in the Métis."[81] kāministikominahikoskahk knowledge keepers, Indigenous intellectuals, trappers, hunters, fishers, teachers, and artists contributed to a social and cultural context where Métis women's artistry flourished into the twentieth century, shaping today's contemporary bead workers, artists, and intellectuals.[82]

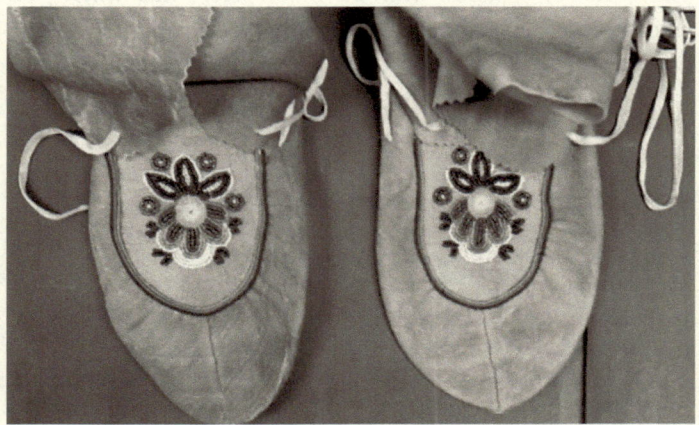

FIG. 7.08. Pointed toe moccasins made by Margaret McAuley, Cumberland House Museum Collection.

The re-matriation of the kāministikominahikoskahk Museum and the 2019 return of the items from the Cotter Family enables members of the local community to restore their relationships to their pasts, and to experience a multisensory engagement with artwork created by their ancestors. In the distinctive curatorial practices of the local committee, the kwecīc Historical Society, mîkisistahikêwin (doing beadwork) to connect generations becomes a metaphor for the loving act of remembering that centres men's and women's labouring. As Sherry Farrell Racette has said, these artworks "are objects encoded with knowledge, although they are sometimes impenetrable and difficult to understand... they also reveal critical information about the worlds and circumstances in which they were created. Connecting to archival records, the oral tradition, and embedded knowledge within First Nations languages greatly enriches our capacity to understand the stories these objects tell."[83] In the community, these objects are no longer isolated and decontextualized but rather placed in conversation with the other pieces that when gathered together tell the story of Métis matriarchs into the twenty-first century.

NOTES

1 Modjeski, "Artifacts Returned to Sask.'s Cumberland House after Decades in BC."
2 Saskatchewan Department of Northern Affairs, *A History of Cumberland House.*
3 Farrell Racette, "Beads, Silk and Quills," 187.
4 Saskatchewan Department of Northern Affairs, *A History of Cumberland House*; Richards, "Cumberland House: Two Hundred Years of History," 108.
5 "About the Delta: Geography & Ecology."
6 Goulet, "Land and Colonization"; "Cumberland House Feature," New Breed Magazine, July–August 2002, 1–40, Archival Collection, New Breed Magazine, 2002, GDI media filename 2002 JulyAug.pdf, Virtual Museum of Métis History and Culture, Gabriel Dumont Institute, accessed December 15, 2023, http://www.metismuseum.ca/media/document.php/04171.2002%20JulyAug.pdf.
7 Richards, "Cumberland House: Two Hundred Years of History."
8 Hearne et al., *Journals of Samuel Hearne and Philip Turnor.*
9 Richards, "Cumberland House: Two Hundred Years of History."
10 Meyer and Thistle, "Saskatchewan River Rendezvous"; Van Kirk, *Many Tender Ties*; Farrell Racette, "Sewing for a Living"; Macdougall, *One of the Family.*
11 Hodge, "'In Want of Nourishment'"; Daschuk, *Clearing the Plains*, 65.

12 Pettipas, "A History of the Work of the Reverend Henry Budd," 68–69.
13 Saskatchewan Department of Northern Affairs, *A History of Cumberland House*, 5.
14 Richards, "Cumberland House: Two Hundred Years of History," 111.
15 Gray, "Rematriation."
16 Armstrong, "Invocation," xi.
17 Armstrong, "Invocation," xii.
18 Farrell Racette, "Looking for Stories and Unbroken Threads."
19 Nixon, "Toward an Indigenous Relational Aesthetics," 195.
20 Nixon, "Toward an Indigenous Relational Aesthetics," 196.
21 Nixon, "Toward an Indigenous Relational Aesthetics," 203.
22 Farrell Racette, "Sewing for a Living," 28–37.
23 Farrell Racette, "Sewing for a Living," 40.
24 Gabriel Dumont Institute in Saskatchewan protects a large collection of Métis art. Métis artist, poet, and writer Gregory Scofield is locating, acquiring, and restoring Métis beadwork that he calls "the Grandmothers" that will one day be housed together in a Métis museum. See Lilley, "Metis Artist's 'Rematriation Project' Hopes to Reunite Vintage Indigenous Wares with Their Home Communities."
25 Farrell Racette, "Looking for Stories and Unbroken Threads"; Farrell Racette, "Sewing for a Living."
26 Farrell Racette with Corbiere and Migwans, "Pieces Left along the Trail," 225.
27 M'Closky, "Art of Craft," 119–20.
28 A selection of her important works include Farrell Racette, "Beads, Silk and Quills"; Farrell Racette with Corbiere and Migwans, "Pieces Left along the Trail"; Farrell Racette, "Looking for Stories and Unbroken Threads"; Farrell Racette, "Sewing for a Living"; and Farrell Racette, "My Grandmothers Loved to Trade."
29 Farrell Racette, "Pieces Left along the Trail," 228.
30 Farrell Racette, "Looking for Stories and Unbroken Threads," 285.
31 Troupe, "Mapping Métis Stories."
32 Troupe, "Métis Women"; Iseke and Desmoulins, "The Life and Work of the Honourable Thelma Chalifoux."
33 MacKinnon, *Metis Pioneers*; MacKinnon, *The Identities of Marie Rose Delorme Smith*.
34 Todd, "Honouring Our Great-Grandmothers," 174.
35 Oster and Lizee, *Stories of Métis Women*.
36 Noel, "Power Mothering," 80.
37 Noel, "Power Mothering," 81.

38 Noel, "Power Mothering," 88.
39 Anderson, *A Recognition of Being*; Anderson, *Life Stages and Native Women*.
40 Anderson, *Life Stages and Native Women*, 4.
41 Anderson, *Life Stages and Native Women*, 7.
42 Anderson, *Life Stages and Native Women*, 103.
43 Anderson, *Life Stages and Native Women*, 104–15.
44 Goulet and Goulet, *Teaching Each Other*; Carriere, *Elders and Teachers Are Cree-Ative Collaborators*, 42.
45 Saskatchewan Department of Northern Affairs, *A History of Cumberland House*.
46 Barron, *Walking in Indian Moccasins*; Quiring, *CCF Colonialism in Northern Saskatchewan*.
47 Waldram, *As Long as the Rivers Run*; Waldram, *Cumberland House and the E.B. Campbell Dam*; Dupuis and Holman, "Indian Claims Commission Cumberland House."
48 Virginia McKay, Jean Carriere, Pierre Dorion, and Marie Deschambeault, "History and Culture Report: Cumberland House," MG 240 box 2 I, R.M. Bone fonds, Northern Sask. Housing Needs Survey, A. General files, Cumberland House, Historical material—1930–1958, 1969–1974—folder 2, University of Saskatchewan Archives and Special Collections.
49 McKay et al., "History and Culture Report: Cumberland House," 60.
50 McKay et al., "History and Culture Report: Cumberland House."
51 McKay et al., "History and Culture Report: Cumberland House," 61.
52 McKay et al., "History and Culture Report: Cumberland House," 64.
53 McKay et al., "History and Culture Report: Cumberland House," 64.
54 McKay et al., "History and Culture Report: Cumberland House," 64.
55 McKay et al., "History and Culture Report: Cumberland House," 64.
56 Farrell Racette, "Looking for Stories and Unbroken Threads," 287–88.
57 Dorion, "Opikinawasowin," 112.
58 Dorion, "Opikinawasowin," 87.
59 Dorion, "Opikinawasowin."
60 Dorion, "Opikinawasowin," 81.
61 Kehte-Hiyak with Agnes Carriere of Cumberland House, Saskatchewan, 00:13:31.
62 Isabelle Impey, interviewed by Leah Dorion-Paquin and Maria Campbell, transcript, July 25, 2001, Virtual Museum of Métis History and Culture, Gabriel Dumont Institute, https://www.metismuseum.ca/media/document.php/06812.Isabelle%20Impey%20Interview.pdf, 6.

63 Isabelle Impey interview, 7.
64 Gabriel Dumont Institute, "Our Shared Inheritance: Traditional Métis Beadwork," 2019, YouTube video.
65 Isabelle Impey, 7.
66 Isabelle Impey interview, 7.
67 Isabelle Impey interview, 8.
68 Isabelle Impey interview, 9.
69 Isabelle Impey interview, 9.
70 Kathy Hodgson-Smith, "An Interview with Irene Morin," *New Breed Magazine*, July–August 2002, 29–31, Archival Collection, *New Breed Magazine*, 2002, GDI media filename 2002 JulyAug.pdf, Virtual Museum of Métis History and Culture, Gabriel Dumont Institute, accessed December 15, 2023, http://www.metismuseum.ca/media/document.php/04171.2002%20JulyAug.pdf, 30.
71 Kathy Hodgson-Smith, "Carrying on the Dorion Traditions: An Interview with Isabelle Impey," *New Breed Magazine*, July–August 2002, 38–40, Archival Collection, *New Breed Magazine*, 2002, GDI media filename 2002 JulyAug.pdf, Virtual Museum of Métis History and Culture, Gabriel Dumont Institute, accessed December 15, 2023, http://www.metismuseum.ca/media/document.php/04171.2002%20JulyAug.pdf., 40.
72 Dorion, "Opikinawasowin," 44.
73 Kehte-Hiyak with Agnes Carriere of Cumberland House, Saskatchewan.
74 Kathy Hodgson-Smith, "John Carriere: If You Look after the Country, the Country Will Look after You," New Breed Magazine, July–August 2002, 8–10, Archival Collection, New Breed Magazine, 2002, GDI media filename 2002 JulyAug.pdf, Virtual Museum of Métis History and Culture, Gabriel Dumont Institute, accessed December 15, 2023, http://www.metismuseum.ca/media/document.php/04171.2002%20JulyAug.pdf., 10.
75 Carrière-Acco, "Ki-Naan'how," 127.
76 Carrière-Acco, "Ki-Naan'how," 128.
77 Carrière-Acco, "Ki-Naan'how," 128.
78 Carrière-Acco, "Ki-Naan'how," 128.
79 Carrière-Acco, "Ki-Naan'how," 129.
80 Carrière-Acco, "Ki-Naan'how," 129.
81 Carrière-Acco, "Ki-Naan'how," 130.
82 Sherry Farrell Racette, interviewed by Leah Dorion-Paquin, transcript, October 17, 2001, Virtual. Museum of Métis History and Culture, Gabriel Dumont Institute, https://www.metismuseum.ca/media/

document.php/06838.S.F.Racette%20interview.pdf. Sherry learned to bead from Cumberland House Matriarch Margaret McAuley. Leah Dorion is the niece of Isabelle Impey, and many cultural resources at the Gabriel Dumont Institute have been developed through the teachings of Isabelle Impey and Sherry Farrell Racette.

83 Farrell Racette, "Looking for Stories and Unbroken Threads," 285.

Eight

Activating Lessons of Care from Family Matriarchs
The Social and Political Work of Nora Cummings

by Cheryl Troupe

I FIRST MET NORA CUMMINGS OVER TWENTY YEARS ago. Although I didn't know her well, I quickly learned that she was a respected lii vyeu, knowledge keeper, and senator of the Métis Nation—Saskatchewan, with a long history of working for her community.[1] I first interviewed her in the early 2000s when I was conducting research for my Master of Arts on Métis women's roles in community formation and how this translated to the development of social and political organizations in Saskatoon in the mid-twentieth century. However, in the past five years, I have gotten to know Nora more profoundly and much differently. In early 2018 she brought together a handful of Saskatoon Métis community members to discuss the potential for reinvigorating Gabriel Dumont Local #11. A local affiliate of the Métis Nation—Saskatchewan, Local #11 had been formed in the late

1960s to represent Saskatoon Métis and remained active until the late 1990s. Nora, her mother, Irene Trotchie Dimick, and her uncle Clarence Trotchie had been instrumental in the Local's founding and although it was no longer active, Nora remained its caretaker. At this meeting, Nora shared the Local's history, including stories of the tremendous amount of work they had done in the organization's early years. She spoke passionately about the need to reengage Local members and educate urban Métis and the public on Métis history, language, and culture. Taking her directive, we agreed as a collective to rebuild the Local, offer Métis educational and cultural opportunities, and work toward creating a stronger sense of community in the city. Since that time, Nora has expressed the desire to share her stories and personal archives with me, and we have engaged in a research project documenting urban Métis perspectives and contributions to the development of the city of Saskatoon. This chapter draws on the culmination of this research and her many stories, which she has permitted me to share.

Nora was born on January 1, 1938, into a large, close-knit, and political family. She has spent her life advocating for Métis people, and for women and children. She is a matriarch in her family and community, generously offering guidance and sharing advice and direction. In the late 1960s, she was drawn into the burgeoning Métis social and political activism around her, dedicating her efforts to bettering conditions for Métis women, children, and families at local, provincial, and national levels. As stated, Nora was actively involved in the formation of Saskatoon's Gabriel Dumont Local #11; she was also the first woman on the Saskatoon Indian and Métis Friendship Centre Board of Directors. By the 1970s, she was one of the Métis Society of Saskatchewan's first provincial field workers advocating for and politicizing Métis women in their communities. In 1972, she became a founding member and first president of the Saskatchewan Native Women's

Movement (SNWM), a grassroots political movement advocating for both Métis and Non-Status Indigenous women, which by 1982 had contributed to the formation of the Native Women's Council of Canada in support of Indigenous women across the country. Nora's activism has been, and remains, guided by foundational teachings of the importance of caring for family and community members modelled by women in her own family and passed on to her by her mother, Irene, and grandmother Justine Landry Trotchie. Through her activism, Nora has cultivated these lessons of care within the Saskatoon Métis community and for Métis people across Saskatchewan and Canada.

Nora grew up living in a road allowance community on Saskatoon's outskirts. Road allowance communities were temporary and often makeshift settlements that sprang up on unoccupied Crown Lands reserved for roads, next to First Nations reserves or at the edge of prairie towns and cities in the late nineteenth and early twentieth centuries. Unique to the Prairie provinces, these communities were formed by Métis in response to forced Métis displacement following the failure of the Dominion Lands policy beginning in the 1870s and subsequent scrip processes to secure Métis land tenure. These were marginalized spaces where there were few economic opportunities. Municipal and provincial governments viewed these road allowances as impediments to development, prompting them to remove Métis from these settlements when the land they occupied became coveted for urban development, cottage and tourist activity, and regional and provincial park development.[2]

The road allowance community formed in Saskatoon in the early twentieth century was located at the southern edge of the city—south of Taylor Street on both sides of Clarence Avenue—in what are now the Adelaide/Churchill and Nutana Park neighbourhoods. While the city had already surveyed this area when Métis families began living there, development had not yet expanded into the vicinity. By the early 1930s, several Métis families moved into the seemingly vacant area, building small, simple log cabins or lumber shacks, or living in tents. Most were recent arrivals to the city, having moved to Saskatoon from the Métis settlement of Round Prairie, south of the city, in search of employment.[3] Some moved directly to the road allowance, while others initially found homes to rent in developed city neighbourhoods and then relocated to the road allowance to avoid the watchful eye of municipal relief agents as the receipt of relief intensified into the 1930s and '40s.[4]

The family was central to Nora's life, and she grew up within a complex web of family and community relationships. There were about forty households in the road allowance community, most of whom were related.[5] In addition to these road allowance families, Nora was also closely related to Round Prairie Métis who were increasingly relocating to the city or had already, taking up residence on Saskatoon's west side in the neighbourhoods of King George, Riversdale, and Holiday Park. Living with her parents and siblings, Nora grew up surrounded by aunts, uncles, cousins, and grandparents. Although poor, it was a vibrant community where cultural traditions were practised and passed on; the Michif language remained strong. Families socialized and celebrated together, and there was always political discussion of Métis history and rights. To a large degree, families lived off the land, hunting, trapping, and harvesting wild plants and medicines, as well as growing large vegetable gardens. For a time, Nora recalls the families planting a community garden on Clarence Avenue at Taylor Street, where Aden Bowman Collegiate now stands. The garden was a space where the community worked together to plant and harvest vegetables collectively. On the city's outskirts, there was relatively little economic opportunity

FIG 8.01. Justine Landry Trotchie and her children in Saskatoon. From left to right: Norman Trotchie and Irvin Trotchie (back row); Clarence Trotchie, Violet (née Trotchie) Livingstone, and Alex Trotchie (middle row); Louise (née Trotchie) Belcourt, Justine Landry Trotchie (Nora's grandmother), and Irene (née Trotchie) Dimick (Nora's mother) (front row).

for men in Saskatoon, particularly during the 1930s. When work was available, it was generally for neighbouring farmers, hauling wood and fence pickets, picking rocks and roots, harvesting fields, and performing various other forms of seasonal and day labour. Sometimes families worked as an economic unit in these tasks, while in other instances women, like Nora's mother, Irene, sought out work as domestics, cleaners, and waitresses in urban homes and businesses. Nora's family lived in this road allowance community until the 1950s when urban development ultimately displaced the Métis who called it home.

Nora had significant responsibilities as the oldest child of Irene Dimick and Jerome Ouellette. She looked after her younger siblings and often babysat her young cousins. She helped her mother around the house and, as she got older, helped her father cut hay and clear fields for farmers. However, one of Nora's most important responsibilities was to help care for her maternal grandmother, Justine Trotchie. Although elderly, Justine remained independent, maintaining her own home close to Nora and her parents. Nora had a close relationship with her Koohkoom Justine and lived with her for a period. She helped Justine with cleaning and household chores and regularly accompanied her when she shopped. On these occasions, Nora negotiated with merchants on her grandmother's behalf because Justine spoke little English. Throughout this period, Justine shared many important cultural teachings with Nora, including lessons about women's roles as caregivers in the family, the importance of caring for children and the elderly, and the significance of visiting and maintaining family, and by extension, community relationships.[6] Nora credits Justine and the cultural values and traditions she shared with teaching her what it means to be Métis.[7]

Nora's extended family recognized Justine as a matriarch. She was treated with respect and regularly sought out for counsel and

FIG. 8.02. Nora and her koohkoom, Justine, in Saskatoon. This photograph was likely taken around 1953.

advice. This matriarchal role was important within Métis families.[8] Matriarchs, most often of advanced age, were held in high esteem for their gifts, knowledge, and expertise, and demonstrated authority within their extended families. They often provided informal leadership within the family and worked hard to ensure cultural traditions were passed on and kinship relationships remained strong. Often, these women acted as healers and midwives. They played an important role in ensuring that cultural celebrations continued and instilled cultural values in the family[9]—behind the scenes, keeping families together and getting along. While city life had brought change to Métis families, the matriarchal role older women such as Justine played in their families continued.[10]

Among the many lessons Justine, Irene, and other women in Nora's family taught her were lessons about motherhood and the importance of caring for children. According to Nora, being a woman and mother is a responsibility given by the Creator: "Babies are gifts from the Creator and as women, we are given the privilege of bringing them into the world. Caring for a baby is especially important."[11] Nora learned these lessons first by watching the older women in her family and then modelling their behaviour, "learning to tenderly handle a baby and to wrap it in its blanket, so it was safe and comfortable."[12] As she got older, she was given more responsibility in looking after her siblings and her cousins. She recalls that for young girls her age, the care and nurturing they provided was understood as more than babysitting but "training to be good moms when our time came."[13] For Nora, these were essential teachings about caring for children that she carried with her when she became a mother.

Nora also learned many important lessons and cultural values from the women in her family about the importance of caring for the family. While Irene and Justine instilled many vital lessons, Nora also credits her godmother Eva Trotchie for preparing her to raise and care for her family. Eva taught Nora cultural values about being generous and hospitable, and to always share food and drink with her visitors. When Nora asked her koohkoom about the practice, Justine explained that providing a meal acknowledges the honour of having the individual visit your home.[14] These practices of visiting and sharing food helped maintain social bonds and reinforced family values of caring for one another and ensuring everyone had something to eat, particularly when times were tough. As a result, visiting across her extended family was common when Nora was young, particularly on Sundays following church and for holiday celebrations including the New Year's celebrations, where families moved from house to house, visiting, dancing, and feasting.[15] Justine and Irene maintained these values and social practices, and it is something Nora has continued.[16]

The women in Nora's family taught her to be strong, courageous, and proud of being Métis. They also taught her about forgiveness. Nora attended St. Joseph's School, quitting when she was fifteen because of the racism she, her siblings, and other Métis faced. They were made to feel humiliated and ashamed and were often punished for not speaking what the nuns considered proper English. At other times, Nora recalled being called "dirty catlicks [Catholics]" by students on the playground, or "dirty, lazy half-breeds" in their everyday interactions with non-Indigenous people.[17] On one occasion, Nora recalls the nuns called her and several other Métis students "*les sauvages*" after being singled out and made to stand at the front of the class. Both Irene and Justine were angry and upset when they learned of this and told Nora to stand up for herself. She was li Michif Niiyinan and should be proud to be a Michif person. This gave Nora the courage to ignore the names and racist epithets and was an important lesson for her in understanding who she is as a Métis woman. Not all nuns, however, treated Nora and other Métis students with such disregard. There was one individual, Sister Elentrude, who Nora recalled treated them with kindness and respect. Like Nora's mother and grandmother, Sister Elentrude encouraged Nora to be proud of who she was, hold her head high, and ignore the name calling.[18] This was an important teaching for Nora about kindness and forgiveness.

As Nora reached her teen years, lessons in caring for the family were firmly ingrained. In addition to looking after Justine, Nora helped her father Jerome, working her own team of horses alongside her father and uncles as they cut and hauled hay for nearby farmers and local businesses. She helped her mother, Irene, with housework and looked after her younger siblings and cousins. She witnessed her mother's hard work, both inside and outside the home, and learned from her mother how to keep a home and work hard herself. According to Nora, "I had to learn. I learned how to become a mom. I learned how to become a cook. I learned how to clean the house. I learned how to work. All those things were instilled in all of us.... That's what my mother taught us."[19] Irene was strong, independent, and hard-working. She took jobs where she could, often travelling around the city on a small bike, to and from work.[20] For a time she worked at a local printing company, Modern Press, but most often she worked as a housekeeper, cleaning the homes of Saskatoon's wealthier residents. This work ethic was ingrained in Nora, who found work at a local café after leaving school, recognizing the importance of bringing income into the family.[21] She worked as a waitress for over a year, quitting to take care of her grandmother Justine when she became ill. Although bringing money into the home was important, Nora's role as a caregiver to her koohkoom was paramount.

Over Nora's lifetime, Justine and Irene modelled important cultural teachings. These lessons have been reinforced throughout Nora's life and she carries them with her today. Nora's close relationship with Justine and the responsibility she had for caring for her grandmother did not end as Nora matured. Rather, it was a lifelong responsibility Nora fulfilled as her koohkoom aged. When Nora married and had her children, Justine moved in with her family. Nora worked to provide Justine with as much independence as possible and allowed Justine to live with and get to know Nora's children, Justine's great-grandchildren. Similarly, as Irene aged, Nora and her husband, Henry Cummings, also welcomed Irene into their home. Irene lived with them until she passed in 2004.

By 1953, city development forced Nora's family and others to move off the road allowance into the more developed neighbourhoods of the city. Many stayed on the east side, finding homes in the Nutana neighbourhood to try and remain close to one another. Despite physical relocation, family and cultural life remained important. The families that had lived on the road allowance maintained social practices of regular visiting and socializing with each other and Métis relatives on the west side of Saskatoon, attending dances, playing cards, and celebrating holidays together. Visiting, storytelling, and the recognition of a shared history were important in keeping these families together.

Nora grew up listening to stories of old Métis buffalo hunters, life at Round Prairie, and her extended family's involvement in the Métis struggle for recognition and protection of land rights that culminated in the 1885 Resistance at Batoche. As a child, she heard stories about her relatives at Round Prairie who, closely related to Métis leader Gabriel Dumont, fought alongside the Métis at Batoche.[22] These included stories of her great-grandmother, Gabriel's sister, Isabelle Dumont Ouellette, and other women of Batoche who supported the fight by cooking and feeding the fighters, caring for the sick and wounded, caring for the children and elderly, and even melting down metal to make bullets for the guns.[23] She also heard stories of the Round Prairie families seeking refuge in Montana after 1885, staying with extended relations and returning to Round Prairie in the early 1900s intent on receiving scrip or homestead and once again take up their lands along the river. Like most Métis communities of the period, farming was hard without financial capital, so most attempted to make a living by working for farmers. By the 1930s, families had already begun leaving the Round Prairie community, trickling into Saskatoon in increasing numbers. They rebuilt a sense of community within the city and lived close to one another to maintain social bonds.[24] These families were inherently political, and while the new urban environment brought new political challenges, it also reinvigorated old ideas about Métis rights and grievances. In the city, they quickly began politically organizing themselves, advocating for education, employment, and land rights.

In the early 1930s, Saskatoon Métis formed their own branch of the Saskatchewan Métis Society, a political organization formed in 1929 in southern Saskatchewan that quickly began to organize across the province. Saskatoon Métis were eager to be involved in the provincial cause and advocate for their rights in the growing urban centre of Saskatoon.[25] Nora's mother, Irene, and Koohkoom Justine both attended meetings of the burgeoning Saskatoon Métis Society and worked alongside other Métis women to organize and host family and community social events that became an opportunity for political meetings. According to author Rita Schilling, these meetings were well attended, often with upwards of sixty people. During this time people were meeting in their homes and while no programs had yet emerged, a spirit of community activism was growing.[26] Women such as Justine and Irene, and others from across the Métis community, often attended these meetings with the men in their families. They also worked behind the scenes, visiting others in their homes, doing informal political work by providing food, encouraging participation, and speaking politically within the confines of the family and the Métis community.[27] Irene recalled that all the women in the community attended these meetings. "We were there right from the start. My mother used to say, 'well, you never know what could happen' so we'd go to these meetings, you know, with the other girls, the other Métis girls. I'd go with them and my mother."[28] As a child, Irene's half-sister Marge Laframboise also attended these meetings with her parents Peter Trotchie and Elizabeth Laframboise. She recalled the organization's creation as something the community was very proud of and eager to be involved in.[29]

These stories, especially those of strong Métis women who got involved politically, spoke out on behalf of their loved ones, and did what was necessary to care for their children, their families, and their homes and lands, left an impression on Nora. As a child, Nora, like her mother, Irene, a generation earlier, attended family gatherings and social events that ultimately became the stage for political activism, witnessing first-hand the stories she heard as a child. This political influence alongside the cultural and storied inheritance from her mother, grandmother, and other women in the family has influenced Nora's activism throughout her life.

Nora married and had children young. As she got older, she was educated into the Métis social and political activist community in Saskatoon and heavily influenced by her mother and uncle Clarence Trotchie. Nora and Clarence had a close relationship. He had served in the Second World War and upon his return, he initially lived with Nora and Justine. He lived away from Saskatoon for a period but returned in 1960 and quickly became a strong leader in the Métis community. The 1960s was a period of intense social and political activism for Indigenous peoples across Canada, and he recognized the need to strengthen ties within the community and give Indigenous people a voice in urban life.

Nora credits Clarence for his role in encouraging her political activism. By the late 1960s, Clarence was actively involved in the new Saskatoon Indian and Métis Friendship Centre that had opened in 1967 to provide a gathering place and services for the city's growing Indigenous population.

FIG. 8.03. Nora (about age fifteen) and her uncle, Clarence Trotchie. This photo was taken in Saskatoon in about 1953.

He and other Métis were having regular political discussions about the social issues of alcoholism, poverty, poor housing, unemployment, and lack of educational opportunities faced by urban Métis in Saskatoon and were eager to make change.[30] Nora was also influenced by her mother who, also encouraged by Clarence, was becoming active in the Friendship Centre movement and regularly attending Alcoholics Anonymous meetings held at the centre.[31] Irene was not unfamiliar with this type of activism as she had also attended Métis political meetings in the 1930s with her mother, Justine.[32] As Nora became politicized, she drew upon cultural values, practices, and lessons of care she learned from her parents, grandparents, and extended family members. These were lessons that she would bring to her social and political activism advocating for Indigenous women, children, and families.

In November 1969, Clarence, Irene, Nora, and other members of the Métis community formed Local #11, one of several provincial Métis Society Locals organizing around the province in these years. Clarence was elected president, with Nora and Irene and others serving as the founding board of directors. The Local initially operated from within the Saskatoon Indian and Métis Friendship Centre. In 1972, the Friendship Centre elected an exclusively Métis board of directors, all of whom were members of Local #11, including Clarence who held the position of Local #11 president and Friendship Centre board chair. The Métis were a growing force within the Friendship Centre but often found themselves at odds with the Centre's structure and priorities, which resulted in the Local splitting from the Friendship Centre.

As the Local was forming, women such as Nora and Irene were increasingly getting politically involved. Nora recalls that it was mostly women who were involved in the early formation of the Local. She and her mother Irene filled positions on the Local's board of directors and also acted as organizers alongside other women such as Vicki Wilson and Betty Roy. Their role was to encourage Métis community participation and raise support for the Local by visiting Métis friends and relatives in their homes.[33] Nora and other women worked hard to develop and maintain a sense of community for urban Métis. They visited around kitchen tables, made telephone calls, and provided transportation to and from meetings.[34]

Like their mothers and grandmothers decades earlier, Nora and other women drew on their cultural values of sharing, hospitality, and visiting to build relationships and maintain social bonds. Through the Local, they planned and hosted cultural activities, social events, and community gatherings such as birthday parties, bingos, dances, and holiday celebrations to help raise funds for the Local, but more importantly to bring people together for political discussion and talk about community needs and priorities. These events were always accompanied by the cultural practice of sharing a meal.[35] It was always important to Nora and others that cultural activities be practised, shared, and passed on.[36] As a result, there was always a lot of activity taking place at the Local's building, such as jigging and square dancing and other activities. According to Nora:

> It was great...we had birthday parties, we honoured the older people, we honoured our people that done something. There was always something happening in that centre. There wasn't a day that something wouldn't happen. On New Year's there was always a big celebration, Christmas parties for the children, and Christmas for the elders and adults. We always found funding. We always found the money. I think the thing that kept the Local strong was the unity that was in it with all of the people. No one ever said, "well gee, I don't think I want to do that. I don't want to get involved in that." It was great![37]

Although cultural activities were an important means of engaging the community, there were also other pressing issues the Local wished to address. Through this form of organizing, they created education and employment programs, programs for women and children, an alcohol treatment centre, and a housing program to meet the needs of the urban Métis community.

Alcohol treatment was an increasingly pressing community issue that intensified after the Second World War and the return of soldiers.[38] Nora grew up seeing alcohol use in her family, and it was often present at extended family gatherings. She recalled that the older women in the family would often curtail excessive drinking and institute consequences for those who caused harm or were destructive or disruptive when drinking. Consequences, Nora noted, were not about punishment, but were done in a way that supported and ensured the good of the family.[39] By the 1960s, Clarence and Nora's mother, Irene, were recovering alcoholics who regularly attended Alcoholics Anonymous meetings and were eager to engage their friends and relatives in the program.[40]

As the Local was becoming established, the provincial Métis Society was working to create an alcohol treatment program. They created the Native Alcohol Council (NAC) in 1969 with fieldworkers hired to assist in the establishment of treatment centres in North Battleford, Prince Albert, Regina, and Saskatoon.[41] Under Clarence's leadership, Local #11 led the development of Saskatoon's NAC house, a thirty-day residential treatment facility that opened in 1973. In the first year, 113 clients had completed treatment.[42] Schilling credits Clarence's leadership with the NAC's success as well as for the inclusion of cultural values that made it more accessible to Indigenous clients.[43]

In the late 1960s and 1970s, men generally filled formal leadership positions in emerging urban Indigenous social and political organizations and took credit for the hard work of building such institutions.[44] A closer inspection, however, reveals that women provided important, although often invisible, behind-the-scenes labour.[45] Although Clarence's leadership in NAC was essential, the program's success should also be attributed to the support and hard work of several women including Clarence's sister Irene, niece Nora, and half-sisters Marge Laframboise, Dorothy Askwith, Kay Mazer, and Bertha Ouellette.[46] These women cooked and cleaned in the centre and looked after day-to-day operations, and they worked directly with clients as fieldworkers making referrals to the program. They also ran other Local programs such as the Follow-Up Program to support clients and their families once the individual left alcohol treatment, the Family Worker Program to advocate for families in dealing with social service agencies, the Court Worker program to help individuals navigate the justice system, and SaskNative housing, a non-profit housing corporation to provide low-income housing for Indigenous peoples in Saskatoon.[47] In their work, these women consistently modelled Métis cultural values of caring for family and community. Nora recalls her mother working very hard as a fieldworker for the NAC centre. As a recovering alcoholic Irene understood what clients were facing, and she treated each with care and compassion, even, on occasion, welcoming clients into her own home "to sober up" for a few days before entering the program.[48]

In addition to those directly involved in these specific programs, there were others, like Nora, who continued to work in the background helping to organize and raise community awareness of the NAC and other Local #11 programs. According to Nora, she was "the gopher" whose role it was to visit with people in their homes, as she had done when organizing the Local.[49] She recalls being sent by Clarence and other Local leadership to visit with the Old People in the community to discuss their needs and priorities, including the creation of seniors housing.[50] Engaging with and gaining support from the community's Old People was important and fitting work for Nora. Drawing on lessons she learned when living with and helping care for her koohkoom Justine, Nora knew well how to engage with Old People in a way that was respectful and honoured their age, experience, and wisdom.

Nora eventually became a family worker for the Local, which in partnership with the provincial Department of Social Services offered a wide range of services to Indigenous people "with emphasis on the prevention of child neglect and abandonment, adjustment to urban life, coping with the law, improving housing and reducing racial discrimination."[51] The program offered similar services to the Local's Court Worker and Follow-Up Programs, resulting in the three programs amalgamating into one, the Family Worker Program.[52] Nora was a family worker for twelve years, often having up to fifty clients at a time. Her job was to advocate for families to get the services they needed and help them find employment and safe, affordable homes. She even helped them find furniture, bedding, and clothing. Nora excelled in this role because she prioritized looking after the family and understood many of the issues her clients faced.[53] She recognized the importance of building strong relationships if she was to truly help her clients. Building trust was paramount, and she treated all her clients with the same care and respect she showed her own family. She often found herself taking on the more challenging clients that none of the other family workers would work with. She spent time getting to know each client, and the time spent paid off. She built such good relationships that often her clients' children would even call her auntie.[54] Nora was honoured to do the work because working with and caring for children, women, and families were values that had been instilled in her.[55] As a family worker, Nora was familiar with clients, knew their difficulties in finding adequate housing and struggles to pay rent, and worked closely with several landlords. This positioned Nora to be involved in the founding of SaskNative Housing in 1974, a program that provided safe and affordable homes to Indigenous people in Saskatoon, many of whom were also accessing NAC treatment and other Local #11 programs.[56]

Working closely in Local programs funded by and often alongside provincial programs, such as social service delivery programs, provided a unique perspective for Nora. She understood her community well and was positioned to work beyond the local level. At the encouragement, and perhaps even insistence, of provincial Métis Society of Saskatchewan president Jim Sinclair, Nora began working as a field worker for the provincial organization in 1971. She was surprised that President Sinclair would have such confidence in her, recalling, "I mean here's me with a grade five education and they want to put me in an office, they're crazy, you know, I mean I can't do this."[57] Despite her hesitance and lack of confidence, Nora recognized it was important for her to be involved, and she had the support of President Sinclair, her uncle Clarence, other Saskatoon Métis leaders, and her family.[58]

Métis leadership recognized her abilities and knew she could do the work of politicizing Métis women on a provincial scale. Accepting the position, she quickly began organizing women across the province in much the same way she had worked organizing in the Saskatoon community. She relied on visiting people's homes and encouraging participation in meetings. In November 1971, Nora and Josephine Pambrum used a provincial Métis Society meeting to gather women to discuss women's issues. Thirty-five women attended, and a temporary committee on women's issues was established with Pambrum as chair and Nora and women from Regina, Ft. Qu'Appelle, Carlyle, and Prince Albert forming a temporary board of directors.[59] The Métis Society then received a grant from the federal government to hire women field workers across the province whose role was to politicize women around issues that were important to them.[60] Women were starting to organize.

The following year they held a meeting in the city of Prince Albert to garner more support and set out planning and fundraising for a second conference. Local women's groups raised money through bingos and bake sales and different fundraisers, attempting to raise enough to cover conference costs.[61] While successful in raising most of the money, they relied on billeting women in others' homes; the Friendship Centre, then led by Clarence and several members of Local #11, provided a banquet, helping to feed conference participants. Over one hundred women from across Saskatchewan attended the 1972 conference, discussing issues that were important to them. They formed a formal women's organization, the Saskatchewan Native Women's Movement (SNWM), with Nora being elected their first president.[62] She held the position for the next five years.[63] At the 1972 conference, the SNWM elected a board of directors and identified eight women from across Saskatchewan to act as fieldworkers who would travel throughout their respective regions, politicizing, organizing, and educating women on the organization's work.[64]

FIG. 8.04. Saskatchewan Native Women's Conference in Saskatoon at the Saskatoon Friendship Centre in 1973. Nora is second from the left, in the centre of the three women.

The SNWM was open to Métis, Status, and Non-Status Indian women. The organization's inclusiveness distinguished it from other provincial organizations representing Indigenous peoples such as the Métis Society of Saskatchewan (now the Métis Nation—Saskatchewan) or the Federation of Saskatchewan Indian Nations (now the Federation of Sovereign Indigenous Nations). The new body prioritized issues that they felt were not being adequately addressed by either organization and were eager to develop programs and services to meet Indigenous women's specific needs. They identified four priority areas, including community health services, halfway houses and counseling for women coming out of jail, daycare centres to support urban working mothers, and cultural programs for women and their families.[65] According to Nora, "we became a force. Our women kind of worked alongside our people at the Métis Nation. Métis and Non-Status, they relied on us. Our women built that nation and we worked hard. We had women's centres, halfway homes. We had people working in the jails—in federal penitentiaries and women's jails. We had people [working] in daycares. Gabriel Housing in Regina—that was done by women, so all of these modern-day programs are in existence because of the women who worked at that level."[66] They applied for and received provincial grants to hire staff, quickly employing fifty people across the province, including in northern and remote communities.[67]

The issues SNWM organized around were those that impacted Indigenous women's daily lives. These issues were in some ways similar to those prioritized by mainstream feminists but also recognizably different. Whereas mainstream feminists challenge sexism, Indigenous women struggle against sexism and racism. Indigenous scholar Kim Anderson argues that Indigenous women have not taken up Western feminism because it is fundamentally about rights rather than about responsibilities and because of its

FIG. 8.05. Opening of "We Care Home" on Spadina Crescent, Saskatoon, 1972. Included in the photo: Saskatoon mayor Bert Sears, Minister Alex Taylor, Nora Cummings, and Irene Dimick.

emphasis on individual autonomy.[68] For many Indigenous women "feminism represents an attack on our responsibilities as women, particularly as mothers. There is also an argument that we cannot apply feminism because it will exclude men from our health and well-being as peoples."[69] For Nora and other women in the SNWM, their issues were linked directly to their roles and responsibilities as women and mothers and to the culturally held value of prioritizing family and family relationships. This included working alongside men to ensure women's issues were addressed. For the SNWM to have their voices heard and help women and children, Nora explained that they needed to work with men and see themselves as "not any higher or lower than our men, we're equal and we work together as equals because we're Métis.... [otherwise] our families struggle, our grandchildren struggle."[70] As a result the SNWM prioritized the creation of programs and services to support women through which they were upholding their culturally held responsibilities to family and community.

When approached by mainstream feminists to become involved in their organizations, Nora recognized that their issues were very different. Mainstream feminist issues seemed "far-fetched" for women in SNWM "because as Indigenous women that's not our way...we were looking at real issues that were affecting us and we wanted those issues to be dealt with."[71] Poverty was a clear difference between these two groups. When approached to be a part of a mainstream feminist "bra-burning" campaign, Nora recognized the difference between non-Indigenous mainstream feminists and the SNWM. She lamented "we can't be doing that.... For goodness' sake, we can't even burn our brassieres because we have to go and buy them at the Salvation Army... it was a hard struggle for us."[72] Despite these differences, Nora acknowledges that many non-Indigenous mainstream feminists supported the SNWM and vice versa when they could.[73]

While Indigenous women's issues were different from those of mainstream feminists, Non-Status and Métis women's issues often, but not always, differed from First Nations' issues, too. When issues overlapped or when they could support one another, the SNWM worked alongside the Saskatchewan Indian Women's Association, an organization for treaty Indian women under the umbrella of the provincial Federation of Saskatchewan Indian organization.[74] Nora recalls they had a good relationship and were supportive of First Nations women's issues but were cautious to never speak on their behalf.[75]

As president of the organization, Nora played a lead role but was mentored and supported by several other women. These women gave her the support she needed to overcome her shyness and build her confidence as a community leader. Older women such as Josephine Pambrum, Mary Ann Lavallee, Florence Desnomie, and Alice Poitras mentored Nora and her peers, encouraging them to work at the grassroots level and to encourage other women to speak up for themselves:[76] "They gave us that support and gave us that strength... It made us feel a lot more at ease because these were older women and they were kind of encouraging us that it was important that as young women we should start doing something not only for ourselves but for our families in the communities."[77] Nora recalls that these women "got me involved and, and they, they were very political."[78] Mary Anne and Josephine encouraged her to approach this work by drawing on her understanding of who she was as a Métis woman and mother and her own experiences and understanding of her family and community. Her mentors recognized that Nora had the skill and ability to fill this role and that she understood her cultural teachings of caring for and supporting women and children.[79]

One of the issues important to Nora and the SNWM was child welfare and adoption. While the creation of support programs was a priority, the SNWM were also not afraid to shy away from public demonstration, particularly on issues such as child welfare and adoption that were directly linked to their roles as mothers and their values of taking care of the family. Before Nora's work with the SNWM, she and other members of Local #11 had actively challenged the provincial government's treatment of Métis children in care. In 1971, along with Métis leader Howard Adams, Vicki Racette, and Clarence's wife Phyllis, Nora contested the removal of Métis children from their homes and subsequent placement in non-Métis homes away from their families and culture. They presented a Métis Foster Home Plan to the provincial government that addressed the high number of Métis children in Saskatoon's Kilburn Hall. As parents, they advocated for placement of Métis foster children with either Métis families or in a group foster home setting under the control and management of Métis people. They reasoned that Métis children in care were disconnected from their culture and subjected to discrimination and racism. They argued that they felt "a sense of racial and cultural responsibility for our children" and wanted these children "to be brought up as Métis."[80]

Two years later, Nora was again moved to act on child welfare when a woman attending a SNWM meeting was brought to tears because she had seen one of her children in an advertisement for the Adopt Indian and Métis (AIM) Program.[81] AIM was a pilot project of the provincial government that began in the late 1960s that used targeted radio, television, and newspaper advertisements to increase the adoption of Indigenous children into non-Indigenous homes. The woman's children had been apprehended years earlier. Recognizing the advertisement was for adoption, Nora, as leader of the SNWM called a public meeting and invited the provincial government officials including the minister of Social Welfare. Over two hundred people attended the meeting, including members of the Métis Society and the SNWM. In events that drew national news attention, activists openly challenged the minister on the removal of Métis children, arguing that the AIM program and government handling of child welfare was detrimental and discriminatory toward Métis children, families, and communities.[82] The SNWM submitted a brief to the Saskatchewan Human Rights Commission and circulated a petition to Métis across the province calling for an end to the AIM program and closure of the AIM offices in Regina because of the unjust way Métis children were being advertised and because Métis people were not given a voice in foster care and adoption decisions.[83] They also objected to Métis children being adopted out of the province. The advertisements were racist and propagated the message that Métis parents were unable to look after their children, that Métis children were inferior or unwanted, and that Métis parents were begging non-Indigenous people to raise their children.[84] While the SNWM's efforts failed to end the AIM program, they were successful in convincing government to shift the program's focus away from race to have the name of the program changed to Aim. Most importantly, they were also able to reconnect the woman with her children who had been taken into foster care in the 1960s.[85] This public demonstration showed the growing strength of the women's organization and its increasing radicalism. Nora argues that they were becoming more radical because that was the only way they were recognized.[86] They needed to speak out for themselves on issues that were important to them.

As the organization's president, Nora also encouraged women to become concerned citizens in their own communities and participate in municipal affairs by joining community organization boards. Nora believed it was important for women to be involved so their voices could be heard and recognized.[87] In 1972, she ran for Saskatoon City Council while her SNWM colleague Vicki Wilson ran for a position on the Saskatoon School Board. Both women recognized the need to educate the wider public on the issues facing Non-Status and Métis women and wanted to demonstrate to other Indigenous women how they might make their voices heard. Nora recalls that "[she] wanted to tell them...we can do things and we're able to do those things and especially women that are educated."[88] Nora was the first Indigenous person to run for Saskatoon City Council, and although unsuccessful, she was pleased with the results. Aiming for fifty votes, she received fifty-one, while Wilson lost in a close race. More importantly, she was excited to see the response from other women and their commitment to campaigning for her and Vicki: "You should have seen the response we got from our women. For our women to go out door-knocking. Our women were all for it. I couldn't believe it. They were a force, it was really something."[89] It was clear that women were becoming active, getting politicized, and making their concerns known.

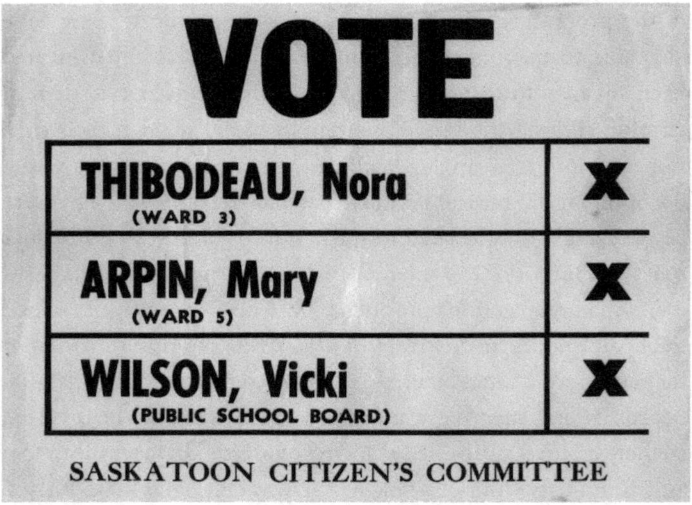

VOTE

THIBODEAU, Nora (WARD 3)	X
ARPIN, Mary (WARD 5)	X
WILSON, Vicki (PUBLIC SCHOOL BOARD)	X

SASKATOON CITIZEN'S COMMITTEE

FIG. 8.06. Saskatoon City Council Ballot, 1972.

Nora's activism and that of the SNWM were creating momentum. In 1974, she was part of the SNWM delegation representing Saskatchewan in organizing the national Indigenous women's organization, the Native Women's Association of Canada (NWAC), and sat on the NWAC's founding board of directors. The organization brought together Status and Non-Status First Nations and Métis women to focus on Indigenous women's issues on a national stage, including inequity for women under the Indian Act. In 1975, the SNWM changed its name to the Saskatchewan Native Women's Association. It was also this year that Nora's contributions to Métis women's leadership and activism were recognized by the City of Saskatoon's Civic Committee of the Status of

Women for International Women's Year in 1975.[90] She was the only Indigenous woman out of fifty recipients to receive this award.

By 1976, the SNWA had over one thousand members and already operated daycare centres, women's counselling and referral centres, programs for women in jail and halfway houses, and emergency shelters for women and children.[91] These houses were full every night, and the programs were deemed a success. Agnes Sinclair of Regina attributed the organization's success to the fact that programs were created by and for Indigenous women as they quickly "earned the reputation of being one of the most dynamic and responsible of Saskatchewan's Native Groups."[92] By 1982, the SNWA had a provincial membership of over three thousand and had locals established across the province, even as far north as Uranium City.[93] They had become the political voice of Saskatchewan Métis and Non-Status women.

Lessons of caring for women and the family instilled in Nora by her mother and koohkoom remained at the centre of her activism. While she credits her family and other women in the organization and leadership of the Métis Society both in Saskatoon and provincially for supporting her to do this work, she recognizes that not all women in the movement were so fortunate. As a result, she took great care to ensure that her colleagues felt supported.[94] She recalls that many of the women who got involved in the organization were dealing with issues such as addiction, poverty, unemployment, and domestic violence. Nora looked up to these women for their strength and courage and saw each of them as role models, valuing them for their experiences and expertise. They spoke from a position of knowing and understanding, she recalls: "We took them, women, under our wing because we felt that was what our issues were. We were dealing with our people that were suffering...we took these women in we brought them on board...we said you're valuable, we need your expertise, we need your knowledge, and we need you to help other young people that are going through this...they were our role models."[95]

FIG. 8.07. Nora in front of the Saskatoon City Transit bus shelter in front of Aden Bowman Collegiate on Clarence Avenue; the shelter is dedicated to the Métis families that lived on the road allowance in the area. The photograph was taken in 2021.

Throughout the 1980s, Nora continued to work on behalf of women through the SNWA and remained active in Local #11. Clarence became ill in 1987 and asked Nora to step in as Local #11's president. It was an honour that Clarence recognized her leadership ability.[96] She remained president until 1993 when she became a senator of the Métis Nation—Saskatchewan.[97] Nora has received much recognition for her work and has been awarded many awards throughout her career. In 2019, she received the Saskatoon Council of Women Hall of Fame Award, and in 2020 she received the Métis National Council's Order of the Métis Nation. The following year she received the Gabriel Dumont Institute's Order of Gabriel Dumont Gold Medal in recognition of a lifetime of outstanding service to the Métis in Canada. Today, she remains involved in the Saskatoon Métis community and Saskatoon civic affairs. She is a regular advisor to city officials, administrators, and community members. She was involved in the dedication of the Saskatoon Public Library's Round Prairie Branch, named for the Métis settlement of which she is a proud descendant. She was instrumental in the creation of a Saskatoon City Transit bus shelter honouring Métis history, culture, and heritage and a series of downtown bike racks that display Métis symbols.

Nora is recognized as a respected leader, mentor, and knowledge keeper and is a matriarch of the Métis community. She is a mother, grandmother, and great-grandmother. For those of us she brought together in 2018 to rebuild Local #11, she is the one who reminds us of our history and who we are as Métis people. She lives the values instilled in her by her mother, Irene, and Koohkoom Justine as well as by other women in her family as she continues to pass on the cultural teachings of sharing, visiting, and caring for one another as a family and a community.

NOTES

1. Lii vyeu means "Old Person" in Michif. I use this term as well as the term "Old People" at the suggestion of Métis community members. It is used as a sign of respect for an individual's age, wisdom, and knowledge.
2. For more on Métis road allowance communities see Campbell, *Halfbreed*; Zeileg and Zeileg, *Ste. Madeleine*; Barron, *Walking in Indian Moccasins*; Campbell, "Foreward: Charting the Way," xiii-xxvi; St. Pierre, *Remembering My Métis Past*; Peters, Stock, and Werner, *Rooster Town*; Troupe, "Mapping Métis Stories"; and Burley, "Rooster Town: Winnipeg's Lost Métis Suburbs."
3. Round Prairie is located on the east side of the South Saskatchewan River approximately thirty kilometres south of present-day Saskatoon. The site had been used by Métis buffalo hunters as early as the 1850s. By the 1860s and '70s, Métis families under the leadership of Charles Trottier were wintering at the site, eventually making it their year-round home as buffalo numbers declined. Numbering about twenty-five nuclear families, they were closely related, and at their core were a group of interrelated Laframboise women. For more on the Trottier hunting brigade at Round Prairie, see Troupe, "Métis Women"; and Macdougall and St-Onge, "Rooted in Mobility."
4. Troupe, "Métis Women"; Kay Mazer, interview by Cheryl Troupe, January 19, 2004; Nora Cummings interview by Cheryl Troupe, October 3, 2021. Oral histories and archival evidence suggest that Métis families faced significant racism and discrimination when accessing relief in Saskatoon. Relief agents were eager to disqualify Métis relief recipients based on their own prejudices. Agents often cut off recipients if they believed they did not truly need assistance or if they were abusing it. Recipients were cut off relief for taking a taxi cab, riding on a street car, or feeding others in their homes that were not their immediate family. In the early 1930s, relief was considered a local responsibility administered by cities or municipalities. This gave them considerable latitude in how relief officials monitored relief recipients and in provision or restriction of relief to those that needed it. For more on relief efforts in Saskatoon see Strikwerda, *The Wages of Relief*.
5. Nora Cummings, interview by Cheryl Troupe, January 14, 2008.
6. Cummings, 2008.
7. Cummings, 2008.
8. Anderson, *Life Stages and Native Women*.
9. Troupe, "Métis Women," 81.

10 Troupe, "Métis Women."
11 Nora Cummings, unpublished memoir, 2021, courtesy of Nora Cummings.
12 Nora Cummings, unpublished memoir, 2021.
13 Nora Cummings, unpublished memoir, 2021.
14 Nora Cummings, unpublished memoir, 2021.
15 Cummings, 2008.
16 Cummings, 2008.
17 Cummings, October 2021.
18 Cummings, October 2021.
19 Cummings, October 2021.
20 Cummings, October 2021; and Cummings, 2008.
21 Cummings, October 2021.
22 The Round Prairie families were closely related to Gabriel Dumont. His parents were Isadore Dumont and Louise Laframboise. Louise was a sister to Jean Baptiste Laframboise, father of Ursule, Angelique, and Philomene. These three sisters were married to Moise Landry and to brothers Charles and Antoine Trottier, all of whom hunted together under the leadership of Charles Trottier. For a time, Isadore and Louise and their children lived and hunted with the Trottier Brigade. See Troupe, "Métis Women".
23 Nora Cummings and Peter Bishop, interview by Ron Laliberte (02), transcript, Saskatoon: Gabriel Dumont Institute, February 28–29, 2004, GDI media filename 05903, Virtual Museum of Métis History and Culture, Gabriel Dumont Institute, accessed September 2022, https://www.metismuseum.ca/media/document.php/05903.C,%20B,%20and%20L%20(02).pdf, 4; Payment, *The Free People*.
24 Troupe, "Métis Women."
25 Schilling, *Gabriel's Children*, 145–48.
26 Schilling, *Gabriel's Children*, 148–49.
27 Troupe, "Métis Women"; Stevenson and Troupe, "From Kitchen Tables to Formal Organization"; Irene Dimick, interview by Judy Thibodeau, transcript, Saskatoon: Gabriel Dumont Institute, February 17, 1984, GDI media filename 01069, Virtual Museum of Métis History and Culture, Gabriel Dumont Institute, accessed September 2022, https://www.metismuseum.ca/media/document.php/01069.Dimick,%20Irene%20(Judy%20Thibodeau).pdf, 39–40.
28 Irene Dimick, interview by Judy Thibodeau, transcript, Saskatoon: Gabriel Dumont Institute, February 17, 1984, GDI media filename 01069, Virtual Museum of Métis History and Culture, Gabriel Dumont Institute,

accessed September 2022, https://www.metismuseum.ca/media/document.php/01069.Dimick,%20Irene%20(Judy%20Thibodeau).pdf, 39–40.

29 Marge Laframboise, interview by Karen Trotchie, transcript, Saskatoon: Gabriel Dumont Institute, February 19, 1984, GDI media filename 01051, Virtual Museum of Métis History and Culture, Gabriel Dumont Institute, accessed September 2022, https://www.metismuseum.ca/media/document.php/01051.LaFramboise,%20Marge%20(K.%20Trot.).pdf., 17. Marge Laframboise's father, Peter Trotchie, was the ex-husband of Justine Trotchie and Nora's grandfather. Justine and Peter were known to have an amicable relationship after they split. Nora credits Justine with teaching her lessons of forgiveness in how she was able to develop a friendly relationship with her ex-husband.

30 Schilling, *Gabriel's Children*, 158.
31 Cummings, 2008.
32 Cummings, 2008.
33 Cummings, 2008.
34 Nora Cummings, interview by Cheryl Troupe, November 12, 2021.
35 Cummings, November 2021.
36 Cummings, November 2021.
37 Cummings, November 2021.
38 Cummings, October 2021.
39 Cummings, October 2021.
40 Cummings, November 2021.
41 Donna Pinay, "Native Alcohol Council," *New Breed Magazine*, February-March 1977, 4, Archival Collection, *New Breed Magazine*, 2002, GDI media filename New Breed (02) February/March 1977, Virtual Museum of Métis History and Culture, Gabriel Dumont Institute, accessed December 1, 2023. https://www.metismuseum.ca/media/document.php/05117.1977%20(02)%20FebMar.pdf.
42 Pinay, "Native Alcohol Council."
43 Schilling, *So Many to Be Remembered*, 42.
44 Kermoal, "Navigating Troubled Political Waters"; Weinstein, *Quiet Revolution West*.
45 Adese, "Restoring the Balance"; Saunders and Dubois, *Métis Politics and Governance in Canada*, 108–9; Troupe, "Métis Women."
46 Troupe, "Métis Women," 119–23.
47 Fred Schoenthal, "Native Alcohol Council," *New Breed Magazine*, October 1974, 7, Archival Collection, *New Breed Magazine*, GDI media filename New Breed (02) October 1974, Virtual Museum of Métis History and Culture, Gabriel Dumont Institute, accessed December 1,

2023, https://www.metismuseum.ca/media/document.php/
04217.1974%20(02)%20October.pdf; Roy Romanow, "Press Release,"
New Breed Magazine, December 1973, 15, Archival Collection, *New
Breed Magazine*, GDI media filename New Breed (09) December
1973, Virtual Museum of Métis History and Culture, Gabriel Dumont
Institute, accessed December 1, 2023, https://www.metismuseum.ca/
media/document.php/04215.1973%20(09)%20December.pdf. Local #11
and Friendship Centre Programs were often offered jointly because
of the overlapping nature of the leadership of these organizations. For
instance, in the early 1970s, Clarence Trotchie was the president of both.
Offering joint programs was an effective and cost-efficient strategy that
avoided the duplication of service delivery.

48 Cummings, 2008.
49 Cummings, November 2021.
50 Cummings, November 2021.
51 Schilling, *Gabriel's Children*, 162.
52 Kay Mazer, interview by Cheryl Troupe, April 27, 2006.
53 Cummings, November 2021.
54 Cummings, November 2021.
55 Cummings, November 2021.
56 Cummings, November 2021.
57 Cummings, November 2021.
58 Cummings, November 2021.
59 Phyllis Trotchie for Nora Cummings, Letter of Invitation to November 1972 Conference, September 26, 1972, courtesy of Nora Cummings; "Women's Answers," *New Breed Magazine*, December 1971, 3, Archival Collection, *New Breed Magazine*, GDI media filename New Breed (12) November–December 1971, Virtual Museum of Métis History and Culture, Gabriel Dumont Institute, accessed December 1, 2023, https://www.metismuseum.ca/media/document.php/148256.New%20Breed%20-%20Nov%20Dec%201971%20Low-Res.pdf.
60 Cummings, November 2021.
61 Nora Cummings and Peter Bishop, interview by Ron Laliberte (14), transcript, Gabriel Dumont Institute, February 28–29, 2004, GDI media filename 05915, Virtual Museum of Métis History and Culture, Gabriel Dumont Institute, accessed September 2022, https://www.metismuseum.ca/media/document.php/05915.C,%20B,%20and%20L%20(14).pdf, 3–4.
62 "Native Women's Movement," *New Breed Magazine*, November 1972, 12, Archival Collection, *New Breed Magazine*, GDI media filename

New Breed (11) November 1972, Virtual Museum of Métis History and Culture, Gabriel Dumont Institute, accessed December 1, 2023, https://www.metismuseum.ca/media/document.php/04203.(07)%201972%20November.pdf.

63 Nora Cummings and Peter Bishop, interview by Ron Laliberte (14), 3–4.
64 "Native Women's Movement," *New Breed Magazine*, November 1972, 12; "Native Women's Movement," *New Breed Magazine*, February 1973, 8, Archival Collection, *New Breed Magazine*, GDI media filename New Breed (02) February 1973, Virtual Museum of Métis History and Culture, Gabriel Dumont Institute, accessed December 1, 2023, https://www.metismuseum.ca/media/document.php/04207.1973%20(02)%20February.pdf. In addition to Nora being elected president, Betty Roy was elected as treasurer, Doris Sparvier as secretary, and Vicki Wilson as coordinator. The Board also consisted of Mary Anne LaVallee, Carlin Goodwill, Lillian Knight, Alice Poitras, Mabel Landry, and Rose Boyer. Hazel Demage was elected as a youth representative and Georgina Fisher as a liaison officer. Leona Blondeau, Irene Dimick, Helen Shingoose, Florence Desnomie, Dianne Tootoosis, Ann Goulet, Doreen Sinclair, Emily Jones, and Glenice Zatorski were elected as provincial fieldworkers.
65 Phyllis Trotchie for Nora Cummings, Letter of Invitation to November 1972 Conference, September 26, 1972.
66 Cummings, 2008. Gabriel Housing Corporation is a Métis-governed non-profit corporation in Regina that provides safe and affordable homes for Métis.
67 Cummings, November 2021.
68 Anderson, "Affirmations of an Indigenous Feminist," 81.
69 Anderson, "Affirmations of an Indigenous Feminist," 81.
70 Cummings, 2008.
71 Cummings, November 2021.
72 Nora Cummings and Peter Bishop, interview by Ron Laliberte (14), 5.
73 Cummings, November 2021.
74 Stevenson and Troupe, "From Kitchen Tables to Formal Organization."
75 Cummings, November 2021.
76 Cummings, November 2021.
77 Cummings, November 2021.
78 Nora Cummings and Peter Bishop, interview by Ron Laliberte (16), transcript, Saskatoon: Gabriel Dumont Institute, February 28–29, 2004, GDI media filename 05917, Virtual Museum of Métis History and Culture, Gabriel Dumont Institute, accessed September 2022, https://

www.metismuseum.ca/media/document.php/05917.C,%20B,%20 and%20L%20(16).pdf, 3.
79 Cummings, November 2021.
80 Nora Thibodeau, Phyllis Trotchie, and Vicki Racette, "Métis Foster Home Plan: Saskatoon," *New Breed Magazine*, November 1971, 5, Archival Collection, *New Breed Magazine*, GDI media filename New Breed (11) November 1971, Virtual Museum of Métis History and Culture, Gabriel Dumont Institute, accessed December 1, 2023, https://www.metismuseum.ca/media/document.php/06958.Binder1.pdf.
81 Cummings, November 2021.
82 Stevenson, *Intimate Integration*, 178–99.
83 Stevenson, *Intimate Integration*; "Native Women's Movement," *New Breed Magazine*, April 1973, 12, Archival Collection, *New Breed Magazine*, GDI media filename New Breed (04) April 1973, Virtual Museum of Métis History and Culture, Gabriel Dumont Institute, accessed December 1, 2023, https://www.metismuseum.ca/media/document.php/04210.1973%20(04)%20April.pdf.
84 Stevenson, *Intimate Integration*.
85 This case has been the focus of the CBC podcast *Missing & Murdered: Finding Cleo*, accessed October 2022, https://www.cbc.ca/radio/findingcleo.
86 Cummings, November 2021.
87 Cummings, November 2021.
88 Cummings, November 2021.
89 Cummings, November 2021.
90 Saskatoon Civic Committee on the Status of Women, "Honouring Outstanding Women of Saskatoon—Program," November 26, 1975, courtesy of Nora Cummings.
91 Leanne McKay, "Saskatchewan Native Women's Association," *New Breed Magazine*, September/October 1976, 5, Archival Collection, *New Breed Magazine*, GDI media filename New Breed (06) September/October 1976, Virtual Museum of Métis History and Culture, Gabriel Dumont Institute, accessed December 1, 2023, https://www.metismuseum.ca/media/document.php/05121.1976%20SepOct.pdf.; "Saskatchewan Native Women's Association," *New Breed Magazine*, April 1975, 5. Archival Collection, *New Breed Magazine*, GDI media filename New Breed (03) April 1975, Virtual Museum of Métis History and Culture, Gabriel Dumont Institute, accessed December 1, 2023, https://www.metismuseum.ca/media/document.php/05116.1975%20(3)%20April.pdf.
92 McKay, "Saskatchewan Native Women's Association," 5.

93   DiLella, "Liberating Community Education and Social Change."
94   Cummings, November 2021.
95   Cummings, November 2021.
96   Nora Cummings and Peter Bishop, interview by Ron Laliberte (31), transcript, Gabriel Dumont Institute, February 28–29, 2004, GDI media filename 06139, Virtual Museum of Métis History and Culture, Gabriel Dumont Institute, accessed September 2022, https://www.metismuseum.ca/media/document.php/06139.C,%20B,%20and%20L%20(31).pdf, 2.
97   Nora Cummings and Peter Bishop, interview by Ron Laliberte (31), 2.

Conclusion

Our goal in this collection has been to complicate the story of Canadian nation building from the perspective of Métis women's lived experiences during the height of the fur trade and into the transitional period that followed. While the featured matriarchs each have unique life histories, their stories speak to the strength of Métis women as matriarchs in their families and the strength of Métis culture, identity, and family networks. Their actions and experiences add perspective on the role and autonomy of matriarchs in Métis communities in the nineteenth and twentieth centuries and expose the myriad responsibilities Métis women had in their families and communities over the course of their lives, particularly as they aged.

While these stories demonstrate the significant presence and impact of the state in Métis lives in the nineteenth and early twentieth century, they reveal the persistence of kinship networks as the fur trade transitioned to a more sedentary industrialized and agricultural economy. These stories also uncover a remarkable picture of resistance, resilience, and cultural survival. They speak to the reality that Métis women utilized their role as matriarchs as they adapted to social, economic, and political changes brought about by development of the West. These women overcame economic changes, political resistance and upheaval, settlement pressure, loss of land, displacement, relocation, family trauma, racism, and loss while consistently adapting, resisting, and challenging the changes they faced. These women responded in dynamic, independent, and extraordinary ways while drawing upon their autonomy as matriarchs to keep their families and kinship networks strong. It is clear from their actions that the well-being of the family was always in mind.

The centrality of family is consistent across these women's lives and is extended to the sources and perspectives from which these biographies emerge. The authors have relied heavily on conversations with Métis family members, personal memoirs, family-held letters and stories, oral histories, photographs, personal papers not held in archival collections, and items of material culture to trace the stories of these women's lives. Each case study demonstrates a commitment to reading and rereading these sources and the existing archival record in new ways, looking for the voices of Métis matriarchs and their families. This family-centred biographical case study approach offers important insights to understanding Métis lived experiences and histories and the role of women and Métis matriarchs as active agents of transition.

This family-centred approach is grounded in relationships each author has to the families of the women they write about, and to the matriarchs themselves. Doris Jeanne MacKinnon and Vanessa Winn's contributions are new interpretations of Matriarchs Marie Rose Delorme Smith and Josette Lagacé Work, who the authors know intimately through the archival record and having written about in the past. Authors Jade McDougall, Gabrielle Legault, and Janice Cindy Gaudet share personal family stories of Matriarchs Caroline McNabb, Julia Lamotte, and Auxile Lepine held in memory and pieced together through traces of family lore, conversation, reminiscences, cherished mementos, and photographs, while authors Madalyn Mandzuik, Allyson Stevenson, and Cheryl Troupe leverage personal relationships, drawing heavily on conversations with family and community members of the matriarch they study and conversations with contemporary matriarchs themselves. Mandzuik writes in close conversation with descendants of nineteenth century matriarch Victoria Belcourt Callihoo, adding their voices in interpreting Callihoo's history, while Stevenson writes in dialogue with Cumberland House community members, matriarchs, and the beaded items of material culture produced in, and ultimately re-matriated to, the community. Last, Troupe draws on long-standing community relationships, ongoing conversations with matriarch Nora Cummings, and on records Cummings has amassed in her social and political activism. Collectively, these authors uplift Métis voices and inspire further research with and about Métis matriarchs.

Marie Rose Delorme Smith and Victoria Callihoo had a desire to leave a written record of their experiences, first while following the buffalo herds and later while taking up land and becoming farmers and ranchers. As MacKinnon and Mandzuik argue, these women navigated changing economies, identities, and geographies, ultimately succeeding to differing degrees in new agricultural and ranching pursuits and in extending their family networks to include non-Indigenous newcomers. This success garnered them significant respect in their respective communities. The contributions Callihoo and Delorme Smith made through their writing was particularly rare in the early twentieth century and remains significant. Indeed, Marie Rose was recently designated by Parks Canada as a person of national historic significance.

Vanessa Winn's exploration of Josette Lagacé Work's life extends our understanding of place to Canada's West Coast, as that westernmost province transitioned from colony into confederation.

Born in 1809, Work's life spanned almost the entire nineteenth century. The child of a fur trade father, Work married an officer in the HBC, adapting to the lifestyle of brigade journeys. She and her family eventually settled on a large estate in colonial Victoria, British Columbia. Referred to as someone who was "strong and elastic as steel," Josette Work's network of ties helped her rise to the position of matriarch who supported a large extended family. After her death in 1896, the premier of British Columbia recognized Josette as an honoured and respected pioneer of the province.

While less publicly recognized than Calihoo, Delorme Smith, or Work, Matriarch Caroline McNabb's legacy is no less significant. Told from the perspective of her great-granddaughter Jade (J.D.) McDougall, McNabb emerges as a strong and powerful figure who demonstrated stewardship for her extended community in the South Saskatchewan River region. Relying on community history publications and oral histories, McDougall asks us to consider what it means to be a matriarch. Although McNabb did not raise a large family of her own, she modelled matriarchs in her own kin circle as she practised adoption and knowledge-sharing. For her great-granddaughter, and for readers, sharing the stories of Caroline's network of descendants provides insights into the dynamics of Métis kinship in the context of geographic mobility and social change.

Author Gabrielle Legault similarly weaves family oral history and archival collections to explore the life of her great-grandmother Julia Fayant Lamotte. Speaking to the importance of material culture in understanding the contributions of Métis matriarchs, Legault notes that items such as pheasant feather hats, cattle-hides, and birchbark baskets converge to piece together the life of "Grandma Julia," intricately linked to place. Legault traces the history of her great-grandmother through the lens of traditional land lost to colonization. For some, this meant settling along the road allowances to extend community into new geographic areas. In detailing the complicated life of her grandmother, Legault demonstrates the often-paradoxical position of Métis women as living "between and among societies," as they transitioned from "old ways" to sedentary lives no longer governed by the cyclical nature of following the herds.

Like McDougall and Legault, Gaudet writes from a personal perspective, exploring the lives and stories of her maymairs and aunties, focusing on her maymair Auxile Lepine to understand the efforts and success of Métis women in resisting patriarchal and racist attitudes. As Gaudet notes, grounded in the connection of kinship love, land, and resistance, the strength of generations of Métis matriarchal resistance emerges to serve as a guiding force for sovereignty, including her own. Arguing that Métis women were born to women of resistance both during and after 1885, and despite the reality that women were increasingly seen as inferior in the face of Victorian patriarchal dominance, Gaudet demonstrates that Métis women actually held household and political authority. Through the lens of women's traditional roles, Gaudet argues that Métis women such as Auxile exercised food sovereignty and entrepreneurship to establish and maintain their roles as matriarchs. In visiting and reconnecting with the lands of her maymair, Gaudet herself experiences and embodies her familial matriarch's sovereignty.

In a broader case study approach, author Allyson Stevenson explores the Métis matriarchs of Cumberland House through the material culture that has been preserved in the Cotter collection. Stevenson's approach helps us to appreciate the historic matriarchal roles that continue to impact the cultural, social, political, and economic lives of Métis communities today. Her study emphasizes the work of artists woven together with scholarship by intellectuals and Indigenous historians in a way that preserves the intergenerational transmission of knowledge and describes its impacts on contemporary artists and community members. As Stevenson notes, oral histories and material artifacts combine to reveal patterns for Métis women in their roles as leaders, knowledge holders, intellectuals, artists, and economic agents.

From a unique and innovative perspective, author Cheryl Troupe introduces readers to community activist and matriarch Nora Cummings. Challenging the patriarchal structures imposed by the state's colonial ideology of patriarchy, Nora re-establishes the historical role of Métis women as central to the political life of Métis communities. Nora, living as a child in a road allowance community, is symbolic of the perseverance of Métis people who, between the late nineteenth and mid-twentieth centuries, were often relegated to the margins by the Canadian state. Acknowledging the abject poverty endured in many of the Métis communities that emerged throughout the Prairies, sharing stories such as Nora's demonstrates the ability of Métis people to preserve and rely on their cultural traditions and kin connections to inspire political and social activism that continues to restore agency to generations of Métis.

These biographies give voice to stories of matriarchs held in memory and esteem by their families and communities. These stories pick up what others, namely Victoria Belcourt Calihoo and Marie Rose Delorme Smith, put down, elevating Métis voices in writing and writing Métis women matriarchs into history, one story at a time. These life stories demonstrate the legacy and enduring significance of Métis matriarchs today. However, as much as this collection provides insight into the lives of strong and resilient Métis matriarchs, it also invites us to further engage in the countless untold stories of Métis women. The family-centred biographical approach and the knowledge gathered about these women suggests that there is much more to be learned about the specific lives, impacts, resilience, and agency of countless other Métis matriarchs.

About the Contributors

Dr. **Janice Cindy Gaudet** is an Auntie, Sister and Kokum who belongs to a strong lineage of Métis women's families along the South Saskatchewan River and from farming communities near Bellevue, Batoche, St. Laurent, St. Louis, and One Arrow, Saskatchewan. She is an Associate Professor at the University of Alberta, and Métis women's expression of sovereignty is at the forefront of her health and well-being research.

Gabrielle Legault is Métis from Saskatchewan, a citizen of Métis Nation BC, and a member of the Kelowna Métis Association. She works as an Assistant Professor of Indigenous Studies at UBC Okanagan in Syilx Territory. Her research centres on community-led collaborations with Métis and Friendship Centres focusing on Indigenous identities, belonging, and well-being.

Doris Jeanne MacKinnon was born on a farm in northeastern Alberta and attended school in the historic town of St. Paul-des-Métis. She has a PhD in Indigenous and post-Confederation Canadian history and an MEd in Adult Education. An independent researcher and postsecondary instructor, she lives in Alberta.

Madalyn Mandziuk holds a BA Hons. in History from the University of Alberta. Madalyn is currently a research assistant at the Institute of Prairie and Indigenous Archaeology and a Juris Doctor candidate at the University of Alberta in the Faculty of Law.

Dr. **Jade McDougall** is a citizen of Métis Nation–Saskatchewan, who recently completed a doctoral dissertation on Métis family narratives within community history volumes from the Red Deer Hill area. Jade is currently an Assistant Professor in the Department of Indigenous Studies at the University of Saskatchewan.

Allyson Stevenson (Métis) is an Assistant Professor in the Department of Indigenous Studies at the University of Saskatchewan and the Gabriel Dumont Research Chair in Métis Studies.

Cheryl Troupe is an Assistant Professor in the Department of History at the University of Saskatchewan. She has a PhD in History and an MA in Indigenous Studies. Cheryl Troupe is Métis from north-central Saskatchewan.

Dedicated to recovering women from the gaps of history, **Vanessa Winn** is the author of two novels portraying real people in nineteenth-century British Columbia and inspired by literature of the era. Featuring primary-source quotes prefacing each chapter and including bibliographies, her novels have been studied in BC university courses and museums.

Bibliography

"About the Delta: Geography & Ecology." Sask River Delta Conservation Initiative. Accessed December 15, 2023. https://www.saskriverdelta.com/geography.

Acoose, Janice. *Iskwewak—Kah' Ki Yaw Ni Wahkomakanak: Neither Indian Princesses nor Easy Squaws*. Toronto: Women's Press, 1995.

Adams, Christopher, Gregg Dahl, and Ian Peach, eds. *Métis in Canada: History, Identity, Law & Politics*. Edmonton: University of Alberta Press, 2013.

Adese, Jennifer. "Restoring the Balance: Métis Women and Contemporary Nationalist Political Organizing." In *A People and a Nation: New Directions in Contemporary Métis Studies*, edited by Jennifer Adese and Chris Andersen, 115–45. Vancouver: UBC Press, 2021.

Anderson, Anne. *The First Metis: A New Nation*. Edmonton: Uvisco Press, 1985.

Anderson, Kim. "Affirmations of an Indigenous Feminist." In *Indigenous Women and Feminism: Politics, Activism, Culture*, edited by Cheryl Suzack, Shari M. Huhndorf, Jeanne Perreault, and Jean Barman, 81–91. Vancouver: UBC Press, 2010.

———. *Life Stages and Native Women: Memory, Teachings, and Story Medicine*. Winnipeg: University of Manitoba Press, 2011.

———. *A Recognition of Being: Reconstructing Native Womanhood*. Toronto: Women's Press, 2016.

Anderson, Kim, Maria Campbell, and Christi Belcourt, eds. *Keetsahnak: Our Missing and Murdered Indigenous Sisters*. Edmonton: University of Alberta Press, 2018.

"Appalled by Fever." *Washington Historical Quarterly* 2, no. 2 (January 1908): 163–64. http://www.jstor.org/stable/40473859.

Armstrong, Jeannette. "Invocation: The Real Power of Aboriginal Women." In Miller and Churchryk, *Women of the First Nations*, ix–xii.

Augustus, Camie. "Métis Scrip." *Our Legacy*. University of Saskatchewan. Last modified 2008. https://digital.scaa.sk.ca/ourlegacy/exhibit_scrip.

Bancroft, Hubert Howe. *Literary Industries*. San Francisco: History Co., 1890.

Barkwell, Lawrence. "Descendants of Daniel Lillie (1780–1858)." Scribd, Inc. No date. Accessed January 13, 2024. https://www.scribd.com/document/369112964/Descendants-of-Daniel-Lillie/.

Barkwell, Lawrence J., and Leah Marie Dorion with Anne Carrière-Acco, eds. *Women of the Métis Nation*. Saskatoon: Gabriel Dumont Institute, 2009.

Barkwell, Lawrence J., Leah Dorion, and Darren R. Préfontaine, eds. *Metis Legacy: A Metis Historiography and Annotated Bibliography*. Winnipeg: Pemmican Publications, 2003.

Barron, F. Laurie. "The CCF and the Development of Métis Colonies in Southern Saskatchewan During the Premiership of T.C. Douglas, 1944–1961." *Canadian Journal of Native Studies* 10, no. 2 (1990): 243–72.

———. *Walking in Indian Moccasins: The Native Policies of Tommy Douglas and the CCF*. Vancouver: UBC Press, 1997.

Belcourt, Herb. *Walking in the Woods: A Métis Journey*. Alberta: Brindle & Glass, 2006.

Berggren, Daisy. "George Kirkness." In Larsen, ed., *A Homesteader's Dream*, 396–97.

———. "John Edward Cook." In Larsen, ed., *A Homesteader's Dream*, 353–34.

Berggren, Daisy, and Clayton Kirkness. "Kirkness, George Thomas and Caroline." In Tait and Olson, eds., *Communities of Courage and Cordwood*, 203–5.

Blanke, Cecile. *Lac Pelletier: My Métis Home*. Saskatoon: Gabriel Dumont Institute, 2019.

Brown, Jennifer S.H. *Strangers in Blood: Fur Trade Company Families in Indian Country*. Vancouver: UBC Press, 1996.

———. "Woman as Centre and Symbol in the Emergence of Métis Communities." *Canadian Journal of Native Studies* 3, no. 1 (1983): 39–46.

Burley, David G. "Rooster Town: Winnipeg's Lost Métis Suburbs, 1900–1960." *Urban History Review* 42, no. 1 (October 2013): 3–25.

Burnett, Kristin. *Taking Medicine: Women's Healing Work in Colonial Contact in Southern Alberta, 1880–1930*. Vancouver: UBC Press, 2010.

Buss, Helen. "Constructing Female Subjects in the Archive: A Reading of Three Versions of One Woman's Subjectivity." In *Working Women's Archives: Researching Women's Private Literature and Archival Documents*, edited by Helen Buss and Marlene Kadar, 23–34. Toronto: York University, 2004.

Calahoo Women's Institute. *Calahoo Trails: A History of Calahoo, Granger, Speldhurst, Noyes Crossing, East Bibly, Green Willow 1842–1955*. 1955. Retrieved from https://digitalcollections.ucalgary.ca/archive/Calahoo-Trail--A-history-of-Calahoo--Granger--Speldhurst--Noyes-Crossing--East-Bibly--Green-Willo--1842-1955-2R3BF1FJW32G9.html.

Callihoo, Mrs. Vital V. "History of the Louis Callihoo Family." In *As the Roots Grow: The History of Spruce Grove and District*, edited by Esther Lunan, 308–10. Spruce Grove, AB: Spruce Grove Public Library, 1979.

Callihoo, Victoria. "The Early Life." *Windspeaker* 6, no. 7. (April 22, 1988): 12–13. https://www.windspeaker.com/sites/default/files/2019-12/April%2022%2C%201988.pdf

———. "Early Life in Lac Ste. Anne and St. Albert in the Early 1870s." *Alberta Historical Review* 1, no. 3 (1953): 21–26.

———. "The Iroquois in Alberta." *Alberta Historical Review* 7, no. 2 (1959): 17–18.

———. "Our Buffalo Hunts." *Alberta Historical Review* 8, no. 1 (1960): 24–25.

Campbell, Maria. *Halfbreed*, 2nd ed. Toronto: McClelland and Stewart, 2018.

——. "Foreward: Charting the Way." In *Contours of a People: Métis Family, Mobility, and History*, edited by Nicole St-Onge, Carolyn Podruchny, and Brenda Macdougall, xiii–xxvi. Norman: University of Oklahoma Press, 2012.

Carpenter, Jock. *Fifty Dollar Bride: Marie Rose Smith—A Chronicle of Métis Life in the 19th Century*. Sidney, BC: Gray's, 1977.

Carrière-Acco, Anne. "Ki-Naan'how, Ki'ghis-Skan, Ni-t'hamhowin Eko Ki-t'haski-Nhow: Ni-Naan Muskay-Ghun Ininiwok Eko Apti-Ghosan Ininiwok, Cumberland Waski-Ghun Ochi Traditional Knowledge and the Land: The Cumberland House Métis and Cree People." In Barkwell, Dorion, and Préfontaine, *Metis Legacy*, 127–34.

Carter, Sarah. *Imperial Plots: Women, Land, and the Spadework of British Colonialism on the Canadian Prairies*. Winnipeg: University of Manitoba Press, 2016.

——. *The Importance of Being Monogamous: Marriage and Nation Building in Canada to 1915*. Edmonton: University of Alberta Press, 2008.

——. "The Montana Memories of Emma Minesinger: Windows on the Family, Work, and Boundary Culture of a Borderlands Woman." In *Recollecting: Lives of Aboriginal Women of the Canadian Northwest and Borderlands*, edited by Sarah Carter and Patricia A. McCormack, 197–221. Edmonton: Athabasca University Press, 2011.

Carter, Sarah, Lesley Erickson, Patricia Roome, and Char Smith, eds. *Unsettled Pasts: Reconceiving the West through Women's History*. Calgary: University of Calgary Press, 2005.

Carter, Sarah, and Patricia A. McCormack. "Lifelines: Searching for Aboriginal Women of the Northwest and Borderlands." In *Recollecting: Lives of Aboriginal Women of the Canadian Northwest and Borderlands*, edited by Sarah Carter and Patricia A. McCormack, 5–25. Edmonton: Athabasca University Press, 2011.

Colpitts, George. *Pemmican Empire: Food, Trade, and the Last Bison Hunts in the Northern Plains, 1780–1882*. New York: Cambridge University Press, 2015.

Cox, Ross. *The Columbia River; Or scenes and adventures during a residence of six years on the western side of the Rocky Mountains among various tribes of Indians hitherto unknown; together with "A Journey across the American Continent."* Edited by Edgar I. Stewart and Jane R. Stewart. Norman: University of Oklahoma Press, 1957.

Crawford, John. "Speaking Michif in Four Métis Communities." *Canadian Journal of Native Studies* 3, no. 1 (1985): 47–55.

Cronlund Anderson, Mark, and Carmen L. Robertson. *Seeing Red: A History of Natives in Canadian Newspapers*. Winnipeg: University of Manitoba Press, 2011.

Crooks, Drew W. "Pierre Lagace: The Life of an Extraordinary Hudson's Bay Company Man." *Occurrences* (Summer 2009). Tacoma, WA.

Daniels, Judy D. ed. *Métis Memories of Residential Schools*. Edmonton: Métis Nation of Alberta, 2004.

Daschuk, James W. *Clearing the Plains: Disease, Politics of Starvation, and the Loss of Aboriginal Life*. Regina: University of Regina Press, 2013.

Dee, Henry Drummond. "An Irishman in the Fur Trade: The Life and Journals of John Work." *British Columbia Historical Quarterly* 7, no. 4 (1943).

Devine, Heather. *The People Who Own Themselves: Aboriginal Ethnogenesis in a Canadian Family, 1660–1900*. Calgary: University of Calgary Press, 2004.

DiLella, Anne-Marie. "Liberating Community Education and Social Change: The Regina Native Women's Group (1971–1986)." MA thesis, University of Saskatchewan, 1989.

Donald, Leland. *Aboriginal Slavery on the Northwest Coast of North America*. Berkeley: University of California Press, 1997.

Dorion, Leah. "Opikinawasowin: The Life Long Process of Growing Cree and Metis Children." MA thesis, Athabasca University, 2010.

Douglas, David. *Journal kept by David Douglas during his travels in North America, 1823-1827: together with a particular description of thirty-three species of American oaks and eighteen species of Pinus, with appendices containing a list of the plants introduced by Douglas and an account of his death in 1834*. London: W. Wesley & Son, for the Royal Horticultural Society, 1914.

Douglas, James. *Fort Victoria Letters, 1846–1851*. Edited by Hartwell Bowsfield. Winnipeg: Hudson's Bay Record Society, 1979.

Dupuis, Renée, and Alan C. Holman. "Indian Claims Commission Cumberland House Cree Nation IR 100A Inquiry." Ottawa: Canada Indian Claims Commissions, March 2005. Government of Canada Publication, https://publications.gc.ca/site/eng/9.687844/publication.html.

Dye, Eva Emery. *McDonald of Oregon: A Tale of Two Shores*. Chicago: A.C. McClurg, 1906.

Elliott, T.C. "Journal of John Work, Dec. 15th, 1825, to June 12th, 1826." *Washington Historical Quarterly* 5, no. 4 (October 1914): 258–287.

Ens, Gerhard J. *Homeland to Hinterland: The Changing Worlds of the Red River Métis in the Nineteenth Century*. Toronto: University of Toronto Press, 1996.

Ens, Gerhard J., and Joe Sawchuk. *From New Peoples to New Nations: Aspects of Métis History and Identity from the Eighteenth to the Twenty-first Centuries*. Toronto: University of Toronto Press, 2016.

Erickson, Lesley. "At the Cultural and Religious Crossroads: Sara Riel and the Grey Nuns in the Canadian Northwest, 1848–1883." MA thesis, University of Calgary, 1997.

———. "'Bury Our Sorrows in the Sacred Heart': Gender and the Metis Response to Colonialism—The Case of Sara and Louis Riel, 1848–83." In *Unsettled Pasts: Reconceiving the West through Women's History*, edited by Sarah Carter, Lesley Erickson, Patricia Roome, and Char Smith, 17–46. Calgary: University of Calgary Press, 2005.

Farrell Racette, Sherry. "Beads, Silk and Quills: The Clothing and Decorative Arts of the Metis." In Barkwell, Dorion, and Préfontaine, *Metis Legacy*, 181–187.

———. "Looking for Stories and Unbroken Threads: Museum Artifacts as Women's History and Cultural Legacy." In *Restoring the Balance: First Nations Women, Community, and Culture*, edited by Gail Guthrie Valaskakis, Eric Guimond, and Madeleine Dion Stout, 283–312. Winnipeg: University of Manitoba Press, 2000.

———. "My Grandmothers Loved to Trade: The Indigenization of European Trade Goods in Historic and Contemporary Canada."

Journal of Museum Ethnography no. 20 (2008): 69–81. https://www.jstor.org/stable/40793871.

———. "Nimble Fingers and Strong Backs." In *Indigenous Women and Work: from Labour to Activism*, edited by Carol Williams. Chicago: University of Illinois Press, 2012.

———. "Sewing for a Living: The Commodification of Metis Women's Artistic Production." In *Contact Zones: Aboriginal and Setter Women in Canada's Colonial Past*, edited by Myra Rutherdale and Katie Pickles, 17–46. Vancouver: UBC Press, 2005.

Farrell Racette, Sherry, in conversation with Alan Corbiere and Crystal Migwans. "Pieces Left along the Trail: Material Cultural Histories and Indigenous Studies." In *Sources and Methods in Indigenous Studies*, edited by Chris Andersen and Jean O'Brien, 223–29. London, New York: Routledge, 2017.

Flaminio, Anna Louisa. "Gladue through wahkotowin: Social History Through Cree Kinship Lens in Corrections and Parole." LLM thesis, University of Saskatchewan, 2013. Harvest, https://harvest.usask.ca/handle/10388/ETD-2013-03-1039.

Foggo, Cheryl. "Assembling Auntie: Illuminating a Long-Forgotten Pioneer." *Alberta Views* 12, no. 1 (January/February 2009): 34–39.

Fortier, Alfred. "Urbain Delorme: L'Homme riche des prairies." *Bulletin de la Societe historique de Saint-Boniface* 3 (1995): 3–8.

Foster, Martha Harroun. *We Know Who We Are: Métis Identity in a Montana Community*. Norman: University of Oklahoma Press, 2006.

Foster, Tol. "Of One Blood: An Argument for Relations and Regionality in Native American Literary Studies." In *Reasoning Together: The Native Critics Collective*, edited by Craig S. Womack, Daniel Heath Justice, and Christopher B. Teuton, 265–302. Tulsa: University of Oklahoma Press, 2008.

Fowke, Edith, ed. *The Penguin Book of Canadian Folk Songs*. Markham: Penguin Books Canada, 1986.

Gabriel Dumont Institute. "Our Shared Inheritance: Traditional Métis Beadwork," YouTube video. Uploaded by @Gabrieldumontinstitute. April 9, 2019. 00:47:42. Accessed January 13, 2024. https://www.youtube.com/watch?v=8GcmH7wnK3c

Gaudet, Janice Cindy. "Collective Memory, Historical Trauma, and Healing." MA thesis, Carleton University, 2007.

———. "Keeoukaywin: The Visiting Way—Fostering an Indigenous Research Methodology." *Aboriginal Policy Studies* 7, no. 2 (2018): 47–64.

———. "Metis Women's Stories." YouTube video. Uploaded by @marcelpetit. February 2019. 00:58:54 Accessed February 15, 2023. https://www.youtube.com/@metiswomenstories4818/featured

Gaudet, Janice Cindy, and Lawrence Martin/Wapistan. "Learning through Conversation: An Inquiry into Shame." In *Power through Testimony: Reframing Residential Schools in the Age of Reconciliation*, edited by Brieg Capitaine and Karine Vanthuyne, 95–112. Vancouver: University of British Columbia Press, 2017.

Gray, Robin R. "Rematriation: Ts'msyen Law, Rights of Relationality, and Protocols of Return." *Journal of the Native American and Indigenous Studies Association* (NAIS) 9, no. 1 (2022): 1–27.

Goulet, Keith. "Land and Colonization: A Nehinuw (Cree) Perspective." PhD diss., University of Regina, 2021.

Goulet, Linda May, and Keith Goulet. *Teaching Each Other: Nehinuw Concepts and Indigenous Pedagogies*. Vancouver: University of British Columbia Press, 2014.

Goyette, Linda, and Carolina Jakeway Roemmich. *Edmonton in Our Own Words*. Edmonton: University of Alberta Press, 2004.

Hall, Norma Jean. "Anne 'Annie' McDermot Bannatyne." In Hall, comp. and ed., *Mothers of the Resistance*.

———. "McNab." In Hall, comp. and ed., *Mothers of the Resistance*.

———. "A 'Perfect Freedom': Red River as a Settler Society, 1810–1870." MA thesis, University of Manitoba, 2003.

———. "Sinclair." In Hall, comp. and ed., *Mothers of the Resistance*.

Hall, Norma Jean, comp. and ed. *Mothers of the Resistance 1869–1870: Red River Métis Genealogies*. Accessed November 14, 2022. https://resistancemothers.wordpress.com.

Halliday McDonald, Lois, ed. *Fur Trade Letters of Francis Ermatinger: Written to his Brother Edward During his Service with the Hudson's Bay Company, 1818–1853*. Glendale: Arthur H. Clark, 1980.

Harpelle, Alix. *My Children Are My Reward: The Life of Elsie Spence*. Winnipeg: Pemmican Publications, 2003.

Healy, William J. *Women of Red River: Being a Book Written from the Recollections of Women Surviving from the Red River Era*. Winnipeg: Russell, Lang & Co, 1923.

Hearne, Samuel, Peter Fidler, Philip Turnor, and Joseph Burr Tyrrell. *Journals of Samuel Hearne and Philip Turnor between the Years 1774 and 1792*. New York: Greenwood Press, 1968.

Hodge, Adam R. "'In Want of Nourishment for to Keep Them Alive': Climate Fluctuations, Bison Scarcity, and the Smallpox Epidemic of 1780–82 on the Northern Great Plains." *Environmental History* 17, no. 2 (2012): 365–403.

Hogue, Michel. *Métis and the Medicine Line: Creating a Border and Dividing a People*. University of North Carolina Press, 2015.

hooks, bell. *All about Love: New Visions*. New York: William Morrow and Company, 2001.

———. *Communion: The Female Search for Love*. New York: HarperCollins, 2002.

———. *Outlaw Culture: Resisting Representations*. London: Routledge, 2006.

———. *The Will to Change: Men, Masculinity, and Love*. New York: Washington Square Press, 2004.

Hua, Anh. "Diaspora and Cultural Memory." In *Diaspora, Memory, and Identity: A Search for Home*, edited by Vijay Agnew, 191–208. Toronto: University of Toronto Press, 2005.

Iseke-Barnes, Judy. "Grandmothers of the Métis Nation." *Native Studies Review* 18, no. 2 (2009): 25–60.

Iseke-Barnes, Judy, and Lisa Desmoulins. "The Life and Work of the Honourable Thelma Chalifoux, White Standing Buffalo." *Canadian Women Studies* 29, no. 1–2 (2011): 24.

Joseph, Bob. *21 Things You May Not Know about the Indian Act: Helping Canadians Make Reconciliation with Indigenous Peoples a Reality*. British Columbia: Indigenous Relations Press, 2018.

Kearns, Laura-Lee. "(Re)claiming Métis Women Identities: Three Stories and the Storyteller." In Adams, Dahl, and Peach, eds., *Métis in Canada*, 59–91. Edmonton: University of Alberta Press, 2013.

"Kehte-Hiyak with Agnes Carriere of Cumberland House, Saskatchewan," You Tube video, Uploaded by @NCI Manitoba, March 4, 2019. 00:13:31. Accessed January 13, 2024. https://www.youtube.com/watch?v=aNJpVD6S-Xc.

Kelm, Mary-Ellen, and Keith Smith. *Talking Back to the Indian Act: Critical Readings in Settler Colonial Histories*. Toronto: University of Toronto Press, 2018.

Kermoal, Nathalie. "Navigating Troubled Political Waters" In *Métis Rising: Living Our Present through the Power of Our Past*, edited by Yvonne Boyer and Larry N. Chartrand, 131–47. Vancouver: Purich Books, 2022.

———. *Un Passé Métis au Féminin*. Québec: Les Éditions GID, 2006.

Kirkness, Arthur. "Cook, John Edward." In Tait and Olson, eds., *Communities of Courage and Cordwood*, 130.

Kirkness, Samuel. "Sam Kirkness, as told by Sam Kirkness." In Larsen, ed., *A Homesteader's Dream*, 397–99.

Ladow, Beth. *The Medicine Line: Life and Death on a North American Borderland*. New York: Routledge, 2002.

Lamotte, Raymond, and Madeleine Lamotte. *The Lamotte Family: Reunion 1894–1994*. Banff: Printing Company of Banff, 1994.

Lang, William L. *Confederacy of Ambition: William Winlock Miller and the Making of Washington Territory*. Seattle: University of Washington Press, 1996.

Larsen, Helen, ed. *A Homesteader's Dream: History of Deer Ridge, Lone Spruce, Mayview, Cookson, Sturgeon River*. Mayview: DMCS History Book, 1981.

LaVallee, Guy. *The Metis of St. Laurent, Manitoba: Their Life and Stories, 1920–1988*. Winnipeg: S.P., 2003.

Legault, Gabrielle. "Stories of Contemporary Métis Identity in British Columbia: 'Troubling' Discourses of Race, Culture, and Nationhood." PhD diss., University of British Columbia, 2016.

Legros, Alta, and Faye Jordan, eds. *Cadillac: Prairie Heritage*. Steinbach: Derksen Printers. 1987.

Leroux, Darryl. *Distorted Descent: White Claims to Indigeneity*. Winnipeg: University of Manitoba Press, 2019.

Lilley, Renée. "Metis Artist's 'Rematriation Project' Hopes to Reunite Vintage Indigenous Wares with Their Home Communities." CBC News. March 21, 2022. https://www.cbc.ca/news/indigenous/indigenous-metis-first-nations-beading-culture-fundraiser-community-1.6388929.

Lugrin, N. de Bertrand. *The Pioneer Women of Vancouver Island, 1843–1866*. Victoria: The Women's Canadian Club of Victoria, 1928.

Lux, Maureen K. *Medicine that Walks: Disease, Medicine, and Canadian Plains Native People, 1880–1940*. University of Toronto Press, 2001.

Macdougall, Brenda. "Knowing Who You Are: Family History and Aboriginal Determinants of Health." In *Determinants of Indigenous Peoples' Health: Beyond the Social*, 2nd ed., edited by Margo Greenwood, Sarah de Leeuw, and Nicole Marie Lindsay, 127–46. Toronto: Canadian Scholars, 2018.

———. *Land, Family and Identity: Contextualizing Metis Health and Well-being*. Prince George, BC: National Collaborating Centre for Aboriginal Health, 2017. https://www.ccnsa-nccah.ca/docs/context/RPT-ContextualizingMetisHealth-Macdougall-EN.pdf.

———. *One of the Family: Métis Culture in Nineteenth-Century Northwestern Saskatchewan*. Vancouver: UBC Press, 2010.

———. "Speaking of Métis: Reading Family Life into Colonial Records." *Ethnohistory* 61, no. 1, (2014): 27–56.

———. "Wahkootowin: Family and Cultural Identity in Northwestern Saskatchewan Metis Communities." *The Canadian Historical Review* 87, no. 3 (September 2006): 431–62.

Macdougall, Brenda, and Nicole St-Onge, "Rooted in Mobility: Métis Buffalo-Hunting Brigades," *Manitoba History* 71 (2013): 21–32.

MacEwan, Grant. *Mighty Women: Stories of Western Canadian Pioneers*. Vancouver: Greystone Books, 1975.

MacKellar, Maggie. *Core of My Heart, My Country: Women's Sense of Place and the Land in Australia & Canada*. Melbourne: Melbourne University Press, 2004.

MacKinnon, Doris J. *The Identities of Marie Rose Delorme Smith: Portrait of a Métis Woman, 1861–1960*. Regina: University of Regina Press, 2012.

———. *Metis Pioneers: Marie Rose Delorme Smith and Isabella Clark Hardisty Lougheed*. Edmonton: University of Alberta Press, 2018.

Macpherson, Elizabeth. *The Sun Traveller: The Story of the Callihoos in Alberta*. Alberta: Musée Héritage Museum, 2004.

Maguire, Hugo. *Stories of the West*. Cochrane: Stockmen's Memorial Foundation Library and Archives, 1938.

Maloney, Alice B. "John Work of the Hudson's Bay Company: Leader of the California Brigade of 1832–33." *California Historical Society Quarterly* 22, no. 2 (1943): 97–109.

M'Closky, Kathy. "Art of Craft: The Paracox of the Pangnirtung Weave Shop." In Miller and Churchryk, eds., *Women of the First Nations*, 113–26.

McCarthy, Martha. *From the Great River to the Ends of the Earth: Oblate Missions to the Dene, 1847–1921*. Edmonton: University of Alberta Press, 1995.

McGuire, Rita. "The Grey Sisters in the Red River Settlement, 1844–1870." CCHA *Historical Studies* 53 (1986): 21–37. http://www.cchahistory.ca/journal/CCHA1986/McGuire.pdf.

McKay-Carriere, Lily. *Elders and Teachers Are Cree-Ative Collaborators! Teaching and Learning Research Exchange*. Saskatoon: Dr. Stirling McDowell Foundation for Research into Teaching, 2009.

McKinnon, Aileen. "Dress in Red River Settlement, 1815 to 1835." MSc thesis, University of Alberta, 1992.

McLean, Don. *Home from the Hill: A History of the Metis in Western Canada*. Regina: Gabriel Dumont Institute, 1987.

Meilleur, Helen. *A Pour of Rain: Stories from a West Coast Fort*. Victoria: Sono Nis Press, 1980.

Meyer, David, and Paul C. Thistle. "Saskatchewan River Rendezvous Centers and Trading Posts: Continuity in a Cree Social Geography." *Ethnohistory* 42, no. 3 (1995): 403–44.

Miller, Christine, and Patrice Churchryk, eds. *Women of the First Nations*. Winnipeg: University of Manitoba Press, 1996.

Miller, Jim. *Compact, Contract, Covenant: Aboriginal Treaty-Making in Canada*. Toronto: University of Toronto Press, 2009.

Millions, Erin Jodi. "'By Education and Conduct': Educating Trans-Imperial Indigenous Fur-Trade Children in the Hudson's Bay Company Territories and the British Empire, 1820s to 1870s." PhD diss., University of Manitoba, 2017.

———. "Ties Undone: A Gendered and Racial Analysis of the Impact of the 1885 Northwest Rebellion in the Saskatchewan District." MA thesis, University of Saskatchewan, 2004.

Mitchell, George. "Lord Selkirk's Baldoon Settlement." In *Kentiana: The Story of the Settlement and Development of the County of Kent*, 37–40. Chatham: Kent Historical Society, 1939. https://electricscotland.com/history/canada/kent4.htm.

Mitchell, Ross. "Andrew Graham Ballenden Bannatyne (1829–1889): First Citizen of Winnipeg." *Manitoba Pageant* 11, no. 1 (Autumn 1965): unpaginated. Manitoba Historical Society. Last modified November 2, 2009. http://www.mhs.mb.ca/docs/pageant/11/bannatyne.shtml/.

Modjeski, Morgan. "Artifacts Returned to Sask.'s Cumberland House after Decades in B.C." CBC News. November 17, 2019. https://www.cbc.ca/news/canada/saskatoon/indigenous-artifacts-returned-cumberland-house-1.5362308.

Moine, Louise. *Remembering Will Have to Do: The Life and Times of Louise (Trottier) Moine*. Regina: Gabriel Dumont Institute, 2013.

Morin, Gail. *Company Men: James Peter Whitford*, vol. 21. Self-published, 2019.

Murphy, Lucy Eldersveld. *A Gathering of Rivers: Indians, Métis and Mining in the Western Great Lakes, 1727–1832*. Lincoln: University of Nebraska Press, 2004.

National Inquiry into Missing and Murdered Indigenous Women and Girls. *Reclaiming Power and Place: The Final Report of the National Inquiry into Missing and Murdered Indigenous Women and Girls*. 2 vols. Ottawa: 2019. Accessed December 15, 2023. https://www.mmiwg-ffada.ca/final-report/.

Nickel, Sarah, and Amanda Fehr, eds. *In Good Relation: History, Gender, and Kinship in Indigenous Feminisms*. Winnipeg: University of Manitoba Press, 2020.

Niemi-Bohun, Melanie. "Colonial Categories and Familial Responses to Treaty and Metis Scrip Policy: The 'Edmonton and District Stragglers,' 1870–88." *Canadian Historical Review* 90, no. 1, (2009): 71–98.

Nixon, Lindsay. "Toward an Indigenous Relational Aesthetics." In Nickel and Fehr, eds., *In Good Relation*, 195–206.

Noel, Jan. "Power Mothering: The Haudenosaunee Model." In *"Until Our Hearts Are on the Ground": Aboriginal Mothering, Oppression, Resistance and Rebirth*, edited by D. Memee Lavell Harvard and Jeannette Corbiere Lavell, 76–93. Toronto: Demeter Press, 2006.

O'Brien, Jean. *Firsting and Lasting: Writing Indians Out of Existence in New England*. Minneapolis: University of Minnesota Press, 2010.

Oster, Bailey, and Marilyn Lizee. *Stories of Métis Women: Tales My Kookum Told Me*. Calgary: Durville & UpRoute Books, 2021.

Parks Canada. "Government of Canada Recognizes the National Historic Significance of Marie Rose (Delorme) Smith." https://www.newswire.ca/news-releases/government-of-canada-recognizes-the-national-historic-significance-of-marie-rose-delorme-smith-889534799.html.

Payment, Diane. "Batoche After 1885: A Society in Transition." In *1885 and After: Native Society in Transition*, edited by F. Laurie Barron and James B. Waldram, 173–88. Regina Canadian Plains Research Center, 1986.

———. *The Free People—Li Gens Libres: A History of the Métis Community of Batoche, Saskatchewan*. Calgary: University of Calgary Press, 2009.

———. "'La Vie en Rose'? Métis Women at Batoche, 1870 to 1920." In Miller and Churchryk, *Women of the First Nations*, 19–38.

———. "Une femme en vaut deux – Strong Like Two People": Marie Fisher Gaudet of Fort Good Hope, Northwest Territories." In *Contours of a People: Métis Family, Mobility, and History*, edited by Nicole St-Onge, Carolyn Podruchny, and Brenda Macdougall, 265–99. Norman: University of Oklahoma Press, 2012.

Pedri-Spade, Celeste. "Waasaabikizo: Our Pictures Are Good Medicine." *Decolonization: Indigeneity, Education & Society* 5, no. 1 (2016): 45–70.

Perry, Adele. *Colonial Relations: The Douglas-Connolly Family and the Nineteenth-Century Imperial World*. Cambridge: Cambridge University Press, 2015.

———. "Historiography that Breaks Your Heart: Sylvia Van Kirk and the writing of Feminist History." In *Finding a Way to the Heart: Feminist Writings on Aboriginal and Women's History in Canada*, edited by Robin Jarvis Brownlie and Valerie Korinek, 81–97. Winnipeg: University of Manitoba Press, 2012.

———. *On the Edge of Empire: Gender, Race, and the Making of British Columbia, 1849–71*. Toronto: University of Toronto Press, 2001.

Peters, Evelyn, Matthew Stock, and Adrian Werner. *Rooster Town: The History of an Urban Métis Community, 1901–1961*. Winnipeg: University of Manitoba Press, 2018.

Petten, Cheryl. "Métis Woman Painted Vibrant Picture of the West." *Windspeaker* 22, no. 7 (October 2004): 30. https://data2.archives.ca/e/e448/e011183946.pdf.

Pettipas, Katherine. "A History of the Work of the Reverend Henry Budd Conducted under the Auspices of the Church Missionary Society, 1840–1875." MA thesis, University of Manitoba, 1972.

Pincher Creek Historical Society. *Prairie Grass to Mountain Pass*. Pincher Creek: Pincher Creek Historical Society, 1981.

Quiring, David M. *CCF Colonialism in Northern Saskatchewan: Battling Parish Priests, Bootleggers, and Fur Sharks*. Vancouver: UBC Press, 2004.

Racette, Calvin. *Métis Development in the Canadian West Book 3: Petitioning for Rights*. Gabriel Dumont Institute, 1987.

Raven, Krystl Dawn. "Beyond the Battlefield: Gabriel Dumont and Métis Leadership (1837–1885)." MA thesis, University of Saskatchewan, 2017.

Ray, Arthur, Jim Miller, and Frank Tough, eds. *Bounty and Benevolence: A History of Saskatchewan Treaties*. Montreal: McGill-Queen's University Press, 2002.

Rich, E.E., ed. *The Letters of John McLoughlin; from Fort Vancouver to the Governor and Committee, Second Series, 1839–44*. London: Champlain Society for The Hudson's Bay Record Society, 1943.

Richards, Mary. "Cumberland House: Two Hundred Years of History." *Saskatchewan History* 27, no. 3 (1974): 108–14.

Riviere, Frances. *Washing at the Creek*. Winnipeg: Pemmican Publications, 2008.

Roan, Chief Wayne, and Earle Waugh. "Relationships." Nature's Laws Project, Heritage Community Foundation, 2004. https://www.albertasource.ca/natureslaws/culture/relational_relationships.html.

Rodney, William. *Kootenai Brown: The Unknown Frontiersman*. Victoria: Heritage House, 2002.

Rollason Driscoll, Heather. "'A Most Important Chain of Connection': Marriage in the Hudson's Bay Company." In *From Rupert's Land to Canada*, edited by Theodore Binnema, Gerhard J. Ens, and R.C. Macleod, 81–107. Edmonton: University of Alberta Press, 2001.

Ruby, Robert H., and John A. Brown. *Indian Slavery in the Pacific Northwest*. Spokane: The Arthur H. Clark Company, 1993.

Saskatchewan Department of Northern Affairs. *A History of Cumberland House: ... As Told by Its Own Citizens, 1774–1974*. Prince Albert: Bicentennial Committee of Cumberland House, Saskatchewan, 1974.

Saunders, Kelly, and Janique Dubois. *Métis Politics and Governance in Canada*. Vancouver: UBC Press, 2019.

Schaeffer, Claude E. "Le Blanc and La Gasse: Predecessors of David Thompson in the Columbian Plateau." *Studies in Plains Anthropology and History* no. 3 (1966): 1–13.

Schilling, Rita. *Gabriel's Children*. Saskatoon: Métis Society Local #11, 1983.

Schilling, Rita. *So Many to be Remembered: By So Few*. Saskatoon: 1978.

Scofield, Gregory. *Louis: The Heretic Poems*. Gibsons: Nightwood Editions, 2011.

Sealey, Bruce D., and Antoine S. Lucier. *The Métis: Canada's Forgotten People*. Winnipeg: Pemmican Publishers, 1975.

Sleeper-Smith, Susan. *Indian Women and French Men: Rethinking Cultural Encounter in the Western Great Lakes*. Amherst: University of Massachusetts Press, 2001.

———. "Women, Kin, and Catholicism." *Ethnohistory* 47, no. 2 (2000): 423–52.

Smith, Dorothy Blakey, ed. *The Reminiscences of Doctor John Sebastian Helmcken*. Vancouver: University of British Columbia Press, 1975.

Smith, Robin Percival. *Captain McNeill and His Wife the Nishga Chief*. Surrey: Hancock House Publishers, 2001.

Smith Parfitt, Mary Hélène. *Prairie Grass to Mountain Pass: History of the Pioneers of Pincher Creek and District*. Pincher Creek Historical Society, 1974.

Société historique de Saint-Boniface. Centre du patrimoine. https://shsb.mb.ca.

St. Louis Local History Committee. *I Remember: A History of St. Louis and Surrounding Areas*. St. Louis, SK: St. Louis Local History Committee, 1980.

———. *History in Print, 1924–1952*. St. Louis, SK: St. Louis Local History Committee, 1980.

St-Onge, Nicole. "Memories of Metis Women of St. Eustache, Manitoba, 1910–1980." *Oral History Forum* 19–20 (March 2000): 90–111.

———. "Of Métis Women and Hunting Brigades." *Canadian Issues* (Spring/Summer 2021): 49–54.

St. Pierre, Edwin. *Remembering My Métis Past: Reminiscences of Edwin St. Pierre*. Saskatoon: Gabriel Dumont Institute, 2012.

Stevenson, Allyson. *Intimate Integration: A History of the Sixties Scoop and the Colonization of Indigenous Kinship*. Toronto: University of Toronto Press, 2020.

Stevenson, Allyson, and Cheryl Troupe. "From Kitchen Tables to Formal Organization: Indigenous Women's Social and Political Activism in Saskatchewan to 1980." In *Compelled to Act: Histories of Women's Activism in Western Canada*, edited by Sarah Carter and Nanci Langford, 218–52. Winnipeg: University of Manitoba Press, 2020.

Strikwerda, Eric. *The Wages of Relief: Cities and the Unemployed in Prairie Canada, 1929–1939*. Edmonton: AU Press, 2013.

Tait, Irene, and Gladys Olson, eds. *Communities of Courage and Cordwood*. MacDowall: MacDowall History Book Committee, 1986.

Taylor, Cora. *Victoria Callihoo: An Amazing Life*. Stony Plain: Eschia Books Inc., 2008.

Teillet, Jean. *The North-West Is Our Mother: The Story of Louis Riel's People, the Métis Nation*. New York: HarperCollins, 2019.

Todd, Zoe. "Honouring Our Great-Grandmothers: An Ode to Caroline LaFramboise, Twentieth-Century Métis Matriarch." In Nickel and Fehr, eds., *In Good Relation*, 171–81.

Thompson, David. *Columbia Journals*. Edited by Barbara Belyea. Bicentennial Edition. Seattle: University of Washington Press, 2007.

———. *David Thompson's Narrative, 1784–1812*. Edited by Richard Glover. Toronto: Champlain Society, 1962.

Thorne, Tanis C. *The Many Hands of My Relations: French and Indians on the Lower Missouri*. Columbia: University of Missouri Press, 1996.

Tierra, Berdhanya Swami. *Mystic Heart: Empowering Unity and Compassion*. Self-published, 2015.

Tolmie, Simon Fraser. "My Father: William Fraser Tolmie." In Tolmie, *The Journals of William Fraser Tolmie*, 385–395.

Tolmie, William Fraser. *The Journals of William Fraser Tolmie: Physician and Fur Trader*. Vancouver: Mitchell Press Limited, 1963.

Tolmie, William Fraser, and George Mercer Dawson. *Comparative Vocabularies of the Indian Tribes of British Columbia: With a Map Illustrating Distribution*. Montreal: Dawson Brothers, 1884.

Troupe, Cheryl Lynn. "Mapping Métis Stories: Land Use, Gender and Kinship in the Qu'Appelle Valley, 1850–1950." PhD diss., University of Saskatchewan, 2019.

———. "Métis Women: Social Structure, Urbanization and Political Activism, 1850–1980." MA thesis, University of Saskatchewan, 2009. https://harvest.usask.ca/handle/10388/etd-12112009-150223.

———. "Re/Storying Métis Road Allowance Communities." Presentation recording. In Rupertsland Centre for Métis Research, "RCMR MÉTIS Talks Fall 2021: Thursday, November 18th, 2021," 58:52 to 1:29:47. YouTube video. Uploaded by @-rcmr9503. 1:49:20. Accessed December 15, 2023. https://youtu.be/THZyuBxCr3U.

Truth and Reconciliation Commission of Canada. *Canada's Residential Schools: The History, Part 1, Origins to 1939*, vol. 1 of *The Final Report of the Truth and Reconciliation Commission of Canada*.

——. *Honouring the Truth, Reconciling for the Future: Summary of the Final Report of the Truth and Reconciliation Commission of Canada, Volume 1, Part 1: The History Origins to 1939*. Montreal: McGill-Queens University Press, 2015.

——. *The Métis Experience*. Montreal: McGill-Queens University Press, 2016.

——. *The Survivors Speak*. Montreal: McGill-Queens University Press, 2015.

Van Kirk, Sylvia. *Many Tender Ties: Women in Fur Trade Society, 1670–1870*. Norman: University of Oklahoma Press, 1990.

——. "Toward a Feminist Perspective in Native History." *Centre for Women's Studies in Education Occasional Papers*, vol. 18 (1987): 377–89.

——. "Tracing the Fortunes of Five Founding Families of Victoria." *BC Studies* no. 115–16 (Autumn/Winter 1997–98): 149–80.

Wade, Mark Sweeten. *The Thompson Country: Being Notes on the History of Southern British Columbia, and Particularly the City of Kamloops, Formerly Fort Thompson*. Kamloops: Inland Sentinel Print, 1907.

Wadsworth, William T.D. "Healing Waters and Buffalo Bones: Using Women's Histories to Challenge the Patriarchal Narrative of Lac Ste. Anne, Alberta." *Pathways* 1 (2020): 13–28.

Waldram, James B. *As Long as the Rivers Run: Hydroelectric Development and Native Communities in Western Canada*. Winnipeg: University of Manitoba Press, 1988.

——. *Cumberland House and the E.B. Campbell Dam: An Economic Impact Study*. Research reports, Centre for Northern Studies, Lakehead University. Thunder Bay: Lakehead University Centre for Northern Studies, 1991.

Wallace, W. Stewart, ed. *Documents Relating to the North West Company*. Toronto: Champlain Society, 1934.

Watson, Bruce McIntyre. *Lives Lived West of the Divide: A Biographical Dictionary of Fur Traders Working West of the Rockies, 1793–1858.* Kelowna: University of British Columbia Okanagan, 2010.

Weinstein, John. *Quiet Revolution West: The Rebirth of Métis Nationalism.* Calgary: Fifth House, 2007.

White, M. Catherine, ed. *David Thompson's Journals Relating to Montana and Adjacent Regions, 1808–1812.* Missoula: Montana State University Press, 1950.

Williams, Christina McDonald. "The Daughter of Angus MacDonald." *Washington Historical Quarterly* 13, no. 2 (1922): 107–17.

Wilson, Charles. *Mapping the Frontier between British Columbia & Washington: Charles Wilson's Diary of the Survey of the 49th Parallel, 1858–1862, while Secretary of the British Boundary Commission.* Edited by George F. G. Stanley. Toronto: Macmillan, 1970.

Wolvengrey, Arok, comp. *Cree–English.* Vol. 1 of nêhiyawêwin: itwêwina / Cree: Words. Regina: University of Regina Press, 2011.

Zeileg, Ken, and Victoria Zeileg. *Ste. Madeleine: Community without a Town, Métis Elders in Interview.* Winnipeg: Pemmican Publications, 1987.

Index

Page numbers with (f) refer to illustrations.

Acoose, Janice, 166
Adams, Elise LaPlante Fayant (Julia's grandmother), 138(f), 139–140, 142–144, 148(f), 149, 154n28
Adams, Howard, 247
Adams, Norbert, 140
Adams, Susie Penner, 142–143
Adese, Jennifer, 149
Adopt Indian and Métis (AIM) Program, SK, 248–249
adoption, customary, 113, 126
African Americans, 19–20, 27n54
agricultural economy. *See* farms and ranches, women as managers
Alberta: Dominion Lands Act, 58n83; Métis Association of Alberta, 47, 61n114; scrip, 58n83. *See also* Callihoo, Victoria Belcourt; Delorme Smith, Marie Rose
Alberta Historical Review, 30, 34, 48–49, 54n26, 55n33
alcohol use and treatment, 53n24, 92–93, 150, 182–183, 236, 238–240, 241

Anderson, Anne, 36–37, 54n32, 55n34, 56n46, 56n49
Anderson, Cronlund, 53n24
Anderson, Kim, xiv, 166, 177–178, 188, 207, 244–245
Anglican Church, 87–88, 110, 200
Anglo-Métis, as term, 126n4
Argon School, SK, 179, 180
Armstrong, Jeannette, 201–202
Askwith, Dorothy, 239
Attig, John and Harriet Stevens, 124, 125
Auxile. *See* Morrison, Auxile Lepine

Baalim, H.G., 11, 12, 18, 23, 25n22
Badger, Elizabeth, 129n57
Baird, Alice Callihoo (Victoria's daughter), 35(f), 58n86, 60n100
Baird, Gerry, 51n1, 53n24, 54n28, 55n33
Baldoon (Selkirk's estate), ON, 109
Ballenden, Eliza, 129n65
Bancroft, Hubert Howe, 63, 97
Bannatyne, Andrew Graham Ballenden, 115, 129n65

Bannatyne, Anne McDermot
    (Caroline's adoptive mother),
    111, 113–117, 114(f), 120, 126,
    129n65
Bannatyne, James, 129n65
Barkwell, Lawrence, 121
Batoche, SK, 171–175. *See also*
    Resistance (1885), Batoche, SK
beadwork and leather: about,
    201–204, 209–211, 213–214;
    devaluation of women's work,
    202; gauntlets, 196(f), 205(f);
    household economy, 14, 203;
    knowledge-sharing, 121, 196,
    210–211; leather work, 2, 3(f),
    8, 12, 85; as loving act, 214,
    217–218; moccasins, 209, 213(f),
    217(f); moosehide preparation,
    209; moss bags, 212; museum
    pieces, 32, 33(f), 195–196,
    196(f), 205(f), 213(f), 217(f);
    relational aesthetics, 202–203;
    styles and patterns, 214
Beardy First Nation, SK, 177
Beaulieu, Catherine, 27n57
Beaulieu, François, 21
Beaver (steamer), 78, 86, 87, 89, 95
Beaver, Rev. and wife, Fort
    Vancouver, 78–79
Belcourt, Alexis (Victoria's father),
    30, 39–40, 56n46
Belcourt, Joseph (Victoria's
    grandfather), 39
Belcourt, Louise Trotchie (Nora's
    aunt), 227(f)
Belcourt, Victoria. *See* Callihoo,
    Victoria Belcourt
Beresford, Charles, 95
Berggren, Daisy Kirkness
    (Caroline's granddaughter), 123
Berube (née Baird), Violet, 35(f)
bison. *See* buffalo hunts

Black, Samuel, 72, 73
Blackfeet hostilities, 41, 70, 76, 77
Blanke, Cecile LaRocque, 135, 137,
    142–149, 152, 154n9
blankets, 212, 214
Bleau, Denica, 138(f)
Blondeau, Leona, 258n64
boarding houses, 2, 9, 12, 19–20,
    21(f)
boarding schools. See residential
    schools; schools
Boucher, Caroline Lesperance
    (Auxile's grandmother), 167–
    168, 170–171, 173, 187(f), 188
Boucher, Jean-Baptiste (Auxile's
    grandfather), 170–171
Boucher, Margaret. *See* Lepine,
    Margaret Boucher (Auxile's
    mother)
Bouvier, Joseph, 27n54
Boyer, Andy, 181
Boyer, Nancy, 174
Boyer, Rose, 258n64
Bremnar, Margaret, 188
British Columbia: boundary party
    (1858), 92; colonial history, 94;
    gold rush, 92, 93–94; Métis
    Nation British Columbia, 64;
    suffrage, 95–96. *See also* Work,
    Josette Lagacé
Brooke, Lionel, 9, 21(f), 22
Brown, Jennifer S.H., xviii, xxiv, 16,
    63–64, 67, 91
Brown, John George "Kootenai," 9,
    9(f), 10, 17, 19, 24n4
buffalo hunts: about, xix–xxi,
    41–43; Blackfeet enemies, 41;
    bone haulers, 142–143; Cypress
    Hills, 136–137; decline of
    herds, xx, 24n10, 42–43; Métis
    brigades, 5, 164, 254n3, 255n22;
    Round Prairie site, 254n3; rules

of the hunt, 163, 185; Salish
hunts, 69; social structure,
41–42; women's labour, xx–xxi,
40–42, 54n26, 163–164
Burnett, Kristen, 17
Buss, Helen, 10
Byrne, Robert and Janet, 26n34

Cabe, Marie Genevieve (Julia's
mother?), 137, 139
Cadboro (schooner), 81–82
Cadillac, SK, 146
California (Rio Sacramento), 77
Callihoo Band, St. Albert area, AB,
30, 43–48
Callihoo, Adolphus B. (Victoria's
son), 58n86, 60n106
Callihoo, Clothilde Hodgson
(Victoria's daughter-in-law),
36, 39(f), 46, 48, 54n27
Callihoo, Felix (Victoria's brother-
in-law), 61n114
Callihoo, John (Victoria's son), 45,
58n86, 59n89
Callihoo, Louis (Victoria's
husband), 43–47, 59n90
Callihoo, Michel (Victoria's father-
in-law), 43
Callihoo, Richard (Victoria's
nephew), 61n121
Callihoo, Victoria Belcourt: about,
xxvi, 29–61, 31(f), 33(f), 35(f),
39(f), 49(f); birth and passing
(1861–1966), 29–30, 51n4;
Catholic faith, 40; convent
school, 40, 60n100; historical
sources, 32, 34, 36–37, 50,
263; languages (Cree, Michif,
English), 36, 48, 54n28; as
a matriarch, xxvi, 32–34, 38,
48–51, 54n28, 55n34, 61n121,
263; Métis identity, 34–36,
48–51, 52n20; personal
qualities, 30–32, 53n24;
transitional period, 44–47;
widowhood, 47
—ABILITIES AND TALENTS:
beadwork and sewing, 32,
33(f); cooking, 44; firearms,
30–31; healer and midwife,
32, 41; household economy,
44–47, 59n90; jigging, 29,
61n121, 238. See also Callihoo,
Victoria Belcourt, writings
and writers
—FAMILY AND COMMUNITY:
about, 35(f), 46–51, 58n86;
Alexis Belcourt (father), 30,
39–40, 56n46; children (list of
13), 58n86; convent schools, 46,
60n100; descendants, 34, 35(f),
39(f), 51n1, 52n18; genealogy,
39–40, 56nn46–50, 58n86;
Hermine "Lizzie" (daughter),
41, 49, 55n34, 58n86; Indian
status, 44, 47, 60n112; Louis
(husband), 43–47, 59n90;
Nancy Rowan (mother),
30, 40–42, 47, 51n7, 54n26,
56nn48–50, 57n70; residential
schools, 46, 47, 60n106; scrip,
40, 44, 51n7, 56n46; siblings
(list of 6), 56n48; social
connections, 47–48; Vital
Victor (son), 30, 32, 36, 39(f),
42, 44, 46, 48, 54n27, 58n86
—HOMES AND TRAVELS: buffalo
hunts, 29–30, 40–43, 48,
54n26; Lac Ste. Anne, 30,
45–46, 51n4; land grants,
60n112; Michel Reserve, St.
Albert area, 30, 44–46, 48;
Youville Home, St. Albert,
55n34

Callihoo, Victoria Belcourt
(continued)
—WRITINGS AND WRITERS: about,
xvi–xvii, xxvi, 30, 32–37, 49–51,
263; *Alberta Historical Review*
articles, 30, 32, 34, 48–49,
54n26, 55n33; authenticity of
her writings, 37; biographies on,
52n20; "Early Life in Lac Ste.
Anne and St. Albert," 43, 46–48;
editing and translations, 36, 37,
54n26, 55n34; G. MacEwan's
relationship, 32, 36, 44, 53n21,
54n26, 55n33; memoirs, 32,
34; motivations, 32, 42, 50;
newspaper articles on, 34–35,
53nn23–24, 54n28; "Our
Buffalo Hunts," 41–43, 51nn4–5

Callihoo, Vital Victor (Victoria's
son), 30, 32, 36, 39(f), 42, 44,
46, 48, 54n27, 58n86

Callihoo, William (Victoria's son),
30, 58n86

Campbell, Maria, 103, 147, 164–165,
168, 176, 181

Canadian Cattlemen (periodical),
xxvi, 2, 10–11, 24n4

Caroline. See Kirkness, Caroline
McNabb

Carpenter, Jock (Marie Rose's
granddaughter), xxvi, 1, 3(f),
6, 17

Carriere, Agnes, xvii, 196, 213(f),
214–217

Carriere, Jean, 200

Carriere, John (Agnes's son),
215–216

Carriere, Pierre, 215–216

Carrière-Acco, Anne (Agnes's
daughter), 121, 216–217

Carter, Sarah, xviii, 24n3, 38, 53n25,
107

Catholicism: anti-Catholic
sentiment, 27n57; community
service, 121; convent schools,
40, 60n100, 116–120, 147; with
Indigenous spirituality, 152;
Mary in kinship worldview,
181; prayer and rosaries, 182;
women as mothers, 178

Chartrand, Dorothy, 38

Chartrand, Marie, 139

childbirth. *See* healers and midwives

children and childcare: child
welfare, 247–248; customary
adoption, 113, 126; family size,
91, 208; foster homes, 247–249,
259n85; household labour, 178–
179; illegitimate children, 139,
140; kinship ethics, 113, 178–
179, 210; matriarchs as cultural
teachers, xiv, 210, 230; moss
bags, 212; teachings on, 113,
210, 230. *See also* mothering

clothing: British styles, 65(f),
92, 107–108, 166; in
commemorative photos,
92, 106(f), 107–108; HBC
cloth, 208; Métis shawls, 43;
mosquito net head bags, 92;
teachings at kitchen tables,
210–211; winter wear, 43,
209, 212. *See also* beadwork
and leather; sewing and
embroidery

colonialism. *See* settler colonialism

Columbia District, 64, 66–67, 69–74

*Communities of Courage and
Cordwood* (Tait and Olson,
eds.), 101, 116

Cook, Adelaide (George Kirkness's
niece), 131n103

Cook, Gilbert (George Kirkness's
nephew), 131n103

Cook, Irene, 214
Cook, John and Catherine Kirkness (George Kirkness's sister), 122, 131n103
Cook, John Edward (Jack) (Caroline's adopted nephew), 122–125, 131n103, 131n114
Cookson, SK, 101, 105, 120, 124
Cotter Collection, Cumberland House Museum, SK, 195–196, 196(f), 199(f), 217, 265–266
country marriages. *See* marriage
Cox, Ross, 70
Crawford, John, 27n48
Cree: Cree language, 8, 127n12, 214–215; Cumberland House area, 198, 209–210, 214–215; language of place, 127n12; Michif as French and Cree dialect, 18; teachings on love, 209–210; wāhkōhtowin (respect and belonging), 104–105, 113, 121–126, 127n12
culture, material. *See* material culture
Cumberland, Lake, 198
Cumberland House (kāministikominahikoskahk), SK: about, xxviii, 195–201, 199(f), 207–209, 217–218; beadwork and embroidery, 205(f), 209–218, 217(f); colonialism in northern SK, 207–208; Cree people, 198, 200, 209–210, 214–215; everyday life, 208–209; history, 197–198, 200–201; location, 198; material culture, 197–198, 201–204, 208–209, 265–266; matriarchs, 196–197, 206–207; migrants from Red River, 200–201; relational ethics, 201, 207; rematriation of cultural items, 195–196, 196(f), 199(f), 213(f), 217–218, 265; schools, 201
Cumberland House (kāministikominahikoskahk), SK, matriarchs: about, xvii, 209–211; Agnes Carriere, 196, 213(f), 214–217; Isabelle Impey, 196, 211–215, 221n82; Margaret McAuley, 196, 216, 217(f), 221n82
Cumberland House Cree Nation, 298
Cumberland House Museum, SK, 195–196, 196(f), 199(f), 201, 205(f), 213(f), 217(f), 265–266
Cummings, Henry (Nora's husband), 233, 235
Cummings, Nora: about, xxviii, 223–225, 229(f), 236(f), 243(f), 245(f), 252(f); awards and recognition, 223–225, 250–253; birth (1938), 224; early life, 224–230, 229(f), 236(f); "firsts," 224–225, 243, 249; historical sources, 263; languages (Michif, English), 226, 231; as a matriarch, xxviii, 223–225, 253, 266; Métis identity, 231–232; personal qualities, 231–232, 253; schools, 231–232
—ACTIVISM: about, 223–225, 235–241; City Council candidate, 249–250; community caregiving, 225, 228, 237–241, 251–252; family worker, 240–242; Friendship Centre, 224, 236–237, 243, 243(f), 256n47; Local #11, Métis Nation, 223–224, 237, 239–241, 243, 247, 253, 256n47; Métis Society field worker, 224, 242–243;

Cummings, Nora—ACTIVISM
(*continued*) NWAC board
of directors, 250; political
family, 233–237; SNWM/SNWA
women's movement, 224–225,
243–252, 243(f); social issues,
236, 238–241, 244–245, 248–
249, 251–252; women mentors,
246–247; women's labour,
239–240
—FAMILY AND COMMUNITY:
about, 226–228, 227(f); alcohol
treatment, 238–240, 241;
ancestors at Batoche, 233–234;
children and descendants, 233,
235, 253; Clarence Trotchie
(uncle), 224, 227(f), 235–240,
236(f), 242–243, 253, 256n47;
families as economic units,
228, 232, 234; food sharing,
226, 228, 231, 238; Henry
(husband), 233, 235; Irene
Dimick (mother), 224–240,
227(f), 245(f), 253, 258n64;
Jerome Ouellette (father),
228, 232; Justine Trotchie
(grandmother), 225, 227(f),
228–236, 229(f), 240, 253,
256n29; Peter Trotchie
(grandfather), 235; Round
Prairie Métis, 226, 233–234,
253, 254n3, 255n22; teachings
of caring and visiting, xxviii,
225, 228–231, 233, 235, 237–238,
240, 242, 247, 253, 256n29
—HOMES: road allowance, south
Saskatoon, 225–228, 233, 266;
Saskatoon, 233, 235–236
customary adoption, 113, 126
Cypress Hills, AB/SK, 136–137,
138(f), 140, 143
Cyr, Yvette Boucher, 170

dances. *See* entertainment
Dease, John Warren, 73, 75
Delorme, Joseph and Norbert
(Marie Rose's uncles), 5
Delorme, Urbain (Marie Rose's
brother), 18
Delorme, Urbain (Marie Rose's
father), 4, 5, 15, 20
Delorme, Urbain, Sr. (Marie Rose's
grandfather), 5
Delorme Smith, Marie Rose: about,
xxvi, 1–4, 3(f), 8–9, 9(f), 13(f),
263; biography, xxvi, 1, 3(f);
birth and passing (1861–1960),
2, 4–5, 12, 23; "Buckskin
Mary," xxvi, 2, 12; early life,
1–6, 3(f); historical sources,
10–11; languages (French,
English, Cree, Michif), 1, 5, 8,
18, 27n48; as a matriarch, xxvi,
1–4, 23, 263; Métis identity, 15,
18, 20, 23; personal qualities,
12, 14–16; recognition, 11, 23,
263; scholarship on, 206;
transitional period, 1–5, 22–23;
widowhood, 2, 9, 20
—ABILITIES AND TALENTS: about,
8–9, 12–13, 20; beadwork and
leatherwork, 2, 3(f), 8, 14;
boarding house manager, 12,
20, 21(f); contract work, 12, 14,
15; healer and midwife, 2, 17–18,
20, 21(f); household economy,
6, 12, 14, 16–17, 20, 26n33;
ranch and homestead manager,
12, 14, 20. See also Delorme
Smith, Marie Rose, writings
—FAMILY AND COMMUNITY:
Charlie Smith (husband), xxvi,
1–2, 5–9, 9(f), 14–16, 20–22;
children (17), 2, 6, 8, 13(f), 14;
community networks, 8–9,

9(f), 19; Cuthbert Gervais (stepfather), 5, 14–16, 18; extended family networks, 18–19; "fifty dollar bride," 1, 6–8; Indigenous relationships, 8–9, 17–20, 24n1; Jock Carpenter (granddaughter), xxvi, 1, 3(f), 6, 17; J.R. "Bob" Delorme (son), 14, 26n34; Marie Gervais (mother), 2, 6–7, 12, 14–16, 18; Mary Hélène Smith Parfitt (daughter), 12, 16–18, 20; settler relationships, 21–22; Urbain Delorme (brother), 18; Urbain Delorme (father), 4, 5, 15, 20
—HOMES AND TRAVELS: about, 1–5; boarding house, 2, 9, 12, 17, 19–20, 21(f); Edmonton, 3, 8; Jughandle Ranch, 8, 9(f), 14, 16, 18, 19; Pincher Creek, xxvi, 2, 8, 9(f), 14, 16, 18, 19, 20, 21(f); property owners, 14–15, 21–22; second homestead, 2, 20; travels, 4–5, 8, 15–16
—WRITINGS: about, xvi–xvii, xxvi, 2, 10–12, 22, 263; archives, 10–11, 25n21, 26n29; audiences, 6, 18; Baalim's interview, 11, 12, 18, 23, 25n22; *Canadian Cattlemen* articles, xxvi, 2, 6–7, 10–11, 24n4; "Eighty Years on the Plains," 6–7, 24n4; fiction, 10, 22–23; on natural remedies, 17; time of writing, 6, 22; on transitional period, 22–23; unpublished manuscripts, 2, 10–11, 25n21, 26n29
Demage, Hazel, 258n64
Deschambeault, Marie, 200
Desnomie, Florence, 246–247, 258n64

Devine, Heather, 24n10, 103–104
Dimick, Irene Trotchie (Nora's mother), 224–240, 227(f), 245(f), 253, 258n64
discrimination. *See* racism and discrimination
diseases. *See* illnesses and injuries
D'Lonais, Olive (Brown's first wife), 17
Dominion Lands Act (1872, 1879, 1885), 22, 44, 58n83, 143–144, 225
Dominion Lands survey, 22, 44, 58n83, 143–144, 165
Dorion, Leah, 210–211, 221n82
Dorion, Pierre, 200
Douglas, Amelia (Josette's friend), 77–79, 85, 88, 91, 94–95
Douglas, David, 86–87
Douglas, James, 77, 88, 94, 95
Douglas, Martha, 94–95
Duck Lake, SK, 164, 171, 175, 176(f), 177, 180–181, 188
Dudar, Grace (Victoria's granddaughter), 51n1, 55n32, 60n100
Dumont, Gabriel, 233–234, 255n22
Dumont, Isadore and Louise Laframboise, 255n22
Dumont Institute, Gabriel, xxix, 211, 219n24, 221n82, 253
Dunbow (St. Joseph's) residential school, AB, 46–47, 60n106
Duncan, William, 85
Dye, Eva Emery, 67–68, 70–72, 76, 85, 91

economy: cash economy, 47; freighting, xx, 43–44; shifting status of women, 118–119; women's continuity with past, 16–17; women's roles, xxii.

economy *(continued)*: *See also* fur trade; Métis women's labour; transitional period (mid-to-late 19th c.)
education. *See* schools
1885 Resistance. *See* Resistance (1885), Batoche, SK
1869–70 Resistance. *See* Resistance (1869–70), Red River, MB
entertainment: jigging, 29, 61n121, 238; "Red River Valley" (song), 23, 27n61; in settlements, 16
Erickson, Lesley, 117–118, 120–121
Ermatinger, Edward (Ned), 72–73, 75, 77, 80
Ermatinger, Francis, 72–73
ethical love. *See* love

family, as term, 171. *See also* Métis kinship relationships
farms and ranches, women as managers, xvi, xx, 12, 14, 20, 146–147, 173(f), 182, 185–186
Farrell Racette, Sherry, 10, 197, 203–204, 217–218, 219n28, 221n82
Fayant, Alex, 143
Fayant, Antoine, 142
Fayant, Caroline (Julia's aunt), 137
Fayant, Jean Louis and Elise LaPlante (Julia's grandparents), 138(f), 139–140, 142–144, 148(f), 149, 154n28
Fayant, Julia. *See* Lamotte, Julia Fayant
Fayant, Marie and Elizabeth, 155n32
Federation of Sovereign Indigenous Nations (was Federation of Saskatchewan Indian Nations), 244, 246
feminism, mainstream, 244–246
Fidler, Peter, 66

Fifty Dollar Bride (Carpenter), xxvi, 1, 3, 3(f), 6
Finlayson, Roderick, 82–83, 88, 90, 95
Finlayson, Sarah Work (Josette's daughter), 75, 78–79, 81–83, 88, 90, 94–95
The First Métis (Anderson), 36–37, 51n7, 56n46, 56n49
Fish Creek, SK, 171
Fisher, Georgina, 258n64
Flaminio, Anna Louisa, 103, 127n12
Flatheads (Têtes-Plattes), as term, 90. *See also* Interior Salish people
Foggo, Cheryl, 27n54
food: food sharing, 174, 226, 228, 231, 238; food sovereignty, 185–186; kitchen table teachings, 210–211
Fort Albany, 109
Fort Colvile, 75–76, 80
Fort Garry, 115, 119–120
Fort Nisqually, 84, 88–90
Fort Rupert, 88
Fort Simpson, 78–88
Fort Stikine, 82–83
Fort Vancouver, 77–79, 85, 87
Fort Victoria, 87–88
Fort William, 109
Foster, Tol, 103
foster homes, 247–249, 259n85
free traders, 5, 20–21, 24n10
freighting economy, xx, 43–44
fur trade: country marriages, 57n52, 69–70; decline of, 45; free traders, 5, 20–21, 24n10; historiography, xviii–xix, 64, 66; illiteracy, 64, 66; marginalization of French-speaking Métis, 20–21; marriage, xviii–xix, 69–72, 74,

87–88, 119; matriarchs, xvi–xvii; Métis identity, xxii, 126n4; as "pioneer of civilization," 15; social hierarchies, 85–86; trade networks, xviii–xix, 72; voyageurs, 64, 66–67; women's labour, xx, 41–43, 203. *See also* Hudson's Bay Company (HBC); North West Company (NWC); transitional period (mid-to-late 19th c.)

fur trade, matriarchs. *See* Callihoo, Victoria Belcourt; Delorme Smith, Marie Rose; Work, Josette Lagacé

Gabriel Dumont Institute, SK, xxix*n*2, 211, 219n24, 221n82, 253

Gabriel Dumont Local #11. *See* Local #11, Métis Nation—Saskatchewan

Gabriel Housing, Regina, 244, 258n64

Gabriel's Crossing, SK, 165, 171

Gairdner, Gary, 51n1

Gareau, Ludgar and Madeleine, 18

Gaudet, Diane. *See* Roy, Diane Gaudet (Auxile's granddaughter)

Gaudet, Janice Cindy (Auxile's granddaughter), xxiii, xxvii–xxviii, 157–193, 162(f), 262, 265, 269

Gaudet, Norma Morrison (Auxile's daughter), 157, 161–162, 179–184, 190

Gervais, Cuthbert (Marie Rose's stepfather), 5, 14–16, 18

Gervais, Marie (Marie Rose's mother), 2, 6–7, 14–16, 18

Gladstone, Robert, 15

Gladstone, William, 9

Gladstone, Zilda (Marie Rose's stepsister), 15

godmothers, 78, 79, 231

gold rush, 92, 175–176

Goodwill, Carlin, 258n64

Goulet, Ann, 258n64

Goyette, Linda, 54n26

Grahame, James Allan, 93

Grahame, Mary Work (Josette's daughter), 80, 88, 93

Grant, Cuthbert, 5, 111

Gravelbourg, SK, 147

Greenleaf-Settee, Elizabeth, 131n103

Grenon, Marguerite, 164, 170

Grey Nuns schools, Red River, MB, 5, 116–121

Gunn, Donald and Julia, 151

Haida, 84, 86, 87, 88

halfbreed, as term, 126n4, 168

Hall, Norma Jean, 109, 116, 131n103

Hardisty, William, 27n57

Harris, Martha Douglas, 94–95

Haudenosaunee matriarchy, 206

Haultain, Frederick, 19

HBC. *See* Hudson's Bay Company (HBC)

healers and midwives: buffalo hunts, 41; Indigenous practices, 17–18; medicinal herbs, xx, 17, 32, 40, 208; midwives, xx, 17, 20, 21(f), 32, 208; resentment by doctors, 20

health, ill. *See* illnesses and injuries

Hearne, Samuel, 198

Helmcken, Cecilia Douglas, 94–95

Henderson, Gloria Jean (Victoria's great-granddaughter), 35(f), 48, 51n1, 55n33

Henry, Julie (Auxile's great-grandmother), 164, 167–168

historiography: about, xviii, 36–39, 55n39; authentic voices, 37; editing and translations, 37; ethical procedures, 153n3; family-centred historical approach, xxiv–xxv, 103–105, 262–263; genealogies, xiv–xv, xxiv, 103–104, 137, 216; male perspectives, xviii, 36, 37, 50, 105; on place, 162, 162(f); settler writing on Indigenous people, 53n25; women's omission from documents, 64, 66, 105, 204
—SOURCES: about, xxii, 262; fur trade archives, 64, 66; material culture, xxii, xxiii, 135, 202–204; memoirs, xvi–xvii; newspapers, 53nn23–24; oral histories, xxii, xxix$n$2, 38, 67–68, 204; photography, 92, 105–108; places, 162, 162(f); postcards, 136(f), 156n83; scrip database, 51n7; stories, xxii, 49–50

Hodgson, Clothilde (Victoria's daughter-in-law), 36, 39(f), 54n27

Hoey, SK, 162(f), 173(f), 179, 188

homestead grants, 24n3, 131n114, 170–171

A Homesteader's Dream (Larsen), 101, 124

hooks, bell, 160

Hudson's Bay Company (HBC): class-crossing marriages, 63, 74; contract to support Indigenous family, 72; family size of officers, 91; free traders, 5, 20–21, 24n10; marginalization of Métis, 5, 20; marriage of clerks to officers' daughters, 64; merger with NWC, 20, 24n10; Sayer Trial (1849), 5, 20–21, 24n10; women's absence in official records, 74; John Work's career, 64, 71–76, 87. *See also* fur trade

Huggins, Edward (Josette's son-in-law), 67–68, 70–71, 76, 91

Huggins, Letitia Work (Josette's daughter), 67, 71, 76, 78, 79–81, 83–89, 91

hunting buffalo. See buffalo hunts

identity. *See* Métis identity

illnesses and injuries: animal encounters, 75; Blackfeet hostilities, 76–77; eye troubles, 75; falls, 80, 83; gunshot wounds, 80; malaria, 76–77, 92; smallpox, 57n70, 79–80, 200; tuberculosis, 91, 94, 123; tumours, 87

Impey, Isabelle, xvii, 196, 211–215, 221n82

Indian Act (1876): about, 59n90; control of reserves, 45, 59n90; enfranchisement, 47; Indian, defined, 58n82; "marrying out," xxx$n$12; status by marriage, 44; unsuccessful petitions for reserves, 136–137. *See also* residential schools

Indigenous peoples: healers and midwives, 17–18, 20; Métis trade with, 24n1; residential schools, 46–47, 60n106, 144–145; settler writings on, 53n25; slavery practices, 83–85; spirituality, 151–152. *See also* Indian Act (1876)

Indigenous Relational Aesthetics (IRA), 202

injuries. *See* illnesses and injuries
Interior Salish people: about, 90;
  buffalo hunts, 69; chastity of
  women, 74; Josette Work's
  family, 64; Kalispel, 69, 70–71,
  93; Têtes-Plattes (Flatheads),
  70, 72–75, 84, 90; Tolmie's
  book of languages, 93
Iroquois, 74, 82–83
Iseke-Barnes, Judy, 38

Jackson, Harriet, 96
Jackson, Margaret Work (Josette's
  daughter), 78–81, 89, 96
Jamieson, Frederick C., 54n26
jigging, 29, 61n121, 238
Jones, Emily, 258n64
Josette. *See* Work, Josette Lagacé
Jourdain, Virginia, 215
Jughandle Ranch, Pincher Creek,
  AB, 8, 9(f), 14, 16, 18, 19
Julia. See Lamotte, Julia Fayant

Kalispel people, 69, 70–71, 93
kāministikominahikoskahk.
  See Cumberland House
  (kāministikominahikoskahk),
  SK
Kamiyistowesit (Beardy) First
  Nation, 177
Kanaquassé, 82–83
Kapeyakwaskonam (One Arrow)
  First Nation, 177
Kearns, Laura-Lee, 38–39
Kennedy, Eliza, 88
Kennedy, Fanny, 80, 84, 85
Kennedy, John Frederick, 80,
  83–85, 87
Kettle Falls post (HBC), 73
Kildaw, Vickie (Victoria's
  daughter), 36, 58n86
Kinnowess (Kininawis), 56n49

kinship. *See* Métis kinship
  relationships
Kirkness, Caroline McNabb: about,
  xxvii, 101–126, 106(f), 264;
  birth and passing (1862–1954),
  101, 113, 125; Catholic faith,
  120–121; convent education,
  101, 116–118, 120, 125; early
  life, 113, 116–122; historical
  sources, 101, 116, 124;
  languages (French, English),
  116, 120; as a matriarch, xxvii,
  101–102, 125–126, 264; photos
  as historical sources, 105–108,
  106(f); wāhkōhtowin (respect
  and belonging), 104–105, 113,
  121–126, 127n12
—ABILITIES AND TALENTS:
  handcrafts, 101, 108, 120–122;
  household economy, 120;
  knowledge-sharing, 102,
  121–122; sewing, 108, 116, 120,
  122, 125
—FAMILY AND COMMUNITY:
  about, 103–105, 264; Anne
  Bannatyne (adoptive mother),
  111, 113–117, 114(f), 120, 126,
  129n65; Charles McNabb
  (father), 110–112, 116–117;
  community service, 120–122;
  customary adoption, 101, 113–
  116, 126; Elizabeth McNabb
  (stepmother), 111–113, 129n57;
  genealogy, 102, 108–113;
  George (husband), 104, 106(f),
  107–108, 119–120, 124–125;
  Jack Cook (adopted nephew),
  122–125, 131n103, 131n114;
  Jade McDougall (great-great-
  granddaughter), xxiii, 102–104,
  262, 264, 270; knowledge-
  sharing, 102, 121–122;

Kirkness, Caroline McNabb—
FAMILY AND COMMUNITY
(continued): Marie Anne
McNabb (mother), 110–111,
113; Mary Kirkness (daughter-
in-law), 122–124; Samuel
(son), 122–124; wāhkōhtowin
(respect and belonging), 104–
105, 113, 121–126, 127n12
—HOMES: Cookson, 101, 105, 120,
124; Prince Albert, 104, 125;
Red Deer Hill, 101–102, 105,
119–120; Red River, 101–102,
105; Shellbrook, 124–126,
131n114
Kirkness, Clayton (Caroline's
grandson), 123, 125
Kirkness, Daisy (Caroline's
granddaughter), 123
Kirkness, George (Caroline's
husband), 104, 106(f), 107–108,
119–120, 124–125
Kirkness, Henry and Catherine
Adams, 131n103
Kirkness, Mary Attig (Caroline's
daughter-in-law), 123–124
Kirkness, Samuel James (Caroline's
son), 122–124
Knight, Lillian, 258n64
knowledge, relational models:
about, 103–104
Kootenai Brown Pioneer Historical
Village, Pincher Creek, AB,
24n4
Kootenay region, 66–67, 69–72, 74
Ktunaxa people, 66
Kullyspel House, Lake Pend
Oreille, 71

La Gassé, Chas, 67
labour, women's. *See* Métis
women's labour

Lac Pelletier, SK, xxvii, 137–138,
138(f), 142–145, 150–152
Lac Ste. Anne, AB, 29, 41–42, 45
Lacombe, Albert, 9, 40
Ladow, Beth, 140
Laframboise, Caroline, xxiii, 206
Laframboise, Jean Baptiste, 255n22
Laframboise, Louise, 255n22
Laframboise, Marge (Nora's
mother's half-sister), 235, 239,
254n3, 256n29
Lagacé, Charles (Josette's father),
64, 66–70
Lagacé, Josette. *See* Work, Josette
Lagacé
Lagacé, Peter (Josette's nephew), 93
Lagacé, Pierre (Josette's brother):
Fort Simpson, 78, 80, 88; gold
on Vancouver island, 88; at
Hillside Farm, 93; illnesses,
80; mother (Emme) and kin,
90, 93; personal qualities, 86;
travels with Josette, 81–82, 88;
uncertainties in history, 67–68,
70–71, 90; wife (Lisette) and
children, 82, 91, 93
Lagacé, Pierre (Josette's uncle), 67
Lagassé, Emme (Josette's mother),
64, 67, 68, 70, 74, 90
Lamirande, Todd, 115
Lamotte, Constantine (Connie)
(Julia's son), 133, 135, 147, 149
Lamotte, Julia Fayant: about, xxvii,
133–153, 141(f), 148(f), 151(f);
birth and passing, 137, 139, 152;
Catholic faith, 151–152; early
life, 136–137, 144–145, 148(f),
151; eye problems (strabismus),
148(f), 150; historical sources,
135–139, 136(f), 152–153, 153n3,
156n83, 264; Indigenous
spirituality, 151–152; languages

(Michif, English, French), 144, 151; as a matriarch, 134, 149–153, 264–265; Métis identity, 145, 149–153; personal qualities, 145–147, 149–153; transitional period, 151–152; uncertainties in history, 137–139
—ABILITIES AND TALENTS: farm and ranch manager, 146–147; healer, 149; household economy, 147, 152; painter, 152; political organizing, 147–149; sewing and needle work, 149–150
—CHILDREN: about, 147, 153; Constantine (Connie), 133, 135, 147, 149; Joseph, 147, 151(f); Josephine, 147, 151(f); Louis, 141(f), 147, 151(f); Louise, 138(f), 147, 151(f); Marguerite (Marge), 133–134, 135, 139, 147, 149, 150–152, 151(f); schools, 147; Theresa (Terry), 133, 135, 147, 151(f)
—FAMILY AND COMMUNITY: Caroline Fayant (aunt), 137; Elise Adams (grandmother), 138(f), 139, 140, 142–144, 148(f), 149, 154n28; Gabrielle Legault (great-granddaughter), xxiii, xxvii, 133–156, 153n3, 262, 264–265, 269; genealogy, 137, 139–143; half-siblings (Nellie and Agnes), 139; Hugo Maguire (biological father), 135, 139–140, 151(f); as illegitimate child, 139, 140, 145; Leon (husband), 145–146, 151(f); Marie Angelique (mother), 137, 139, 156n83
—HOMES: about, xxvii, 136–137; The Farm, 138(f), 145; Lac Pelletier, xxvii, 137–138, 138(f), 142–145, 150–152; map, 138(f); Saskatchewan Landing, 137, 138(f), 142; Val Marie, 145

Lamotte, Leon (Julia's husband), 145–146, 151(f)
Lamotte, Louise, 138(f)
Lamotte, Tova (Julia's daughter-in-law, Connie's wife), 133, 135, 146, 153
land titles, 22–23
Landry, Mabel, 258n64
Landry, Moise, 255n22
languages: Cree language, 127n12, 214–215; language of place, 127n12; Tolmie's book of languages, 93. *See also* Michif
LaPlante, Elise. See Fayant, Jean Louis and Elise LaPlante (Julia's grandparents)
Larsen, Helen, 101, 124
Lavallée, Madeleine, 137
Lavallee, Mary Ann, 246–247, 258n64
leather. See beadwork and leather
Leblanc, Bertha Lepine, 176, 176(f)
Leblanc, Oscar, 176(f)
Lebret (Qu'Appelle) Industrial School, SK, 144–145
Legault, Gabrielle (Julia's great-granddaughter), xxiii, xxvii, 133–156, 153n3, 262, 264–265, 269
Lepine, Ambroise, 172
Lepine, Auxile. See Morrison, Auxile Lepine
Lepine, Josephte (Josette) Lavallée (Auxile's grandmother), 172–174, 181(f), 188
Lepine, Margaret Boucher (Auxile's mother), 159(f), 168, 170–172, 174–177, 188

Lepine, Maxime, Jr. (Auxile's father), 168, 170–172, 174–177, 188
Lepine, Maxime, Sr. (Auxile's grandfather), 167, 172–174
Lepine Flats, SK, 174
Leslie, Rev. and wife (Willamette), 79, 81
Lesperance, Alexis (dit Bonami) and Marguerite Grenon (Auxile's great-grandparents), 170
Lesperance, Caroline. *See* Boucher, Caroline Lesperance (Auxile's grandmother)
Lessard/Lacerte, Angelique Azure, 111
Lesser Slave Lake region, AB, 40
L'Hyrondelle, Catherine (Victoria's grandmother), 39, 56n46
L'Hyrondelle, Jacque (Victoria's great-grandfather), 56n46
Liboiron, Marge, 133
Livingstone, Violet Trotchie (Nora's aunt), 227(f)
Lizee, Marilyn, 38
Local #11, Métis Nation—Saskatchewan, 223–224, 237, 239–241, 243, 247, 253, 256n47
Lougheed, Isabelle Clark Hardisty, 206
love: about, 160–163, 201–203; beauty in aesthetics, 197; Cree teachings, 209–210; defined, 160; as female power, 201–202; kinship love, 160, 162–164; in Métis world view, 160–161, 210; as resistance practice, 173, 186; in women's creations, 213–214
Lugrin, N. de Bertrand, 85
Lux, Maureen, 17
Lynch-Staunton, Emma, 11–12
Lynch-Staunton, Frederick W., 9

Macdougall, Brenda, xix, 55nn39–40, 103–104, 111, 127n12, 163–164
MacEwan, Grant, 32, 36, 44, 53n21, 54n26, 55n33
MacKellar, Maggie, 10
MacKinnon, Doris Jeanne, xxiii–xxiv, xxvi, 1–27, 55n40, 206, 262–263, 269
Macleod, James, 9, 19–20, 27n54
Macleod, Mary Drever, 19–20, 27n54
Macpherson, Elizabeth, 47
Maguire, Hugo (Julia's biological father), 135, 139–140, 151(f)
Mair, Charles, 115
malaria, 76–77, 92
Mandziuk, Madalyn, xxiii, xxvi, 29–61, 263, 270
Manito Sakahigan (Lac Ste. Anne), AB, 29, 30, 41–42, 45
Manitoba: Dominion Lands Act, 58n83; road allowance communities, 144; scrip, 58n83, 167–168. *See also* Red River, MB; Resistance (1869–70), Red River, MB
Manson, Donald, 72, 73
Marie Rose. *See* Delorme Smith, Marie Rose
Markwart, Mona Gaudet (Auxile's granddaughter), 182, 184
marriage: acculturated ideal in transitional period, 119; bride price, xix, 72; chastity, 74; class-crossing practices, 74; country marriages, 57n52, 69–70; of daughters to father's junior officers, 88, 119; endogamy, 174–175; genealogies in oral history, xiv–xv, 216; legitimacy, 71–72, 87–88; marriage brokers, 216;

"marrying out," xix, xxx*n*12; for networks, xiv–xv, xviii–xix, 72
Mary Dare (ship), 89
material culture: about, 197–198, 203–204, 264–265; devaluation of women's work, 202; economic benefits, 203; matriarchal social relations, 197–198; oral history, 204; relational aesthetics, 201–203; rematriation, 197–198, 201, 204, 217–218; research methods, 204; symbols of frontier, 203; undervalued in fur trade era, 203. *See also* beadwork and leather; museums; sewing and embroidery
Mazer, Kay, 239
McAuley, Margaret, xvii, 196, 216, 217(f), 221n82
McCargar, Donald (Marie Rose's great-grandson), 3(f)
McCargar, Shirley-Mae (Marie Rose's granddaughter), 3, 17
McCartney, Barry (Marie Rose's great-grandson), 17
McDermot, Anne. See Bannatyne, Anne McDermot (Caroline's adoptive mother)
McDermot, Sarah Mary McNab (Caroline's aunt), 113, 115
McDonald, Duncan, 71
McDonald, Finan, 68–74, 78
McDonald, John, 68
McDonald, Margaret, 69–71, 78
McDougall, Jade (Caroline's great-great-granddaughter), xxiii, 101–132, 262, 264, 270
McDougall, Marie Anne, 172
McDougall, Sophie Boyer, 170, 174
McDougall, Terry, 175–176
McGuire, Rita, 117

McKay, Virginia, 196, 200
McKenzie, Dougal, 215
McKenzie, Old Bill, 215
McKinnon, Aileen, 107
McLeod, Antoine and Joseph, 111
McLeod, Marie Anne, 111
M'Closky, Kathy, 203
McLoughlin, John, 78–79, 82–83, 85, 87
McLoughlin, John, Jr., and wife, 82–83, 87
McLoughlin, Marguerite, 78
McNab/McNabb family, Red River, 108–113
McNab, John (Caroline's great-grandfather), 118
McNab, Sarah Mary (Caroline's aunt), 113
McNabb, Caroline. *See* Kirkness, Caroline McNabb
McNabb, Charles (Caroline's father), 110–112, 116–117
McNabb, Elizabeth Badger Cameron (Caroline's stepmother), 111–113, 129n57
McNabb, Marie Anne McLeod (Caroline's mother), 110–111, 113
McNeill, William and Mathilda, 86, 88, 95
Medicine Line (US/Canada border), 137, 138(f), 139
Métis, as term, 126n4
Métis identity: about, xxii–xxiii, 126n4; authority of women, 178; collective vs. individual, 178; Eurocentric norms, 166; fluidity and diversity, xxii–xxiii, 126n4; genealogical links for citizenship, 137; pride in, 134; rejection of victimhood, 158; sovereignty, 157, 163–164, 185, 188–190, 265;

Métis identity *(continued)*:
stigma, 150, 165–166; stories and storytelling, 50, 157–160, 233–234

Métis kinship relationships: about, xiii, 103–105, 121–122, 161; across time and space, 161; all life as sacred, 210; community service, 120–122; family, as term, 171; genealogies, xiv–xv, xxiv, 103–104, 137, 216; intergenerational continuity, 103–104; kinship circles, 103–104; knowledge-sharing, 120–122, 125–126; matriarch's knowledge, xiv–xv; Mother Mary as kinship, 181; mothering as collective well-being, 206; non-human world, 209; relational aesthetics, 202–203; responsibilities, xiii, 121–122; sharing ethic, 171; time concepts, 49; wāhkōhtowin (respect and belonging), 104–105, 113, 121–126, 127n12. *See also* love

Métis language. *See* Michif

Métis matriarchs: about, xiii–xvi, xxiii–xxv, 188, 201–202, 206–207, 261–267; agents of transition, xv–xvii; authority of, xxv, 178, 190, 202, 206–207, 210; case study overview, xxv–xxix; community resilience, 196; cultural teachers, xiv; economic participation, xiv, xx; governance, xiv, 216–217; identity as fluid, xxii–xxiii; multiple identities, xvi; social stability, xv; sovereignty, 157, 163, 185, 188–190, 265; spiritual stability, 189–190; work ethic, xvi. *See also* love; Métis kinship relationships; Métis women's labour; transitional period (mid-to-late 19th c.)

Métis visiting: about, 161, 186, 188; beadwork with tea and stories, 213–214; keeoukaywin (Michif), 186; as kinship love, 161; teachings of caring, 225, 228–231, 233, 235, 237–238, 253. *See also* stories and storytelling

Métis women's labour: about, 147; buffalo hunts, 41–42, 54n26, 163–164; domestic help, xxi, 145; everyday life, 208–209; farm and ranch managers, xvi, xx, 12, 14, 20, 146–147, 173(f), 182, 185–186; fur trade era, xx, 41–43, 203; healers and midwives, xx; political participation, 223–225, 235–241; road allowance communities, xxi, 145; scholarship on, xxi; transitional period, xx, 44–45, 118–119; work ethic, 216. *See also* beadwork and leather; children and childcare; clothing; food; healers and midwives; sewing and embroidery

Métis Nation—Saskatchewan: Cummings as senator, 223; Lamotte family organizers for, 147, 148; Local #11, 223–224, 237, 239–241, 243, 247, 253, 256n47; name change, 244

Metlakatla, BC, 85

Michel Band, St. Albert area, AB, 30, 43–48

Michif: French and Cree dialect, 18; halfbreed, as term, 168;

Métis, as term, 126n4; road allowance communities, 144, 226; shame in schools, 231
—WORDS: keeoukaywin (visiting), 186; lii vyeu (Old Person), 223, 254n1; mataants and moonoocs (aunts and uncles), 162; Maymair and Paypair (grandmother and grandfather), 160, 180
midwives, xx, 17, 20, 21(f), 32, 208
Mighty Women (MacEwan), 36, 53n21, 54n26
Milk River, AB, 137, 138(f), 142
Minesinger, Emma, 38
Moine, Louise Trottier, 143
moosehide, 209
Morin, Gail, 139
Morin, Sharon, 51n1
Morrison, Auxile Lepine: about, xxvii–xxviii, 157–193, 159(f), 169(f), 173(f), 176(f), 189(f); birth and passing (1908–1985), 157, 164, 176; Catholic faith, 181–182, 184; early life, 159(f), 164–165, 169(f), 175, 177, 180–181; historical sources, 162, 162(f); languages (Michif, French, Cree, English), 177, 182; as a matriarch, xxvii–xxviii, 157–164, 183–184, 188–190, 265; personal qualities, 180–182, 186; school, 180–181
—ABILITIES AND TALENTS: family piano, 179–180, 186; farm manager, 173(f), 182, 185–186; food sovereignty, 185–186; household economy, 179–180, 185–186; turkey shoots, 186
—CHILDREN: Christina, 179, 186; disabilities, 180, 182, 184; Doug, 178–179; Duncan, 178–179, 186; infant deaths, 176; Ken, 178–180, 182; Norma, 157, 161–162, 179–184, 190; schools, 179–180, 184; twins (Marilyn and Evelyn), 176(f), 179
—FAMILY AND COMMUNITY: Diane Roy (granddaughter), 178–180, 183, 185–186; genealogy, 167–174, 188; Janice Gaudet (granddaughter), xxiii, xxvii–xxviii, 157–193, 162(f), 262, 265, 269; kinship care, 178–180; list of kinship ties, 171; Margaret Lepine (mother), 159(f), 168, 170–172, 174–177, 188; Maxime Lepine, Jr. (father), 171–172, 174–177, 188; Norman (husband), 176(f), 180, 182–184, 188; siblings, 176, 176(f), 179; turkey shoots, 186; visiting, 186, 188
—HOMES: Duck Lake, 164–165, 175, 176(f), 177, 180–181; Hoey homestead, 162, 162(f), 173(f), 179–180, 185–186, 188; road allowance community, 165; Saskatoon, 180
Morrison, Christina (Auxile's daughter), 179, 186
Morrison, Doug (Auxile's son), 179
Morrison, Duncan (Auxile's son), 177, 179, 186
Morrison, Jack and Margaret Bremner (Auxile's mother-in-law and father-in-law), 188
Morrison, Ken (Auxile's son), 178–180, 182
Morrison, Leo, 190
Morrison, Norman (Auxile's husband), 176(f), 180, 182–184, 188
moss bags, 212

mothering: authority of women, 210; Catholic role of women, 178; as collective wellbeing, 206; language of the home, 214–215; shaping of political life, 206; teachings at kitchen table, 210–211; women's responsibilities, 178, 244–245. *See also* children and childcare
Moyer, Bertha, 138(f)
Moyer, Edna, 138(f), 153, 156n83
Moyer, Genna and Andrew, 153
Moyer, Raymond, 138(f)
Moyer, Robert, 138(f)
Moyer, Ronald, 138(f)
Murphy, Lucy Eldersveld, xviii
Musée Héritage, St. Albert, AB, 32, 33(f)
museums: recognition of Métis works, 203; rematriation of items, 195–196, 196(f), 199(f), 213(f), 217–218, 265; re-storying of items, 195–196. See also Cumberland House Museum, SK
music. *See* entertainment

namesakes, 78
Native Alcohol Council, Saskatchewan (NAC), 239–240, 241
Native Women's Association of Canada (NWAC), 250
Native Women's Council of Canada, 225
Nez Perce, 68, 70–71
nicknames, 149
Nipissing, Archange (Victoria's grandmother), 40
Nipissing, Ignace (Victoria's great-grandfather), 40

Ni-ti-mous (Kootenai Brown's wife), 17, 19
Nixon, Lindsay, 202
Noel, Jan, 206–207
North West Company (NWC): country marriages, 57n52, 69–70; illiteracy, 64; Kootenay region, 66–67, 69–72, 74; merger with HBC, 20, 24n10; Spokane House, 70–75. *See also* fur trade
North-West Territory: as provinces, xxv; scrip, 58n83
NWC. See North West Company (NWC)

Oblate missionaries, 21, 179
Ogden, Julia Rivet, 68
Ogden, Peter Skene, 68, 71–73, 75, 76, 82
Ogden, Sarah Julia, 79
Old People, as term, 254n1
One Arrow First Nation, SK, 177
oral history: in family-centred historical approach, xxiv–xxv, 262; genealogies, xiv–xv, xxiv, 103–104, 137, 216; as historical sources, xxii, xxixn2, 38, 67–68, 204; on marriage xxx, xiv–xv, 216; on material culture, 204. *See also* stories and storytelling
Oregon territory, 75–76
Oregon Treaty (1846), 89
Oster, Bailey, 38
Ouellette, Bertha, 239
Ouellette, Isabelle Dumont (Nora's great-great-grandmother), 233–234
Ouellette, Jerome (Nora's father), 228, 232
Our Lady of Lourdes Shrine, SK, 181

Pambrum, Josephine, 242, 246–247
parenting. *See* children and
    childcare; mothering
Parfitt, Mary Hélène Smith (Marie
    Rose's daughter), 12, 16–18, 20
patriarchy, resistance to, 161–163,
    166–167
Payment, Diane, 18–19, 147, 162,
    164, 171–174, 178
Pedri-Spade, Celeste, 105
pemmican, 42
Pend Oreille, Lake, Idaho, 70, 71
Perry, Adele, 64, 66
photography, 92, 105–108, 106(f)
Piikani people, 66
Pilon, Agnes Lepine, 176, 176(f)
Pilon, Charles, 176(f)
Pilon, Josephte (Victoria's great-
    grandmother), 56n46
Pincher Creek, AB, xxvi, 2, 8, 9(f),
    14, 16, 18–20, 21(f), 22, 24n4
Point Ellice House, Victoria, 94
Poitras, Alice, 247, 258n64
political organizing. *See*
    Cummings, Nora
political resistance. *See* Resistance
    (1869–70), Red River, MB;
    Resistance (1885), Batoche, SK
Ponteix, SK, 133, 147
Prince Albert, SK, 102, 104, 125,
    126n3, 179, 185
Prince of Wales hotel, Waterton,
    AB, 8
Pruden, John, 111, 129n49
Pryor, Montana, 156n83

Qu'Appelle (Lebret) Industrial
    School, 144–145
Qu'Appelle Mission, 142, 154n28

Racette, Sherry. *See* Farrell Racette,
    Sherry

Racette, Vicki, 247
racism and discrimination: by
    families in mixed marriages,
    145; fur traders' wives in US,
    89; ideologies of race, 119,
    166; negative representations
    of women, 166; relief
    administration, 254n4;
    transitional period, 119
Raven, Krystl Dawn, 104
Red Deer Hill, SK, 101–102, 105,
    119–120
Red River, MB: about, 5, 110–113,
    115; customary adoption, 113,
    126; economic uncertainties,
    118; Fort Garry, 115, 119–120;
    free traders, 5, 20–21, 24n10;
    Grey Nuns schools, 5, 116–121;
    kinship networks, 111–113,
    115; McNab/McNabb family,
    108–113; political resentments,
    22–23, 115; scholarship focus
    on politics and military,
    55n39; scrip or treaty status,
    112; social hierarchy, 117–118;
    St. Clements parish, 110; St.
    François Xavier parish, 4,
    111, 154n28, 168, 170. *See also*
    Resistance (1869–70), Red
    River, MB
"Red River Valley" (song), 23, 27n61
Redvers, 145
Regina, SK, 244, 258n64
Reid, John, 27n57
religion and spirituality. *See*
    Anglican Church; Catholicism;
    spirituality
rematriation, 197–198, 201, 217–218
research on matriarchs: case study
    overview, xxv–xxix. *See also*
    historiography; historiography,
    sources

residential schools: Dunbow (St. Joseph's) school, High River, 46–47, 60n106; Lebret (Qu'Appelle) school, 144–145; transportation to, 145
resilience. *See* resistance and resilience
Resistance (1869–70), Red River, MB: about, 22–23, 167–168; land dispossession, 22–23, 167–168; migrations, xxvii, 142–143, 168, 170–172, 200; participants, 5, 20, 170, 172; punishments, 172; women's lives, 170, 172–175
Resistance (1885), Batoche, SK: about, 167–168, 172–173; economic instabilities, 175; land dispossession, 22–23, 167–168; migrations, 18–19, 168, 171–172, 175–177, 188, 234; participants, 5, 20, 233–234; women's lives, 172–178, 188, 233–234
resistance and resilience: about, 158–161, 188; collective identity, 161; food sharing, 174, 226, 228, 231, 238; matriarchal sovereignty as, 157, 160–161, 163, 185, 188–190, 265; power of love, 160–164, 201–203; publishing as act of, 50; relational aesthetics as, 202; road allowance communities as, 165; storytelling and stories, 157–158, 166–167, 233–235. *See also* Métis kinship relationships
return of objects to communities. See museums
Riel, Louis, 5, 20, 172
Riel, Louis, Sr., 5, 24n10

Rio Sacramento, 77
road allowance communities: about, xx–xxi, 143–144, 165, 225–228; forced displacements, 143–144, 165, 175, 225, 228, 233, 265; kinship networks, xxi, 144, 233–234; land surveys unused portions, 165; poverty, 165, 225, 266; recognition of, 252(f); as resistance, 165; scholarship on, 254n2; south Saskatoon, 225–228; subsistence economy, xxi
Robertson, Carmen L., 53n24
Rochfort Bridge Museum, Lac Ste. Anne, AB, 32
Roemmich, Carolina Jakeway, 54n26
Roman Catholic. *See* Catholicism
Round Prairie settlement, SK, 226, 233–234, 253, 254n3, 255n22
Rousset, Louis and Blanche Lepine, 176, 176(f)
Rowan, Antoine (Victoria's grandfather), 40, 56nn49–50
Rowan, Nancy (Victoria's mother), 30, 40–42, 47, 51n7, 54n26, 56nn48–50, 57n70
Rowand, Ignace and Louise (Victoria's great-grandparents), 40
Rowand, John, 40, 51n7, 56n50
Roy, Betty, 237, 258n64
Roy, Diane Gaudet (Auxile's granddaughter), 178–180, 183, 185–186
Rozyk, Amanda, 121
Russian territory, 81–83

Salish. *See* Interior Salish people
Sanderson, Elsie, 210
Sanderson, Solomon, 215

Saskatchewan: colonialism in northern areas, 207–208; road allowance communities, 144; scrip, 167–168. *See also* Regina, SK; Saskatoon, SK

Saskatchewan, matriarchs. *See* Cumberland House (kāministikominahikoskahk), SK, matriarchs; Cummings, Nora; Kirkness, Caroline McNabb; Lamotte, Julia Fayant; Morrison, Auxile Lepine

Saskatchewan Indian Women's Association, 246

Saskatchewan Landing, 137, 138(f), 142

Saskatchewan Métis Society, Saskatoon, 234, 237, 239

Saskatchewan Native Alcohol Council (NAC), 239–240, 241

Saskatchewan Native Women's Conferences (1972, 1973), 242–243, 243(f)

Saskatchewan Native Women's Movement (SNWM), 224–225, 243–250, 243(f)

Saskatoon, SK: activism, 234–235; bus shelter, 252(f), 253; community gardens, 226–228; Local #11, Métis Nation, 223–224, 237, 239–241, 243, 247, 253, 256n47; racism and discrimination, 231–232, 248–249, 254n4; recognition of Métis, 252–253, 252(f); relief administration, 254n4; road allowance communities, 225–228, 233; Round Prairie Métis, 226, 233–234, 253, 254n3, 255n22. *See also* Cummings, Nora

Saskatoon Indian and Métis Friendship Centre, 224, 236–237, 243, 243(f), 256n47

Saskatoon Métis Society, 234, 237, 239

SaskNative Housing, 240, 241

Saunders, Annie, 19–20, 27n54

Sauteuse, Lizette (Victoria's great-grandmother), 40

Sayer Trial (1849), 5, 20–21, 24n10

Schilling, Rita, 234–235, 239

schools: about, 116–119, 121; Anglo norms, 116–117, 119, 121; for boys, 179; convent schools, 116–119, 147; curriculum, 116–117, 119; day schools, 117, 119; fear-based schooling, 180–181; Indian residential schools, 46–47, 60n106, 144–145; sexual abuse, 78–79; shaming of Michif speakers, 231; social hierarchy, 117–119

schools, locations: Fort Vancouver, 78–79; Fort Victoria, 87–88; High River, 46–47, 60n106; Prince Albert, 179; Qu'Appelle, 144–145; Red River, 5, 116–121; St. Albert, 46

Scofield, Gregory, 219n24

scrip: about, 44, 58n83, 167–168; database, 51n7; denial as punishment, 172; few permanent settlers, 144; imcompetent management, 168; land dispossession, 143–144, 167, 225; locations, 58n83, 167; Order in Council for, 58n83; scrip or treaty status, 44, 112

Sears, Bert, 245(f)

Selkirk, Earl of, 109

settler colonialism: assimilation, 166–167, 180–181; removal of female authority, 202; settler gaze on Métis "in the past," 36. *See also* Indian Act (1876); road allowance communities; scrip; transitional period (mid-to-late 19th c.)

sewing and embroidery: Anglo norms, 121–122; blankets, 212, 214; economic benefits, 203; English fashion, 107(f), 108; HBC cloth, 208; knowledge-sharing, 121–122; school curriculum, 116, 119; silk thread, 205(f), 209; winter wear, 209, 212

Shaunavon, SK, 140

shawls, 43

Shellbrook, SK, 124–126, 131n114

Shingoose, Helen, 258n64

Simpson, George, 72, 73, 82, 86, 87

Sinclair family (Julia's ancestors), 139

Sinclair, Agnes, 139, 251

Sinclair, Doreen, 258n64

Sinclair, George (Julia's father), 139

Sinclair, Jim, 242

Sinclair, Marie Angelique Fayant (Julia's mother), 137, 139

Sinclair, Nellie, 139, 156n83

Sinclair, Thomas, 139

Sinclair, William and Marie Chartrand (Julia's grandparents), 139

Sion convent, Prince Albert, 179

Sitka, 81–83

slavery, 83–85

Sleeper-Smith, Susan, xviii

smallpox, 57n70, 79–80, 200

Smith, Charlie (Marie Rose's husband), xxvi, 1–2, 5–7, 9, 9(f), 14–16, 20–22

Smith, J.R. "Bob" (Marie Rose's son), 14, 26n34

Smith, Marie Rose Delorme. *See* Delorme Smith, Marie Rose

Smith Parfitt, Mary Hélène (Marie Rose's daughter), 12, 16–18, 20

smoking ki-ni-kin-nik, 149

SNWM/SNWA (Saskatchewan Native Women's Movement/ Association), 224–225, 243–252, 243(f)

songs. *See* entertainment

South Branch post (HBC), 174

sovereignty in matriarchy, 157, 160–161, 163, 185, 188–190, 265

Sparvier, Doris, 258n64

Spicer, Norma, 57n69

spirituality: connections with ancestors, 134–135; Indigenous spirituality, 151–152; matriarchal service, 161; premonitions, 152; seers, 183; spiritual stability of matriarchs, 189–190

Spokane House, 70–75

St. Albert, AB, 32, 33(f), 43, 48

St. Albert convent, AB, 46, 60n100

St. Boniface, Red River, MB, 5, 116–121

St. François Xavier, Red River, MB, 4, 111, 154n28, 168, 170

St. Joseph's (Dunbow) residential school, High River, AB, 46–47, 60n106

St. Joseph's School, Saskatoon, SK, 231–232

St. Laurent, SK, 171, 174–175, 181

St. Louis, SK, 126n3, 165, 170–171, 174–175, 188

St. Patrick's school, Prince Albert, SK, 179

Staines, John, 87–88

stereotypes, 166
Stevenson, Allyson, xxiii, xxviii, 195–222, 263, 265–266, 270
Stobbart School, Duck Lake, 180–181
St-Onge, Nicole, 55nn39–40, 111, 163–164
stories and storytelling: about, xxii, xxixn2, 157–158, 177–178, 233–234; in family-centred historical approach, xxiv–xxv, 262–263; genealogies, 216; matriarchs as cultural teachers, xiv, 210–211; in Métis identity, 50, 157–160, 233–234; of resistance, 166–167, 177–178, 233–235; re-storying objects in museums, 195–196; visiting with tea and stories, 213–214. *See also* oral history
Strand, Paulette (Julia's granddaughter), 133, 135, 137, 149, 151(f), 152–153
Swift Current, SK, 142–143, 145, 147–149

Taillon, Adolphe (Victoria's stepfather), 40
Tall Creek, 57n70
taxidermy, 86–87
Taylor, Alex, 245(f)
Taylor, Cora, 52n20, 56n50
Teillet, Jean, 143–144, 168, 171, 186, 188
Têtes-Plattes (Flatheads), as term, 90. *See also* Interior Salish people
Thompson, David, 66–71, 74, 90
Thorne, Tanis, xviii
Thorp, Isabella Cameron, 112, 129n57
Todd, Zoe, xxiii, 161, 206

Tofte, Barb (Julia's granddaughter), 135, 153, 153n3
Tolmie, Ettie (Josette), 96
Tolmie, Jane Work (Josette's daughter), 75, 78–79, 81–82, 88–89, 93–96
Tolmie, Jean (Josette's granddaughter), 91
Tolmie, Simon Fraser (Josette's grandson), 95
Tolmie, William Fraser (Josette's son-in-law), 79, 82, 86, 88–89, 93, 95
Tootoosis, Dianne, 258n64
transitional period (mid-to-late 19th c.): about, xix–xx, 175–176; decline of buffalo, xx, 24n10, 42–3, 46–47; economic participation, xix–xx, 44–45; farms and ranches, xvi, xx, 12, 14, 20, 146–147, 173(f), 182, 185–186; ideologies of race, 119, 166; matriarchs as agents in, xv–xvii, 22–23; migrations after resistances, xxvii, 18–19, 142–143, 168, 170–172, 175–177, 188, 200–201, 234; settlements, xix–xxi, 143; shifting status of women, 118–119; women's labour, xix–xxii, 44–45, 118–119
treaty status or scrip, 44, 112
Trotchie, Alex (Nora's uncle), 227(f)
Trotchie, Clarence (Nora's uncle), 224, 227(f), 235–240, 236(f), 242–243, 253, 256n47
Trotchie, Eva (Nora's godmother), 231
Trotchie, Irene. *See* Dimick, Irene Trotchie (Nora's mother)
Trotchie, Irvin (Nora's uncle), 227(f)

Trotchie, Justine Landry (Nora's grandmother), 225, 227(f), 228–236, 229(f), 240, 253, 256n29
Trotchie, Norman (Nora's uncle), 227(f)
Trotchie, Peter (Nora's grandfather), 235, 256n29
Trotchie, Phyllis (Nora's aunt), 247
Trottier hunting brigade, 164, 254n3, 255n22
Troupe, Cheryl, xxiii, xxviii, 164, 165, 167, 223–260, 263, 266, 270
Tsimshian, 80, 81, 82, 84, 85
tuberculosis, 91, 94, 123

urban matriarchs. *See* Cummings, Nora
US/Canada border (Medicine Line), 137, 138(f), 139

Van Kirk, Sylvia, xvi, xviii–xix, 63–64, 66, 88, 91, 95, 107–108, 165–166
Vancouver Island, 88
Vandale, Maria, 183
Vandale, Sonny, 180
Vandelle, Hermine "Lizzie" Callihoo (Victoria's daughter), 41, 49, 55n34, 58n86
Victoria, BC: Fort Victoria, 87–88; Hillside Farm, xxvi–xxvii, 63, 87–88, 89(f), 90–96; Works as a founding family, 95–97. *See also* Work, John (Josette's husband); Work, Josette Lagacé
Victoria Belcourt. *See* Callihoo, Victoria Belcourt
violence, gendered, 165–166
visiting. *See* Métis visiting

wāhkōhtowin (respect and belonging), 104–105, 113, 121–126, 127n12
Wait, Calvin William, 35(f), 51n1, 55n33
Walker, Anna M., 55n34
Wallace, Catherine (Kate) Work, 83, 93–94
Wallace, Charles Wentworth, 93–94
Walsh, Billy, 9
Waterton Lakes National Park, AB, 8, 10, 14, 19
Whitman, Narcissa, 85
Willamette River valley settlement, 79, 81, 85
Williams, Christina McDonald, 71
willow, red (ki-ni-kin-nik), 149
Willow Bunch, SK, 137, 138(f), 142, 145
Wilson, Charles, 92
Wilson, Vicki, 237, 249–250, 250(f), 258n64
Winn, Vanessa, xxiv, 63–100, 262, 263–264, 270
Wolvengrey, Arok, 127n12
women: Catholic views of, 178; colonial violence, 165–166; homestead rules, 24n3; mainstream feminism, 244–246; shawls as feminine symbols, 43. *See also* Métis kinship relationships; Métis matriarchs; Métis women's labour; transitional period (mid-to-late 19th c.)
Woodhouse, Chase Going (Josette's granddaughter), 96
Work, Henry (Josette's son), 91
Work, John (Josette's husband): about, 75, 90, 92–95; Anglican, 87–88, 90; birth and passing (c. 1792–1861), 67, 75, 92; brother David, 80; career in HBC, 64,

71–76, 87; farmer, 88, 90–91; as father, 75, 86, 87, 92; historical sources, 72–73, 76, 84; illnesses and injuries, 75, 77, 80, 82, 87, 92; Irish background, 75, 90; landowner, 90–93, 95; Legislative Council member, 95; marriage legitimacy, 71–72, 87–88; personal qualities, 75–76, 80–81, 83, 86, 92; property owner, 95; travels, 87

Work, John (Josette's son), 89, 92–93

Work, Josette Lagacé: about, xxvi–xxvii, 63–97, 65(f), 89(f), 263–264; Anglican, 87–88, 90; birth and passing (1809–96), 63, 96; descendants as BC founding family, 95–97; early life, 63–64, 68–73; historical sources, 64, 66, 67–68, 76; illnesses and injuries, 77, 83; Indigenous relationships, 87; languages (Kalispel, French, English, Chinook trading patois), 71, 74, 78; marriage to John, 63, 71–72, 74, 87–88; as a matriarch, xxvi–xxvii, 64, 65(f), 93–97, 263–264; names, 69, 90–91; personal qualities, 63, 76, 80–81, 92, 94, 264; recognition, 64, 66, 264; uncertainties in early life, 68–73; widowhood, 92–93, 96–97. See also Work, John (Josette's husband)

—ABILITIES AND TALENTS: farming, 75, 88; firearms, 83; healer, 75, 80, 81, 94; leather and beadwork, 85; sewing and cooking, 83–84, 92; taxidermy, 86–87; teaching, 83–84

—CHILDREN: Catherine (Kate) Wallace, 83, 93–94; Henry, 91; Jane Tolmie, 75, 78–79, 81–82, 88–89, 93–96; John, 89, 92–93; Letitia Huggins, 67, 71, 76, 78, 79–81, 83–89, 91; Margaret Jackson, 78–81, 89, 96; Mary Grahame, 80, 88, 93; Sarah Finlayson, 75, 78–79, 81–83, 88, 90, 94–95; Suzette, 90, 94

—FAMILY AND COMMUNITY: about, xxvi–xxvii, 64, 90–97; abuse, 78–79; Amelia Douglas's friendship, 77–79, 85, 88, 91, 94–95; Charles Lagacé (father), 63–64, 66–70; descendants as BC founding family, 95–97; Emme (mother), 64, 67, 68, 70, 74, 90, 93; godmothers and namesakes, 78; illnesses, 77, 79–80; against Indigenous slavery, 83–85; Kalispel kin, 64, 70, 90, 93; kinship care, 93–97; political participation, 95–97; schools, 78–79, 81, 87–88; social hierarchies, 85–87, 94; suffrage support, 95–96; uncertainties in history, 63, 66–73. See also Lagacé, Pierre (Josette's brother); Work, John (Josette's husband)

—HOMES AND TRAVELS: *Beaver* (steamer), 78, 87, 89, 95; brigade journeys, 63; Fort Colvile, 75–76, 80; Fort Nisqually, 84, 88–90; Fort Simpson, 78–88; Fort Vancouver, 77–78; Oregon territory, 75–76, 89; Snake River area, 75–76; Spokane House, 70–75; travels to California, 77; Victoria (Hillside Farm), xxvi–xxvii, 63, 87–88, 89(f), 90–96

Work, Letitia. *See* Huggins, Letitia Work (Josette's daughter)
Work, Margaret. *See* Jackson, Margaret Work (Josette's daughter)
Work, Suzette (Josette's daughter), 90, 94

world view. *See* Métis kinship relationships

York Factory, 118

Zatorski, Glenice, 258n64

Cheryl Troupe is an Assistant Professor in the Department of History at the University of Saskatchewan and has a PhD in History and an MA in Indigenous Studies. Cheryl is Métis from north central Saskatchewan.

Doris Jeanne MacKinnon was born on a farm in northeastern Alberta and attended school in the historic town of St-Paul-des-Métis. She has a PhD in Indigenous and post-Confederation Canadian history and an MEd in Adult Education. An independent researcher and postsecondary instructor, she lives in Alberta.